The Jewish Search for a Usable Past

THE HELEN AND MARTIN SCHWARTZ LECTURES IN
JEWISH STUDIES, 1998

Sponsored by the
Robert A. and Sandra S. Borns
Jewish Studies Program
Indiana University

DAVID G. ROSKIES

The Jewish Search for a Usable Past

INDIANA UNIVERSITY PRESS

Bloomington and Indianapolis

This book is a publication of

Indiana University Press
601 North Morton Street
Bloomington, IN 47404-3797 USA

http://www.indiana.edu/~iupress

Telephone orders 800-842-6796
Fax orders 812-855-7931
Orders by e-mail iuporder@indiana.edu

The paper used in this publication meets the minimum requirements of American National Standard for Information Sciences—Permanence of Paper for Printed Library Materials, ANSI Z39.48-1984.

Manufactured in the United States of America

Library of Congress Cataloging-in-Publication Data

Roskies, David G., date
   The Jewish search for a usable past / David G. Roskies.
        p.   cm. — (The Helen and Martin Schwartz lectures in Jewish studies)
   Includes bibliographical references and index.
   ISBN 0-253-33505-1 (alk. paper)
   1. Jews—Civilization. 2. Jews—Persecutions. 3. Memory—Religious aspects—Judaism. I. Title. II. Series.
DS112.R755 1999
909'.04924—dc21   98-46951
1 2 3 4 5   04 03 02 01 00 99

To the Memory of
Gerson D. Cohen ז״ל
(1924–1991)
Who Built a Jewish Memory-Site
Second to None

Contents

at all than to reopen that politically sensitive chapter of Polish-Ukrainian relations, especially now that Ukraine had been liberated.

There was no overlap between Tishevitz and Tyszowce. Even the map that the mayor produced from the parish archives bore not the slightest resemblance to the one I had drawn on the basis of Jewish memories. No *shul*, no heders, no house of study, no hasidic *shtiblekh*, no ritual bath. It was a good thing I had not visited this town twenty years before. The discrepancy between "our" town and "theirs" was simply too great. I did not possess then, nor did I possess at this time, tools adequate to bridge that abyss. All I could do with my books and interviews was conjure up a vicarious and precarious mini-Jewish state called the "shtetl." My informants, most of them Labor Zionists, would have had it no other way. Besides, the textbook was written in Jerusalem, in the wake of the Yom Kippur War.

For my Polish counterpart, still worried about the status of his home, the dead, peace-loving, and powerless Jews posed no immediate threat. The Ukrainians did. That is why he created a seamless and heroic past. Each of us, I realized, had used the past to compensate our losses. Each of us did so by a colossal act of reinvention.

The one remaining question was this: Was a three-way competition for this godforsaken piece of real estate really worth the effort? When I left Tyszowce, the romance of the shtetl died within me.

Like my journey that summer in the southeastern part of Poland, this book obeys the peculiar logic of a map. We begin by drawing a historical map through modern Jewish memory, and follow a roundabout route, from Germany, to Eastern Europe, to North America. The next four chapters revisit those parts of the Old World that remained stubbornly old. "The Golden Peacock" (chapter 6) charts the momentous ocean crossing, followed by two chapters that explore different memory-sites in the United States and Canada. We come full circle in chapter 9, which tries to locate both the Old World and the New in the Land of Israel. Do the pieces, we ask, still fit together on a Jewish map?

Like that summer in Poland, this book is animated by a dialectic of loss and retrieval. Each object found along the way is at one and the same time a memory-site and an emblem of loss: a torn scripture, a ghettoscape, a shtetl, a rabbinic role model, a repertory of Yiddish songs, a row of graves, a school, a protocol of Old Tel Aviv. A memory-site, this book argues, is fashioned from the prior awareness of loss. But should the loss be too great, all one is left with is apocalyptic rage.

Isaac Babel, a fellow traveler, was adept at finding lost treasures. In "The Story of My Dovecot," he unpacks his Uncle Lev's large trunk, shipped

Preface and Acknowledgments

There had not been so hot a summer since 1939. In some parts of Poland, the mighty Vistula was reduced to a stream. In Warsaw, the asphalt was melting.

This was also the summer of anniversaries. For the first time in fifty years the true story of the Warsaw Uprising could be told, Soviet betrayal and all. Memorial concerts and exhibitions were being held in all the major cities; the scouts and veterans were out in full force.

But in the sleepy town of Tyszowce, near the Ukrainian border, a young local historian was preparing for a different anniversary: fifty years since the founding of the local high school. As the school's principal, he had been commissioned to write its history. On that hot summer's day in 1994 he came running to meet his Jewish counterpart who, twenty years earlier, had written a textbook about Jewish life in the town—a town the Jews called Tishevitz when they made up 55 percent of the population.

We compared notes. Mine were drawn from *Pinkes Tishevitz* (the Tishevitz memorial book); from Yekhiel Shtern's classic monograph about traditional Jewish education; from a novel by his brother, Jacob Zipper; from a travelogue by the great Yiddish writer I. L. Peretz and a demon-monologue by his heir, Isaac Bashevis Singer; from extensive interviews conducted in Montreal among former Tishevitzer. Their story—and mine—was mostly about the transformation of Jewish life in the town between the two world wars.

The principal began his in 1655, when Tyszowce played host to the confederation against the Swedes. The town, he explained, lost its historic significance following the last partition of Poland, in 1795. As for the years between World War I and the liberation of the town by the Red Army, the local historian had left them blank.

The bastard, I thought, has erased the whole period to avoid the tragic fate of the Jews. But I was wrong.

"I had to," he explained, "on account of the Ukrainians."

Between 1945 and 1947, Tyszowce had been part of a huge contested area along Poland's eastern border. Better not to mention the interwar years back to Odessa by the Los Angeles police. "In this trunk there were dumbbells, locks of female hair, Uncle's prayer-shawl, horsewhips with gilt knobs and flower tea in boxes decorated with cheap pearls." In Babel's most poignant tale, "The Rebbe's Son," Lyutov discovers the scattered belongings of Red Army soldier Ilya Bratslavsky: portraits of Lenin and Maimonides lying side by side; a strand of female hair placed inside a book of the resolutions of the Sixth Party Congress, and in the margins of communist leaflets crooked lines of Ancient Hebrew verse; "pages of the Song of Songs and revolver cartridges."

I too would like to believe that there is something in this book of mine for everyone. I have kept the diction as nonacademic as possible, hoping to provide the adventuresome tourist with a vacation in Jewish lands. Alternatively, every chapter treats a different subject, in a kind of scavenger hunt with multiple prizes. The notes are for the hiker looking for graded trails. Rousseau has taught that the life story of each individual is utterly unique. But the Torah teaches that the life of each Jew is essentially the same. One map serves all.

The invitation to take my map and carry it west of the Hudson was issued by Professor Alvin Rosenfeld of Indiana University. In their present form, "The Jewish Search for a Usable Past" and "The Golden Peacock" were delivered as the Martin and Helen Schwartz Lectures in Jewish Studies at Indiana University, March 23–24, 1998. I owe an additional debt of thanks to my editor, Janet Rabinowitch, for the opportunity to whip these essays into coherent shape and for shepherding the guidebook so skillfully on its way.

"The Library of Jewish Catastrophe" originally appeared in *Holocaust Remembrance: The Shapes of Memory*, ed. Geoffrey H. Hartman (Oxford: Blackwell, 1994). Copyright 1994 by Basil Blackwell Ltd. and reprinted with permission.

"Ringelblum's Time Capsules" is an expanded version of "*Landkentenish:* Yiddish Belles Lettres in the Warsaw Ghetto," which originally appeared in *Holocaust Chronicles: Individualizing the Holocaust through Diaries and Other Contemporaneous Personal Accounts*, ed. Lucjan Dobroszycki and Robert M. Shapiro (Hoboken, N.J.: Ktav, 1998). Copyright 1997 by Yeshiva University and reprinted with permission.

"A City, a School, and a Utopian Experiment" is my favorite essay; it has appeared three times before, in different versions and venues. As "Yiddish in Montreal: A Utopian Experiment," it first appeared in *An Everyday Miracle: Yiddish Culture in Montreal*, ed. Ira Robinson, Pierre Anctil, and Melvin Butovsky (Montreal: Véhicule Press, 1990).

"Zionism, Israel, and the Search for a Covenantal Space" was originally delivered at a conference on "Makkom: Spirit and Space in Modern Israel," sponsored by the Ginor Chair in Israeli Culture and Society at the Jewish Theological Seminary.

New York City
March 2, 1998

The Jewish Search for a Usable Past

1 The Jewish Search for a Usable Past

I know that the way things are done in this world, and the way they have
always been, Genesis comes before Exodus, but in this case the Amalekites
came first. And I suggest you listen to the lesson they taught me, because it
may come in useful some day.

—Sholem Aleichem (1914)

Once upon a time, everything a Jew needed to know about the world was
locatable in the Universal Jewish Encyclopedia known as *Mikra'ot gedolot*.
The deep past, covenantal, codified at Sinai, was laid out in the Torah,
Prophets, and Writings; the surrounding commentaries provided the up-
date. For greater convenience and affordability, the entire usable past was
anthologized in the Five Books of Moses, the Five Scrolls, the Sabbath and
Festival prayer books, the *Ein Ya'akov*, and the *Book Jashar*. Local events
were recorded in the communal *pinkas*. Most of their contents were known
by heart, through constant recital.

"Memory" per se was not even an operative category in Judaism. Rather,
Jews in each period had their master metaphors, organized around saints,
sanctuaries, and sacred times. In this way, each generation of Jews shaped
the model life, the model community, and the model time. In times of
crisis, the function of Jewish memory was to transcend the ruptures of history. Anger was the tenor, sacrilege was the vehicle. At such times the pre-
cise levers of inner-Jewish transformation were the historical archetypes
that embodied the covenantal relationship between God and Israel: God's
command of Lekh-lekho to Abraham; the Akedah, the Exodus, Sinai, the
Mosaic Curses, the Ḥurban or Destruction of the Temple, the Valley of
the Dry Bones, the Battle of Gog, the Megillah of Purim, the martyrdom
of the Ten Harugei Malkhut.[1] And so the chronicler, preacher, or synagogue poet could either invoke any of the relevant archetypes, reminding
God, as it were, both of His promise and of Israel's steadfastness in the past,
or, more boldly, could engage in "sacred parody," playing the present sacrilege off the past. In the face of national catastrophe, the Jewish response
is dialectical: the worse the present expulsion order, or massacre, or blood
libel, the more it recalls the most sacrilegious event of the past.[2]

The Great Nineteenth-Century Kulturkampf

By the beginning of the nineteenth century, the message of Jewish memory—if not yet the medium—went up for grabs. At the meeting of East and West, the great Kulturkampf began between the religious pietists, the Hasidim, who were taking Jewish Eastern Europe by storm, and the Maskilim, the undercover agents of modernity, two in a city, ten in a province. The landscape was transformed, not so much by Napoleon as by the Baᶜal Shem Tov (ca. 1700–1760), whose legendary biography appeared in 1815.[3] Here was a new type of normative zaddik: a lowly, obscure individual who went from a state of hiddenness to self-revelation to political and cosmic action. The central plot-line of this (literally) marvelous book, *Shivḥei haBesht*, is the story of *hitkarvut*, how Israel Baᶜal Shem orchestrated the "drawing near" of his chief disciples, without their even knowing who he was. The new model of community was of male disciples spread far and wide who owed allegiance to the zaddik, the main intercessor between heaven and earth. Most radical from a religious perspective was the model of time, made explicit in the book's preface: *nes gadol haya po*, a great miracle was wrought for Israel right here, both in the great urban centers of Brody and Lemberg, and in the Ukrainian outback of Shepetovka, Mezhbizh, Shpole, Sdey-Lovon, Chechelnik, Kaminka.

Meanwhile, the Baᶜal Shem Tov's great-grandson had just died, leaving behind several utterly unique works, among them, his *Sipurey mayses*, which marked the beginning of modern Yiddish and Hebrew storytelling.[4] Behind his fantastically elaborated tales about abducted princesses and grotesque beggars, Reb Nahman of Braslav (1772–1810) had composed a fiercely polemical work. Each story dramatizes the contest between the seeker-wanderer and the forces of evil, disguised, more often than not, in innocent garb. The figure of the Maskil comes in for special ridicule, bested, in a long and complicated story, by the simple piety of the *tam*, by a "real Baᶜal Shem," and finally, by the Devil himself. Included within these thirteen canonical tales is an exquisite example of Jewish historical fiction, set in Spain or Portugal, the "Tale of the King Who Decreed Conversion." Secular history for Reb Nahman was a hieroglyphic of the holy. In the story's blazing climax, the forces of evil are burned to a crisp, the community of praying Jews remains protected behind a wall of fire, but the Marrano minister returns to a life of hiddenness in the royal court—a stunning self-portrait of the zaddik who must continue to wage the redemptive battle in the world of falsehood.

In addition to spreading the new gospel by means of sermons and stories,

Hasidism spawned a major revival of Jewish song, the memory-sites that would ultimately travel the farthest and longest. (See chapter 6.) Some were *dveykes-niggunim*, melodies without words; others were mantra-like songs set to the Book of Psalms or the Sabbath and Festival liturgy; still others were the Yiddish songs attributed to Reb Levi Yitskhok of Berdichev; and most innovative were the songs of pilgrimage to the rebbe. For Hasidism laid claim to Jewish space: to the court of the living rebbe or to his holy grave.

The Haskalah waged its battle for reform on every possible front, but first and foremost in the field of education. Here and there the Maskilim established their own schools, where the talmudic past was delegitimated, the arcane customs of the Ashkenazic present were burlesqued, and the future belonged to German high culture. Aaron Halle Wolfsohn (1754–1835) delivered on all three counts in his German-Yiddish *lustspiel*, *Leichtsinn und Frömellei* (Frivolity and hypocrisy), performed in lieu of the yearly *Purim-shpil* in his Königlicher Wilhelmshule, in 1794.[5] Here the drunken King Ahasuerus is recast as an arch-conservative, Yiddish-speaking merchant. Esther is his flighty, superficially educated daughter, and her Uncle Mordecai is played by the dashing, German-preaching Maskil, Marcus. To round out the biblical plot, Haman is the venal, ignorant Polish Hasid, Reb Yoysefkhe. Molière would have felt right at home, seeing Haman-Tartuffe-Reb Yoysefkhe unmasked in a whorehouse. (On Purim, anything goes, even among straight-laced German Maskilim.)

Once the search for a usable past was being waged through new venues and institutions—the rebbe's court with its tales and songs, the modern school with its parodies and plays—the structure of remembrance began to change as well. It became ever more contrapuntal, as choosing one set of memories entailed actively opposing another set. Remember that in the older scheme, there was the communal reminding of God or the personal reminding of the community. Either way it meant the restoration or recycling of memories already there; disassembling the present in terms of the eternal past. But something more creative was happening now, as every act of retrieval was simultaneously an act of rejection: the Haskalah vs. Jewish medievalism, Hasidism vs. the Haskalah.

We need more active parts of speech to render the new dynamic. "The *Turn* to History in Modern Judaism," so ably charted by Ismar Schorsch, doesn't quite do the trick.[6] In point of fact, his is a map of polemical highroads and byroads. And he finds them everywhere: from the new Reform liturgy and synagogue architecture to the spanking new works of secular fiction. Ludwig Philippson's enormously popular historical novels, he shows, do double duty. "Drawn from the stockpile of Sephardic history,"

they idealize the past of Spanish Jewry so as to efface and replace the igno-
minious legacy of medieval Ashkenaz.[7] Far more subtle in its polemic is
Heinrich Heine's *The Rabbi of Bacherach* (1824), the first bona fide historical novella on a Jewish theme.[8] On the surface, there is nothing the least
bit parodic about the noble, ascetic figure of Rabbi Abraham, the young
prodigy of Bacherach. That Heine implausibly sends him off to study in
Spain, where Rabbi Abraham is infected by the healthy bug of Sephardic
aestheticism, reveals the new ideological agenda of German Jewry. But
Heine's impetus to breathe new life into the dry bones of the Jewish past
by restoring its passion and pain was derived from someone very close at
hand: Eduard Gans, the chief theoretician of the *Verein für Cultur und
Wissenschaft der Juden* in Berlin. Heine's animus was fueled, according to
Schorsch, by his friend's attempt to reduce the story of the Jews to abstract
philosophical formulations. One way or the other, the affirmation of Judaism evinced by the heroes of Schorsch's narrative entails a large amount of
rejection.[9] All memory is fast becoming counter-memory.

By the 1830s, the message of the Jewish historical imagination was being greatly radicalized as the medium was changing apace. Only a heretic
would write a novel about Baruch Spinoza and portray him as the father
of Enlightenment philosophers. As Berthold Auerbach did, in 1837. Only
a budding socialist would write *The Holy History of Mankind* and place
Spinoza's social philosophy at its very center. As Moses Hess did, also in
1837. Only a professional historian would produce a scholarly monograph
on Rashi in order to hoist the enemy on its own petard. As Leopold Zunz
did, in 1822. By historicizing the greatest of all medieval Ashkenazic com-
mentators ("Salomon ben Isaac, gennant Raschi"), Zunz made biography
into a weapon against those who claimed Rashi's mantle—the rabbinic establishment of his own day and age.[10]

The same politics of emancipation that turned past into present could
turn the living present into a thing of the past. This is how the shtetl, where
the majority of Yiddish-speaking Jews still struggled, studied, and sang, became the subject of quaint and sentimental ghetto stories. Introduced into
literature by Leopold Kompert for the sake of his fellow German Jews, the
ghetto was then repackaged for the sake of gentile readers by Karl Emil
Franzos.[11] Whether the shtetl was represented as a paradise lost or as a true
species of the medieval ghetto, now being consigned to the dustbin of history, lox, stock, and bagel, the emancipatory message came through loud
and clear: there was no stopping the March of Time. (See chapter 4.)

Nor was there any stopping the march of historical thinking. Indeed,
thanks to Shmuel Feiner's *Haskalah and History* (1995), which traces the
hundred-year intellectual saga of the Haskalah in German, Hebrew, and

Yiddish, it is now possible to see, for the first time, how the writing and reading of history broke down the barriers between East and West, scholarship and belles lettres, the intellectuals and the folk, and even between Jewish men and women.[12]

Picking up on Feiner's story in the very middle, with Russian Jewry during the reforms of Alexander II, we see the making of a caravan route whereby historical narratives are being imported from the West for resale in the East. The Maskilim used these narratives to argue, in three different ways, that the past was unlivable: whether it be the Jewish past, the exotic past of other religious and national groups, or the past of Mother Russia.

First came the Kovno-born Maskil Abraham Mapu (1818–1867), who simultaneously invented the modern Hebrew novel and reinvented the biblical past.[13] History, for Mapu, was crisis, and the only constant was the unbroken chain of idolatry, backwardness, and immorality, which stretched from the Priests of Baal and the Priests of Beth El all the way to the followers of Shabbetai Zvi and beyond. The modern Hebrew novel thus became the ledger of rotten legacies. Never again would Russian Jews read about the siege of Jerusalem in the time of Sennacherib without being "reminded" of the idolatrous Hasidim who still lived in their midst. Once they were convinced of the need to segregate the rotten past from the present, the rescue operation could proceed apace. For Mapu's historical novels were also designed to foster the revival of the Hebrew language; to acquaint readers with the flora and fauna of the Land of Israel and, by extension, with the joys of nature; and to extoll productive labor on the soil. All these shards of the ancient past were restorable, moreover, not by dint of divine intervention but through human effort alone.

Exotic historical themes became the province of the first homegrown school of popular writers: Isaac Meir Dik in Yiddish, Kalman Shulman in Hebrew. With a speed that market forces helped to generate, historical fiction in German and Hebrew designed primarily for men was reworked into Yiddish for the sake of the women. The fair sex could thrill, for example, to the Massacre of St. Bartholomew in 1572 through *Di blut hokhtsayt fun Pariz* (The bloodbath of Paris; 1870), or to the race across the ice in *Uncle Tom's Cabin*, through its Yiddish adaptation, *Di shklavery oder laybeygnshaft (podanstvo)* (1868). Should Russian-Jewish readers miss the contrast between the benevolent rule of Tsar Alexander II and the evils of the antebellum South, the preface reminded them of the liberation of the serfs in Mother Russia. Finally, there was the study of Russian history proper, just the thing to instill patriotism and faith in the ultimate triumph of emancipation: Mikhl Gordon's *Di geshikhte fun Rusland*, "dertseylt in prost yidish loshn" (1869), and Shlomo Mandelkern's multivolume *Sefer divrei yemei Rusia* (1875). And so the choices that history offered were simple and straightforward: one could live in the right place at the wrong time (ancient Judea during the time of Sennacherib); the wrong place at the wrong time (France or the American South during times of persecution); or the right place at the right time (Russia in the present century).

Was any of this hoopla for secular history actually penetrating the Yiddish outback? Was the ebb and flow of Jewish collective memory in any way affected by the insurgent notion of linear, ameliorative, time? Though the data is far from complete, we do know this. The first, traumatic event in the lives of ordinary Russian Jews was the forcible drafting of their underage sons into Cantonist brigades.[14] The *kahal*, the local Jewish council, was authorized to fill the quota. The folk responded to the new historical challenge in three ways: (1) by appealing to a higher authority than that of the tsar; (2) by calling for the consolidation of group norms; and (3) by issuing its appeal both in the Holy Tongue and the vernacular:[15]

> Oy, *av horakhamim, shoykhen bamroymim*
> du bist a foter iber ale yesoymim.
> Beser tsu lernen khumesh mit Rashi
> eyder tsu esn di soldatske kashe.
>
> . . . .

> O GOD OF MERCY, WHO LIVEST IN THE HEAVENS,
> You are the father of all the orphans.
> Better to study Bible and Rashi
> than to eat the soldier's mush.
> Better to snooze on a Study House bench
> than to make a friend in a trench.
> Better to wear a *tallis* and *kitl*
> than to sport a sword round your middle.

Alternatively, they could sing this:[16]

> Trern gisn zikh in ale gasn
> In kindershe blut kenen mir zikh vashn.

> The streets flow with our tears
> You can bathe in the blood of children dear.
> . . . .
> Little children are torn from their lessons
> And pressed into coats with soldiers' buttons.

Our rabbis, our bigshots are in cahoots
Teaching our children to be recruits.

These songs, transcribed two generations after the Cantonist brigades were already abolished, illustrate the creative ways in which the folk reconciled new themes and challenges to the deep structure of Jewish collective memory. Rhetorically, the new historical forces were absorbed into a neat contrapuntal structure: "Better A than B." Some of the anger was redirected inwardly, at one brother who sold another into slavery. But the deep structure continued to work much the same way it always had. It could be one of two things: either covenantal or anticovenantal. Either it could *invoke* God's promise to Israel in the grammar of remembrance, or it could *provoke* God's response by throwing the present sacrilege in His face. Though there now existed a public venue for remembrance outside the synagogue, these historical songs continued to prey upon Scripture and the liturgy.

And so, the repertory of available pasthoods had been greatly expanded during the nineteenth century, by the introduction of new forms, new forums, and even new languages of Jewish self-expression. While for the mass of consumers it was still business as usual, for the writers and reformers in the modernist camp, the embarrassment of riches came at a price. It underscored the ever-growing ideological rift between secular history and covenantal memory.

No one was more aware of the radical absurdity of attributing something called "history" to the Jews than the veteran Hebrew-Yiddish Maskil Sholem-Yankev Abramovitsh (1835–1917). Addressing a fictional group of fellow intellectuals, among whose number was the young historian Simon Dubnov, Abramovitsh protested the absurdity of holding up Jewish corporate existence in Russia-Poland to Western criteria:

> None of us ever did anything to set the world on fire. Dukes, governors, generals, and soldiers we were not; we had no romantic attachments with lovely princesses; we didn't fight duels, nor did we even serve as witnesses, watching other men spill their blood; we didn't dance the quadrille at balls; we didn't hunt wild animals in the fields and forests; we didn't make voyages of discovery to the ends of the earth; we carried on with no actresses or prima donnas; we didn't celebrate in a lavish way. In short, we were completely lacking in all those colorful details that grace a story and whet the reader's appetite.[17]

The crotchety gentleman was up to his old tricks. Abramovitsh knew full well that the history of Russian Jews, however colorless, powerless, and banal, had already been written—by him—using the realistic novel, allegory, and narrative poetry. What's more, he himself had bridged the gap between history and collective memory through *Di klyatshe*, the Mare, his allegorical stand-in for the long-suffering Jews of the Diaspora, who had entered into Yiddish folkspeech, thanks to her ironic resonance with chapter 1, verse 9, from the Song of Songs, "I have likened you, my darling, / To a mare in Pharaoh's chariots."[18] Why, this very diatribe was itself but the preface to Abramovitsh's requiem on the shtetl, which he began to write in 1897. But what "Reb Shloyme" did not let on to his anonymous interlocutors is that the dukes, governors, generals, and soldiers; the duels, quadrilles, and animal hunts—in fact, the whole arsenal of romantic exploits—had made real inroads into the Yiddish landscape, not only through the pages of Jewish pulp fiction but, more spectacularly, on the Yiddish popular stage.

It was Abraham Goldfaden (1840–1908), a Maskil of the moderate camp, who gave Russian Jews a past both unlivable and usable. He did this by taking the traditional Purim plays and swallowing them whole. In his satires he lampooned Jewish superstition and forced marriages, while in his historical operettas, like *Shulamis* and *Bar Kochba*, he paraded Jewish kings and generals across the stage, choreographed Jewish marching music, and orchestrated men and women singing duets. (See chapter 6.) Goldfaden's copies were better than the folk original not only because he raided the ancient past for its as yet unsung heroes and heroines but also because he betrayed that past in the name of an imagined future. The seat of that future was Zion.

Of all the new ideologies that Jews would henceforth live by, none took out a stronger lease on the past than Zionism. However revolutionary the Zionist impulse to take history into one's own hands, to reclaim the Land, drain the swamps, and build agricultural communes such as existed nowhere else on earth, the cultural arm of Zionism fought for a restorative program: the revival of Hebrew as a spoken language; *kinnus*, or the ingathering and preservation of the Diaspora through creative anthologies; the fashioning of new national symbols out of old.[19] In a culture of poverty Zionism was extremely ecological. Why invent new festivals when Hanukkah, Purim, and Passover could all serve as days of national liberation? What's more, every genre of historical writing, from Mapu's *The Love of Zion* to Graetz's *History of the Jews*, was itself a valuable exercise in national self-definition. Folk belief and custom, vilified only yesterday as ossified remains of the medieval past, were now reclaimed as folklore, the sine qua non of nationhood. And yes, the stocks of the vernacular language, Yiddish, also rose accordingly.

Socialists and anarchists, even if they were so inclined, had a much harder time kidnapping the Jewish symbols and festivals. It required great homiletic skill to recast the concepts of surplus value, class conflict, and alienation of labor into recognizably Jewish terms. Between Moses and Spinoza, it was difficult to locate another proto-socialist Jew. The Jewish socialist calendar, only recently expanded to include Bastille Day and May Day, otherwise celebrated only the Exodus from Egypt. And not until the assassination of Tsar Alexander II could the local arm of the revolutionary movement boast of any Jewish martyrs.

By the 1880s, the battle lines were being redrawn, with the nationalists in one camp and the internationalists in another. Just then the field itself was abandoned, as millions of Jews began to move: from the shtetl to the cities; from Eastern Europe to the West; from Europe to the Americas. The New World was especially rich in new means of commemorative production. The Yiddish theater, banned in Russia before it could become firmly established, become professionalized on the East Side of London and the Lower East Side of New York. A satellite industry of sheet music and gramophone records came into being. Socialists and anarchists, hounded, jailed, and hanged in the Old World, were free to organize and propagandize in the New. But whether they owed allegiance to Moses or to Marx, to Benjamin Disraeli or Benjamin Zeev Herzl, the majority of Jews were to experience a profound sense of loss and dislocation.

Then, and only then, at the tail end of the nineteenth century and with increasing urgency during the decades to come, did the search for a usable past become a game of high stakes. For the past was dying, left and right, as one memory vein after another was being severed: communal, behavioral, linguistic, geographic. But as they say in Yiddish: "Got shikt tsu di kelt nokh di kleyder," God sends the cold winds after sending the clothes. A triple revolution had occurred in the German-speaking lands—on the ideological, aesthetic, and historical fronts. When these were imported and adapted in the Yiddish-speaking lands, they gave rise to a complex network of new institutions. These institutions—literature, journalism, theater, education, politics, philanthropy, and scholarship—were now ready to be shipped overseas. And not a moment too soon, because henceforth and in perpetuity, the only usable past was an isolated, segregated, repackageable past.

The Example of Sholem Aleichem

If the lone historian is the hero of Yosef Yerushalmi's bleak narrative about the inevitable decline of Jewish memory,[20] and the rabbi-scholar is the hero of Schorsch's more inspirational tale, the engagé writer is the hero of my revolutionary parable. My roster or pantheon includes many names, but as this story of mine is already burdened with far too many details, one writer will have to suffice: Solomon Rabinovitsh, a.k.a. Sholem Aleichem (1859–1916). Elsewhere, I described how this Russian-Jewish Maskil and intellectual reinvented himself as a teller of semitraditional tales.[21] It seems that whatever I do, whatever subject I choose, I keep coming back to Sholem Aleichem. And this essay is no exception.

Solomon Rabinovitsh was a child of the cultural revolution who played the Kiev stock market by day and wrote realistic novels and literary criticism by night. Such a man no longer had any truck with Jewish covenantal memory. But Sholem Aleichem of Yehupetz, who spent his summers in Boiberik, could bring to life a character who did. Enter: Tevye, fresh from the Ukrainian outback of Shepetovka, Mezhbizh, Shpole, Sdey-Lovon, Chechelnik, and Kaminka. And with barely a heder education, what this paterfamilas can do! He can disassemble all events, no matter how devastating or new, into the covenantal drama of God-Reb-Israel-and-the-Community-of-Israel. Tevye has no "historical" memory, in the secular sense, to speak of. The sum total of his book learning is from Scripture, the Siddur, the Five Scrolls, and some Yiddish story books. He is your classic teller of local traditions, an old-fashioned Histor, rooted in personal memory and the archetypal past. Through his daughters and their suitors, however, Tevye is confronted with new emotional crises that test his faith. Gradually, over a twenty-five-year period, Tevye becomes a Jobian figure fated to experience all of Russian-Jewish history in the flesh. What's more, he himself comes to recognize that this is the case.[22]

1905. Chava, his third daughter, has just taken refuge with the local priest in advance of her marriage to her Ukrainian lover, Khvedka. "I thought my head would burst from trying so hard to figure things out," says Tevye to himself on his way home from the priest's.

> Ma pishi uma khatosi—was I really the world's greatest sinner, that I deserved to be its most-punished Jew? God in heaven, mah onu umeh khayeynu—who am I that You don't forget me even for a second, that You can't invent a new calamity, a new catastrophe, a new disaster, without first trying it out on me? (p. 75)

Behind this litany, punctuated with the words of Jacob to Laban and a snippet from the morning prayers, there stands a lone man of faith struggling with the forces of modernity. But because Tevye does God's will, because the covenantal contract itself is never in question, God is also the source of all his rage, disappointments, and subversions. Never have memory and historical reality worked in concert so well as here, in the folkspeech of the last Jewish patriarch on Russian soil.

A year later, the south of Russia, where Tevye lives, is awash in pogroms and Jews are running every which way, because, as Tevye says, "It's an old Jewish custom to pick up and go elsewhere at the first mention of a pogrom. How does the Bible put it? *Vayisu vayakhanu, vayakhanu vayisu*—or in plain language, if you come hide in my house, I'd better go hide in yours . . . " (p. 83). Yes, the Children of Israel are in the desert once more, only instead of "journeying and camping" on their way to the Promised Land, they are like rats trapped in a maze. One of them is about to land on Tevye's doorstep and will deliver his daughter Shprintze a fatal bite.

Thinking that Tevye's woes had run their course by 1909, Sholem Aleichem sent his wife Golde off to an early grave and sent old Tevye off to the Land of Israel. Then history itself intervened to provide an alternative ending. *Vayehi bimey Mendel Beilis*, says Tevye with even heavier irony than usual, "it happened back in the time of the Beilis case, when Mendel Beilis was atoning for all our sins by going through the torments of hell and the whole world was talking of nothing else" (p. 122). If the blood libel trial dragging on in nearby Kiev-Yehupetz was a throwback to the Middle Ages, how much more so the tsarist decrees ordering the wholesale expulsion of Jews from the villages. Sholem Aleichem, I believe, brought Tevye back from retirement not only to complete the portrait of him as the personal embodiment of Jewish historical fate but, much more importantly, to have Tevye instruct the Jews of Russia on how they might still be able to cut history down to size by using the time-honored methods.

Sholem Aleichem did precisely what Yerushalmi thought to be impossible: he recast the historical predicament of the modern Jew into the language of fatalism and faith. In Tevye's eyes, the current manifestations of political reaction are an almost exact replay of two well-known biblical chapters, Lekh-lekho and Balak, the one about Abraham being sent forth from the Land, the other about the Amalekites trying to curse and destroy Israel. "I know that the way things are done in this world, and the way they have always been," he says, "Genesis comes before Exodus, but in this case the Amalekites came first. And I suggest you listen to the lesson they taught me, because it may come in useful some day" (p. 120).

Tevye was indeed Sholem Aleichem's most useful historical fiction, partly by literary design, partly by historical accident. For Sholem Aleichem died before he could decide whether Tevye literally talked his way out of being expelled from the village, or whether he and his reconstituted family (Chava having returned to the fold in the eleventh hour) were sent packing, with their final destination left open. Sholem Aleichem's death, in turn, coincided with the redrawing of the map of Europe. Tevye's world was no more. The East European Jewish past was dead. Long may it live! Each successive generation of Tevye's offspring was now free to decide what piece of it was still relevant; what, if anything, could serve as a myth of origins. This is how Tevye was reborn again and yet again: in Maurice Schwartz's Yiddish Art Theater production of 1919 and later film version of 1939; in the 1957 production of "Tevye and His Daughters"; in the Broadway musical and later film version of "Fiddler on the Roof"; in the Israeli film version of 1967; and in the Ukrainian-language production of "Fiddler" in 1989. Tevye was so eminently usable that each production could pick and choose among his misadventures for the ones that fit best (Israelis, for instance, could delight in the get-rich scheme of Tevye's relative Menakhem-Mendl), and each ended with the family setting out for a different destination: Baltimore, Israel, and even, in the Ukrainian version, nearby Berdichev. Meanwhile, for American Jews, the whole of Eastern Europe had been turned into a single *lieu de mémoire*, or memory-site, called a "shtetl," and so the Broadway musical moved Tevye out of his glorious isolation in the village into the nearby town of Anatevke, thereby turning Tevye into a man for all sentimental seasons.[23]

For some, the Tevye of history became part of a new covenantal narrative of shtetl-pogrom-and-flight-to-freedom. For others, his historical particularity was brought back to life thanks to new ways of mediating the past. A new translation of the Yiddish original, such as the one I have been quoting from, by Hillel Halkin, restored to Tevye's folkspeech some of its Judaic literacy. The restoration of Maurice Schwartz's 1939 film by the National Center for Jewish Film allowed audiences familiar only with Zero Mostel and Topol to see a radically recontextualized Tevye on the videoscreen. Meanwhile, thanks to scholars working behind the scenes to unravel the textual history of the novel and the Americanization of its central protagonist, David Roskies can add his own voice to the *Mikra'ot gedolot* of modern Jewish culture.[24]

Just as Sholem Aleichem became a household presence on both sides of the Atlantic, so the institution of literature, and its ancillary branches of journalism, drama, criticism, and translation, brought multiple and competing pasthoods into every Jewish home, even the extremely ascetic home of Rabbi Pinchas Menachem Singer of 10/12 Krochmalna Street in Warsaw, where Yiddish newspapers apparently did not penetrate until World War I. To be sure, not every branch of literature was equally hospitable to explorations of the distant, severed, past. Some genres—the historical novel, the family saga, the epic poem, the ballad, tragedy, the creative anthology—were ideally suited for this purpose, while others, like the short story, the lyric, the monologue, the reportage, were not. Autobiography gained prominence in Jewish culture precisely when the immediate past seemed in danger of disappearing, due to wars, immigration, or emancipation. Some *isms* were more past-friendly than others. Realism, romanticism, and more recently, magic realism, were obvious candidates. Symbolism and expressionism encouraged a revival of interest in myth, symbol, underground traditions, and premodern literary forms. Writers of a naturalist bent, in contrast, gave primacy to the present in all its social density, while literary impressionists were partial to passive heroes and heroines flitting in and out of drawing rooms.

Some institutions were more rooted in the past than others. The traditional heder more than the modern secular school. The Zionist school more than the socialist school. The landsmanshaft more than the labor union. The art theater more than Vaudeville. WEVD ("the station that speaks your language") more than WNBC. (See chapters 7 and 8.)

Some political cultures stimulated literary-historical activity more than others. To follow the peregrinations of Jewish writers from one country to another is to follow the byways of collective memory and collective amnesia. While still living in Poland, a place of fiercely competing and exclusionary nationalisms, Isaac Bashevis Singer (1904–1991) boned up on Polish-Jewish history in preparation for writing his brilliant first novel, *Satan in Goray* (1933). But once he came to America, and after a feverish few months spent researching a sequel on Jacob Frank in the New York Public Library, Singer fed off personal memory alone, and the only concession he made, late in life, was to ask a young female admirer to send him a map of prewar Poland. Denuding his Yiddish originals of their cultural specifics for the sake of translation was the price Singer was willing to pay for access to the society at large.[25]

Nowhere was the game of historical memory played for such high stakes as in the brave new world of Soviet power. The Yiddish writers who moved back there from Weimar Germany, Poland, Palestine, and the United States were forced to eliminate from their work all vestiges of petit bourgeois nationalism. Even such innocent words as *goy* and *sheygets* were expunged. It was easy enough for the Soviet regime to obliterate all collective memories and unassimilable pasts. Abolish all independent Jewish institutions, and the DNA of Jewish memory was destroyed as well. What remained was a deracinated, proletarian folk culture, Yiddish in form, socialist in content.[26] Conversely, no sooner did the evil empire collapse than the amoeba cells of Jewish memory began to re-form, ever so slowly.

Kiev 1989. I am teaching a group of native-born, Yiddish-educated Soviet pensioners. We are reading I. L. Peretz's neo-folktale, "The Conjuror," in the Yiddish original, a story about a magician who comes to town on the eve of Passover. When his true identity is revealed and a seder is literally conjured up at story's end, the students look at me with blank stares. No one has ever heard of Eliyohu hanovi (Elijah the Prophet), and only one elderly woman can explain to her classmates that *novi* has something to do with the *profet* of the Old Testament. But the youngest student in class does know what a seder is, having played in a recent revival of Sholem Aleichem's "It's Hard to Be a Jew," which ends with the tsarist police disrupting a family seder . . . in Kiev. Little could Sholem Aleichem have imagined that his works would someday embody the entire retrievable past of Russian-Ukrainian Jewry.

In Eastern Europe, Jewish historians themselves, not just their subjects, were in the direct line of fire: S. Ansky crisscrossing the Eastern war zone in World War I; Eliyohu Tcherikower in a Kiev torn by civil war; Emanuel Ringelblum, Rabbi Shimon Huberband, Rachel Auerbach and the whole Oyneg Shabes archive in Nazi-occupied Warsaw—all of them laboring day in, day out to record and to rescue every scrap of paper so that the world would at least know what the Jews had suffered. Following Ansky's example, they saw it as their task to supply both the facts and the meaning of the facts. Huberband not only compiled a fact sheet of Jewish martyrdom; he redefined the meaning of Kiddush Hashem in the light of the Final Solution. Rachel Auerbach not only documented the social history of Warsaw Jews in extremis; she composed a secular liturgy to commemorate the six weeks during which they were erased from the earth. And, most famously of all, the dean of Russian-Jewish historians, Simon Dubnov, went to his death enjoining the Jews of Riga to record, record, record. The amount of writing that survived the Nazi Holocaust was directly proportional to the vision and archival skills of professional and lay historians. (See chapter 2.)

A Free Market of Pasthoods

We are nearing the end of my revolutionary parable about loss and renewal, about loss as the *precondition* of renewal. Its heroes—the purveyors of Jewish memory—are the surveyors of a new Jewish life. If anything, the services of these writers and scholars are in ever greater demand. For all of Jewry is now divided along ideological lines, and each ideology has carved out a different piece of the past. Reform Judaism lays claim to the biblical, archeological past, the seat of the Judeo-Christian heritage. Conservative Judaism lays claim to the early rabbinic period, when the rabbis replaced the prophets and priests, when the law and the liturgy replaced the biblical cult, and when Hellenism coexisted peacefully with Rabbinism in ancient Palestine. Modern Orthodoxy lays claim to the Middle Ages, when Halachah reigned supreme and the Rambam (Moses Maimonides) labored valiantly for legal hegemony and philosophical complexity. Hasidism and right-wing Orthodoxy lay claim to Jewish Eastern Europe. Reconstructionism lays claim to modernity, particularly as played out in America. Non-Jewish Jews, meanwhile, who affiliate mostly with universities, lay claim to Freud, Kafka, and Walter Benjamin, and support pilgrimages to Vienna, Prague, and Berlin. The latest *ism*, feminism, lays claim to a heretofore totally neglected past, the wholesale revision of which is something to behold.

Here is *Bat Mitzvah*, a handbook for "Jewish Girls Coming of Age," published in 1995.[27] Part One contains the entire usable feminist Jewish past in capsule form, beginning with Judith Kaplan's bat mitzvah in early May 1922 and working backwards in time. "What had been the role of the Jewish woman for thousands of years was changing," claims the author as she brings the story back to modern times.

> And the few who had set precedents in the centuries before, like Bruriah, and Doña Gracia, and Sarra Coppio Sullam, were being joined by many others. More and more women pushed to be heard through their writings, their action, their perseverance, abilities, and creativity. (p. 36)

Such a statement would have been unthinkable even a decade ago, not only because the enfranchised Jewish woman had not yet become fully mainstreamed, but because the Bruriahs, Doña Gracias, and Sarra Sullams had not yet been recovered.

The end result of the multiple revolutions in Jewish consciousness that we have been following is that Jews do not want to share the same past anymore. Every denomination has carved out a different piece of it, and thank God, there's enough to go around. Only when one or more groups lay claim to the same past does it start getting dicey. The Holocaust is an obvious case in point, because within Judaism, destruction is always fraught with covenantal meaning. I have attended any number of scholarly colloquia on the Holocaust that ended with the lecturer at the podium engaged in a shouting match with the Holocaust survivors in the audience. For the historian, the Holocaust is a segregated past. For the survivor, it is everything. More recently, with the collapse of communism, Poland has become a hotly contested Jewish memory-site. While some hasidic groups have rebuilt the holy graves of their zaddikim, thus essentially denying that the Holocaust ever happened, the Jewish educational establishment has organized mass pilgrimages to the Polish death camps, with Auschwitz, Treblinka, and Majdanek marking out the Stations of the Cross. One member of my own family became observant upon his return from just such a pilgrimage.

And so the revolutions have come full circle. No longer is Judaism an ideological bulwark against the vagaries of history. History has become the ideological foundation for various offshoots of Judaism. At the threshold of a new millennium, the institutional base of Jewish memory has shifted back from the secular to the sacred realm.

2 The Library of
Jewish Catastrophe

> Tear down their altars, smash their pillars, put their sacred posts to the fire,
> and cut down the images of their gods, obliterating their name from that
> site. Do not worship the LORD your God in like manner.
>
> —Deut. 12:3–4

In the Jewish experience of the twentieth century, one cycle of violence
rapidly gave way to another: the Kishinev pogrom of 1903 that ushered
in the century with more deaths (49) than all the previous pogroms combined; World War I, where untold numbers of civilians were murdered,
robbed and deported along the Eastern Front; the Civil War in the Ukraine
which claimed between 60,000 and 250,000 civilian Jewish lives, and the
Holocaust. The immediate problem facing the survivors of these catastrophes was not how to mourn but simply how to preserve a record of the
unfolding disaster. For it was now possible for the modern nation-state to
wipe out entire populations and hide the fact. Something that the Rabbis
could never have anticipated had been added to the landscape of Jewish
catastrophe: that the state would control all lines of communication as well
as the lives of all its citizens. Whereas once, in Hadrianic times, the Rabbis
had coined the phrase *bishᶜat hashemad* to designate a time of religious
persecution, one could now speak of a new category, *bishᶜat hahashmada*,
"in times of mass extermination."[1] Whereas *bishᶜat hashemad* the Rabbis
had enjoined the masses to perform Kiddush Hashem, to sanctify God's
Name in acts of martyrdom, now, in a time of mass extermination, the
latter-day rabbis enjoined the masses to preserve every scrap of evidence;
to consider these documents as if they were *sheymes*—sacred fragments
that bore the *shem* or Name of God.[2]

I wish to illustrate how painstaking and courageous was the making of a
new literature of destruction.[3] The first chapter was written in the wake of
the Kishinev pogrom, when Jews in London and New York staged mass
rallies in support of the victims and to denounce the tsar, and when members of the ad hoc Hebrew Writers' Union of Odessa called on their fellow
Jews (in Hebrew) to mobilize Jewish self-defense units throughout Russia:

Brothers! The blood of our brethren in Kishinev cries out to us! Shake off the dust and become men! Stop weeping and pleading, stop lifting your hands for salvation to those who hate and exclude you! Look to your own hands for rescue![4]

This group of Hebrew writers dispatched one of their number, thirty-year-old poet Hayyim Nahman Bialik, to collect eyewitness accounts from the survivors. While Bialik returned from Kishinev with several notebooks worth of survivor testimony that remained unexploited, his pogrom poem, "In the City of Slaughter," transformed the way modern Jews perceived catastrophe. Published under the code name "The Oracle at Nemirov," as if it were recounting the seventeenth-century Cossack revolt, Bialik's epic poem dethroned the Jewish God of History and vilified the survivors for their passivity.[5] Forty years later, in the ghettos of Warsaw, Vilna, and Lodz, Bialik's poem would be constantly cited to measure the distance from pogrom to Final Solution.[6] Thus, on the third day of the Great Deportation, which marked the beginning of the end in the Warsaw ghetto, diarist Abraham Lewin would link Kishinev to Warsaw with this famous line: "The sun is shining, the acacia is blooming, and the slaughterer is slaughtering."[7]

A discrete and brutal event, Kishinev became an international *cause célèbre* that gave rise to new forms of political action and poetic response. Then came the first total war in history. The war had barely begun when three leading Jewish intellectuals in Warsaw—I. L. Peretz, Jacob Dinezon, and S. Ansky—issued this appeal to their fellow Jews:[8]

Woe to the people whose history is written by strange hands and whose own writers have nothing left but to compose songs of lament, prayers and dirges after the fact.

Therefore, we turn to our people that is now and evermore being dragged into the global maelstrom, to all members of our people, men and women, young and old, who live and suffer and see and hear, with the following appeal:

BECOME HISTORIANS YOURSELVES! DON'T DEPEND ON THE HANDS OF STRANGERS!

Record, take it down, and collect!

All relevant documents and photographs were to be mailed—C. O. D., if necessary—to the Jewish Ethnographic Society in Petrograd.

Though it was early in the war, it was already too late, for in July 1915 the tsarist government closed down the entire Jewish-language press, imposed strict censorship on all news from the war front, and banned the use of the Hebrew alphabet in the mails. It was left to Ansky himself to launch a one-man rescue operation to save the lives, livelihoods, letters, and legends of Jews victimized by the war.

Ansky's four-volume chronicle of the war was the second major contribution to the modern Library of Jewish Catastrophe. Titled *Khurbm Galitsye* (The destruction of Galicia), its subtitle defined the geographic, temporal, and generic scope of this extraordinary document: *The Jewish Catastrophe in Poland, Galicia and Bukovina, from a Diary, 1914–1917*. In marked contrast to the celebrated European war memoirs and semifictional novels that were to appear, from Henri Barbusse's *Le feu* to Erich Maria Remarque's *All Quiet on the Western Front* to Jaroslav Hašek's *The Good Soldier Schweik*, Ansky used his personal experience to document the fate of an entire collective. Having traveled widely before the war through the backwoods of Volhynia and Podolia on a celebrated ethnographic expedition, he possessed intimate knowledge of Jewish folkways and foibles. As a Russian socialist-revolutionary and one-time Narodnik (populist), he had access to the minds and inner reaches of the Russian military command. As a poet, playwright, and journalist, his "diary" would be a literary document in its own right.[9]

Ansky redefined the Literature of Destruction both vertically and horizontally, viz. both in relation to what had come before in Jewish culture and what European gentile survivors and chroniclers of the Great War were doing in their respective languages. No more would Jewish writers be satisfied with composing "songs of lament, prayers and dirges after the fact." Henceforth the Literature of Destruction would draw on eyewitness accounts, would render the concrete and sensual particulars of modern violence, would spare neither victim nor victimizer, and would seek the causality of war, revolution, and pogrom not in heaven but on earth. In contrast to the European and Anglo-American literature of war, however, the modern Jewish texts would continue to present the catastrophe in terms of the ancient archetypes of Akedah, Ḥurban, Kiddush Hashem.[10] (New to the repertory as of 1907 was the crucifixion, now reinterpreted as an icon of Jewish suffering.)[11] Thus, the modern Library of Jewish Catastrophe both grew out of Jewish collective memory and fed back into it. To the ancient and medieval songs of lament, prayers, and dirges were added panoramic chronicles written in the first person but encompassing the fate of the collective.

Ansky represents the new voice of collective memory to emerge from

World War I and a new generation of secular intellectuals with roots in other cultures as well as their own. In the catastrophe that followed, his mantle was assumed by the Russian-Jewish historian Elias Tcherikower. Like Ansky, Tcherikower was an active player in the very events that he would chronicle. Tcherikower, recently returned from America, moved to Kiev at the end of 1918 to assume a central role in the Jewish National Secretariat. But no sooner had the Ukraine proclaimed its independence and no sooner had the Jews been granted national autonomy than civil war erupted, and the Jews were caught between all the warring factions: the Whites, the Reds, the Poles, the Ukrainians. Even as Kiev kept changing hands, Tcherikower organized an archive to collect and research materials on the Ukrainian pogroms. The terse Yiddish circular issued in May 1919 began with an invocation of the *Tokheha*, the Mosaic Curses: "Jews!" it read, "a terrible pogrom-Tokheha has befallen our cities and towns, and the world does not know; we ourselves know nothing or very little about it. [Knowledge of] this must not be suppressed!"[12]

Tcherikower and his staff left several important legacies: three out of a projected seven-volume series of historical monographs on the pogroms, as well as Rokhl Feigenberg's *Chronicle of a Dead Town*, a documentary novel of destruction in which the anatomy of a single pogrom was recreated in excruciating detail. Their most lasting legacy of all, however, was the archive itself—as model and metaphor. For the archive was never safe from the hands of those who wished to see all evidence of this crime destroyed. Copies of every important document were therefore made in triplicate and two of them deposited elsewhere for safekeeping. And a good thing, too, for when the Soviets succeeded in annexing the Ukraine, they made the destruction of the archive a top priority. Tcherikower managed to smuggle the archive out of the Soviet Union and reassembled it in Berlin as the Ostjüdisches Historisches Archiv. When Hitler came to power, Tcherikower divided the archive into two, shipped the lion's share to the YIVO Institute in Vilna, and took the rest with him to Paris. And when the Nazis occupied northern France, Tcherikower fled to the south, abandoning his archive in Paris where, at the end of 1940, it was rescued by the historian and former French Foreign Legionnaire Zosa Szajkowski, who was dropped behind enemy lines by the U.S. Air Force to aid the French resistance. As for the bulk of the archive in Vilna, the Nazis destroyed it in 1942.

The legacy of this archive on the pogroms, then, is nothing less than a redefinition of the law of sheymes: under extreme conditions every scrap of paper becomes sacred.

The sheer scope of historical catastrophe had made the old methods of chronicling obsolete. Besides issuing appeals for all primary sources to be preserved and collected, East European Jewish historians began to generate their own primary sources using the tools of social science. Foremost among them was the analytic questionnaire, first used by I. L. Peretz back in the 1890s when he conducted a statistical expedition through the Tomaszow region of Poland, then perfected by S. Ansky's ethnographic expedition on the eve of World War I. But it was Max Weinreich of the YIVO Institute in Vilna who introduced the latest social scientific methods in order to study the long-range effects of trauma, discrimination, and poverty on Jewish adolescents. (Weinreich even coined the Yiddish term for "adolescent.") Under the YIVO's auspices, Polish-Jewish adolescents began submitting their autobiographies—a new genre for the Jews—for Weinreich and others to examine, while an army of amateur *zamlers*, or collectors, worked the ethnographic and linguistic field on YIVO's behalf.[13] While the Polish government was intent upon eliminating the Jews from all walks of life, the zamlers, students and scholars associated with YIVO came to see self-study as the route to emancipation.

Most research projects had barely gotten off the ground by the time the German tanks rolled into Poland, but the ideology and methodology behind a modern Jewish archive were now firmly in place. It should therefore come as no surprise that within a month of the German invasion, an underground archive, nicknamed for clandestine purposes Oyneg Shabes (Enjoyment of the Sabbath), was already being established in Warsaw.[14] By design of its founder and organizational genius, thirty-nine-year-old Emanuel Ringelblum, the Oyneg Shabes archive was to be a decidedly *modern* library that drew upon the cumulative experience of contemporary East European Jewry. Ringelblum, a YIVO-affiliated scholar, began by choosing for his staff young men and women with prior training in the study of Jewish life; with reliable political (read: Labor Zionist) credentials; and already involved in the life of the collective. Here is how Ringelblum described the hiring process:

> Of the several dozen full-time staff, the great majority were self-educated intellectuals, mostly from proletarian parties. We deliberately refrained from drawing professional journalists into our work, because we did not want it to be sensationalized. Our aim was that the sequence of events in each town, the experiences of each Jew—and during the current war each Jew is a world unto himself—should be conveyed as simply and faithfully as possible. Every redundant word, every literary

gilding or ornamentation grated upon our ears and provoked our anger. Jewish life in wartime is so full of tragedy that it is unnecessary to embellish it with one superfluous line. (p. 389)

Thus Ringelblum also broke with the time-honored practice that favored archetypal embellishment over temporal details, sacred text over historical context. He wanted to let the facts tell their own story. Finally, in contrast to the rabbinic strategy of preserving only one, timeless version of events, Ringelblum went out of his way to gain multiple perspectives—that of young and old, religious and secular—and to cover the entire range of Jewish experience in wartime. "We tried to have the same events described by as many people as possible," he wrote. "By comparing the different accounts, the historian will not find it difficult to reach the kernel of historical truth, the actual course of an event." To this end, the ghetto population was divided up by age, gender, class, religious persuasion, and place of origin; detailed questionnaires were drawn up to cover every conceivable aspect of Jewish life and death; autobiography contests were announced, and amateur field-workers were coopted to work alongside the professionals. The YIVO mandate was being carried out against all odds.[15]

Yet for all its hard-nosed historical positivism, and for all its desire to leave nothing out, Oyneg Shabes's work of recording, compiling and synthesizing the data of Jewish destruction had become, as Chaim Kaplan put it, *melekhet hakodesh*, a sacred task analogous to the building of the Tabernacle. The turning point came with the Great Deportation in the summer of 1942 when 275,000 Jews were shipped off to Treblinka in cattle cars:

> The work of O[yneg] S[habes], along with the whole of our social and economic life, was disrupted. Only a very few comrades kept pen in hand during those tragic days and continued to write about what was happening in Warsaw. But the work was too sacred and too deeply cherished in the hearts of the O[yneg] S[habes] coworkers; the social function of O[yneg] S[habes] too important for the project to be discontinued. We began to reconstruct the period of the Deportation and to collect material on the slaughterhouse of European Jewry— Treblinka. On the basis of reports made by those who returned from various camps in the province, we tried to form a picture of the experiences of Jews in the provincial cities during the time of the deportation. At the moment of writing, the work is proceeding full force. If we only get some breathing space, we will be able to ensure

that no important fact about Jewish life in wartime shall remain hidden from the world. (ibid.)

A life of extremity—there was to be no breathing space—made absolute demands. What's more, those few who survived the Great Deportation had to become both historians and threnodists, had to supply the facts as well as their meaning. Despite their scientific objectives, the chroniclers of the Warsaw ghetto were thrown back to the age-old models of commemoration—to the liturgy. The most dramatic example was Rokhl Auerbach, a staff member of Oyneg Shabes almost from its inception and the one, along with Hirsh Wasser, who dug up part of the archive in 1946.

Like the best of her generation, Rokhl Auerbach was equally at home in Yiddish, Hebrew, and Polish. She had been a close friend of leading Jewish intellectuals and writers, such as Dvora Fogel and Bruno Schulz, and a one-time companion of Yiddish poet Itzik Manger. But both in the ghetto and on the Aryan side of Warsaw she devoted her energies to documenting the catastrophe—in Polish. While Polish, however, was the language most accessible for historical documentation, Yiddish remained the language of collective memory. And so she composed, while in hiding on the Aryan side, and at great personal risk, a Yiddish prose epic of the ghetto's destruction titled "Yizkor, 1943."[16]

What unlocked the memory of those weeks of unsurpassed terror, and what probably enabled her to write in the first place, was the liturgy. From a Jewish woman's perspective, this liturgy began with Hannah's prayer in 1 Samuel and ended in the recitation of *yizkor* four times a year in her grandfather's synagogue back home in Galicia. Here is the penultimate part of her lament:

> Not long ago, I saw a woman in the streetcar, her head thrown back, talking to herself. I thought that she was either drunk or out of her mind. It turned out that she was a mother who had just received the news that her son, who had been rounded up in the street, had been shot.
>
> "My child," she stammered, paying no attention to the other people in the streetcar, "My son. My beautiful, beloved son."
>
> I too would like to talk to myself like one mad or drunk, the way that woman did in the Book of Judges who poured out her heart unto the Lord and whom Eli drove from the Temple.[17]
>
> I may neither groan nor weep. I may not draw attention to myself in the street.

> And I need to groan; I need to weep. Not four times a year. I feel the
> need to say *Yizkor* four times a day. (p. 464)

Here was a secular Jew who had to play all roles at once because she might turn out to be the sole survivor. Warsaw was Jerusalem and she its witness-as-threnodist, composing a new Book of Lamentations. She was the last living member of her family who must name the names of all the dead. She was the witness-as-eyewitness who must conjure up before it is too late the face of a murdered people—young and old, rich and poor, noble and corrupt. The memorial prayer served Auerbach as a measure of how much had changed; of the losses that *had* no possible measure. In lieu of the ancient and medieval dirges recited at fixed times and within a sacred space—hers was a private lament with no fixed addressee. Indeed, she chose not to publish it until twenty years after it was written. Inasmuch as Auerbach perceived the Holocaust to be the culmination of all catastrophes that came before, her memorial had to encompass all the bereaved mothers-daughters-wives-and-lovers who perished along with their men.

That unbelieving Jews would transmit the traditional response to catastrophe—in however dialectical a way—is consistent with the collective ethos of East European Jewry. That the techniques of Jewish collective memory were still viable, even as the whole culture of East European Jewry was being destroyed, testifies to the power of that fusion of sacred and secular. The eyewitness chroniclers of modern Jewish catastrophe—Bialik, Ansky, Tcherikower, Ringelblum, Auerbach, and others—found new and even subversive means to merge the events they witnessed into an ongoing saga. Despite their loss, or lack of faith in a God of History, they revived the archetypal reading of that history.

The efforts of these activist-historians demonstrates that the will to bear witness had to be cultivated. It did not arise in mystical fashion out of the Holocaust and its aftermath. Oyneg Shabes and other archives like it drew on forty years of organized and politicized activity to make the chronicling of events a tool of Jewish self-emancipation. Questionnaires, contests, and collectors made the act of memorializing a grassroots phenomenon. There is likewise no mystery about the amount of documentation that survived. The greater the perceived destruction, the greater the effort to preserve every documentatory scrap. That is precisely why these *sheymes* written *bishʿat hahashmada* deserve special status.

They also help to refute the commonly held belief that an adequate response to the Holocaust could only emerge one generation after the event. A careful reading of the Oyneg Shabes archive, itself but one part of the vast Library of Jewish Catastrophe written during the Nazi occupation, shows that a new archetype of catastrophe emerged even as the events were unfolding. Whatever area of post-Holocaust consciousness one mines— whether historiography, theology, social psychology, literature, the graphic arts, or music—one discovers the core of that new consciousness in the midst of the Nazi terror.

The encyclopedic scope, the way this body of writing combines fact and fiction or modern and traditional forms of Jewish self-expression, makes it comparable to that other great collective document of the Diaspora—the Talmud. Ringelblum is to Oyneg Shabes as Rav Ashi was to the Babylonian Talmud. The ghetto and concentration camp archives, moreover, exist like the Talmud in various recensions. Oyneg Shabes is as distinct from the *Lodz Chronicle* as the diverse holdings of the Zonabend Collection from Lodz are distinct from the Sutzkever-Kazcerginski Collection from Vilna. And the various ghetto archives compiled over a three-four- and even five-year period of occupation are utterly different from *The Scrolls of Auschwitz* written by members of the *Sonderkommando* in between the gassings of whole "transports" in 1943–1944.

Like the Talmud, this literature *of* the Holocaust requires a mental curriculum of languages, history, theology, fiction, folklore, and then some, to master. Many of the relevant documents are still undeciphered and unpublished even in their original languages. As opposed to the writing *on* the Holocaust that will go on being produced for generations to come, these documents composed during the Holocaust are finite and therefore (like the Talmud) constitute a closed canon. Because of their insistence on the knowability of the destruction—that one could, in Ringelblum's words, convey as simply and faithfully as possible, the sequence of events in each town, the experiences of each Jew—they require a separate hermeneutics.

Perhaps they are sacred, too. Sacred in the way that any Torah-related text or seyfer is hallowed by the faithful—who obey a strict hierarchy of what seyfer may be placed on top of another, and if any page is torn out, that sheyme is accorded proper burial. But since they arise out of a secular and revolutionary consciousness that taught Jews to make history by knowing their history, their sanction does not come from God. They derive their authority from the dead whose deeds they chronicle; from those who preserved and buried every scrap of evidence so that the Nazis would not vanquish Jewish memory even as they destroyed the Jews of Europe; and from the living who publish, translate, and teach these memorial texts.

3   Ringelblum's Time Capsules

If we only get some breathing space, we will be able to ensure that no important fact about Jewish life in wartime shall remain hidden from the world.

—Emanuel Ringelblum, January 1943

These are the truths I hold to be self-evident:

There exists a closed canon of wartime writings that testifies to the historical reality of what later came to be known as "The Holocaust."

This literature *of* the Holocaust, written primarily in Yiddish, Polish, and German, but also in Hebrew, French, Russian, Italian, and other continental languages, is distinct from the literature *on* the Holocaust, which will go on being written for generations to come, primarily in English and Hebrew, but also in all the languages of Europe and of the Slavic countries recently liberated from bondage. In each of these languages, moreover, the meaning of the Holocaust will increasingly be shaped not so much by the record of past events as by changing forms of literary expression, the *Zeitgeist*, and the political reality on the ground.[1]

For the time being and for the foreseeable future the primary responsibility of scholars and teachers of the Holocaust is to those who were murdered. As moral compensation for the indignity visited upon them when they lived, we must approach their surviving literary remains with special historical precision.

I call this approach to the destruction of European Jewry *landkentenish*, familiarity with the landscape, and take as my guide the thirty-three-year-old historian Emanuel Ringelblum, who, as editor of a journal by that name, went on to become the cartographer of a tiny piece of Jewish real estate in the heart of Warsaw, in the General Government of Poland.[2] Of particular interest are the claims made by Ringelblum himself as to the historical veracity of the six thousand documents that he and his hand-picked staff of chroniclers, statisticians, ethnographers, and social scientists would ultimately collect, copy, and bury underground. Inside the ten tin boxes and two milk canisters to be unearthed after the war by the sole surviving members of the Ringelblum Archive, code name "Oyneg Shabes," would be eyewitness accounts and diaries; letters and postcards; sermons and songs; epic and lyric poems; novels, short stories, and plays; essays, questionnaires, and autobiographies; and an almost complete set of the Jewish underground press. Consistent with Ringelblum's scholarly agenda and the literary conventions of the given medium, each individual item offers a different perspective on Jewish life in wartime. Each makes a different truth claim, based on its different placement at the intersection of Jewish tradition and European culture. Thus, if *kentenish* of the *land* was a prerequisite for chronicling the life and death of European Jewry, then those who study these writings today must also be schooled accordingly. This essay lays out part of the mental curriculum required to properly decipher and evaluate the documents found in Ringelblum's time capsules.[3]

The Function of Social Realism

Most accessible are the songs. These were the first to be collected, edited, published, and performed. Much is currently being learned about the provenance of ghetto songs in particular, and the interplay of language, melody, and lyrics.[4] Most neglected is the one literary genre that seems in retrospect to have been the most prevalent inside the Nazi-occupied ghettos, and later, in some of the death camps: the reportage, or journalistic sketch. Part memoir, part eyewitness account, and part fiction, the reportage derived its authority from its real or implied narrator.[5] This is what Solomon Rabinovitsh discovered when he fashioned the all-knowing and irrepressible "Sholem Aleichem," Mr. How-Do-You-Do, to narrate his satires and travelogues back in the 1880s and 1890s. Alternatively, I. L. Peretz grounded his own "Impressions of a Journey through the Tomaszow Region" (1891) within the tormented psyche of a citified traveler.[6] For Yiddish readers, there was no felt contradiction between a subjective point of view, an intimate narrative voice, and strict adherence to observable reality. If songs were the form of self-expression that traveled best, the reportage was the preferred vehicle of the Truth mediated through the presence of a trustworthy witness.

In both the Lodz and Warsaw ghettos, there lived a writer whose reportages encompassed the whole epoch, from before the establishment of the ghetto until the eve of its liquidation, and its whole social panorama, from the typhus-ridden tenements to the upper echelons of the Judenrat. Both men kept writing as if under deadline, covering the length and breadth of their respective ghettos; and this despite the fact that they never saw a single one of these pieces published. In Lodz, it was Yozef Zelkowicz (1897–1944), whose voluminous writings have yet to be collected, but whose excruciatingly detailed chronicle of the mass deportations, *In yene kosh-marne teg* (In those nightmarish days), is unsurpassed.[7]

In Warsaw, the major practitioner of the genre was Peretz Opoczynski (1895–1943). Among the first whom Ringelblum handpicked to staff the underground Oyneg Shabes Archive, Opoczynski was valued both for his politics (as a lifelong Labor Zionist) and his prewar accounts of Polish-Jewish poverty and spiritual decline. The latter distinguished Opoczynski from the yellow sheet journalists whom Ringelblum categorically excluded from his inner circle. During wartime especially, when each Jew was "a world unto himself" and Jewish life was "so full of tragedy," Ringelblum instructed his staff to avoid "every redundant word, every literary gilding or ornamentation" and to replicate the sequence of events "as simply and faithfully as possible."[8] And so it was that Opoczynski, an engagé writer whom Ringelblum trusted implicitly, produced what is probably the major corpus of Yiddish reportages in the Warsaw ghetto.[9]

The courtyard on 21 Wołynska Street where he lived served as Opoczynski's microcosm of the ghetto.[10] Among its seven hundred tenants crammed into fewer than one hundred apartments, he found a ready-made cross-section of professions and personalities whose changing fortunes he followed from the outbreak of the war through a two-year period. As in the ghetto itself, there were powerful forces pulling away from the center, militating against solidarity: the chance to flee eastward across the new Soviet border; hunger, disease, death, corruption, and a unique form of oppression called the *paruvke*, which could hit at any time.

No sooner do they hear the dreaded call *Paruvke!* than the women of the courtyard try to gather up their bedding and carry it to safety to the nearest building. But the Polish police, the so-called Blue Boys, have already blocked off all the exits and the disinfection is on; this, despite the doctor's thorough-going inspection the day before and despite the bribe money collected by the tenement committee. Only the wealthy can buy their way out now. As for the rest, all of them, including the children, are led away to the public bath on Spokojna Street, to the "slaughterhouse," as everyone calls it. There follows a detailed description, complete with dialogue, of the long wait outside the bathhouse, of the beatings on the inside, the brutal shaving of all one's hair, including that of women and pious men, the medical inspection, and finally the hot bath itself. At two in the morning they return home, hungry, tired, and depressed, to a wet, fumigated apartment stripped of its bedding. Even so, there's a joke for the occasion. *Lekhayim!* shouts one Jew to another. "We've been kashered and rendered pure. So where's the challah and the fish?" (p. 422).

On the one hand, Opoczynski remains scrupulously true to the facts, due to his prior journalistic training and to the stern eye of Emanuel Ringelblum. Names, dates, and statistics are supplied wherever possible. On the other hand, Opoczynski's ideological-artistic slant is everywhere apparent, especially in his enthusiasm for the people's adaptability to suffering. Note that the whole episode of the paruvke decree ends with a self-deprecating joke.

One of Opoczynski's better-known reportages (based on first-hand experience) follows the fortunes of "The Jewish Letter Carrier." Initially welcomed by the ghetto population as the first in Poland's history, he must eventually bear witness to the people's despair. The opening paragraph resembles nothing so much as a story of Sholem Aleichem:[11]

> A yidisher potshar? Ay, gezunt zolt ir mir zayn. Zogt nor, tsu vemen darft ir, vemen zukht ir, mir veln shoyn alts vayzn, ir vet nisht lang darfn zukhn. Ir zet, yidn, mir hobn shoyn mit mazl a yidishn potshar, take vi in Palestine.

> A Jewish mailman? Oh, I can't believe my eyes! Tell me, who are you looking for? at what address? We'll show you, you won't have to waste time looking. Jews, will you get a load of this: we've got a Jewish mailman, just exactly as if we were in Palestine!

This ironic sense of living "in Palestine" pervades the writings of many ghetto chroniclers, most notably those of Chaim Kaplan, though for him the analogy is always sardonic. In contrast, by invoking the Sholem-Aleichem-type monologue, Opoczynski conjures up a shtetl-like environment where Jews are all on intimate terms with one another; and this model of solidarity, in turn, becomes the foil for unmasking the *shmendrikes*, the self-hating assimilationist Jews, the corruption, and the apathy that take hold of the ghetto population. Thanks to the modern Yiddish classics that he knew so well, Opoczynski has a ready-made model of the shtetl as collective hero, especially in time of crisis. This he exploits most brilliantly, I think, in his reportage "Smuggling in the Warsaw Ghetto."[12] Here the implicit model of Kozia Alley with its strict hierarchy of smugglers, middlemen, porters, and guards, who support "tens of thousands of Jews who even with money in their pocket would die of hunger if the alley did not serve as their granary" is not Sholem Aleichem's Kasrilevke but Sholem Asch's famous Kola Street. Yiddish literature's longstanding romance with the Jewish gangster, or *ba'al-guf*, as he is called, represents a well thought-out ideological position. Whereas both Zionist Chaim Kaplan and the ghetto's Bundist leadership considered the smugglers to be scum of the earth, Ringelblum and his staff saw in them proof of Jewish vitality and adaptability.[13]

The keen sense of Polish-Jewish social reality, complete with the argot and lexicon unique to each neighborhood and social grouping; the view of group behavior as being of paramount importance, offset by deep divisions along class and ideological lines; the blurring of boundaries between journalism and fiction—all this harkens back to earlier developments in Yiddish narrative prose, especially in Poland between the two world wars. The corpus of Yiddish belles lettres contained in the Oyneg Shabes Archive resonates not only with the writings of Sholem Aleichem, Peretz, and Asch, but also and particularly with the social realistic prose fiction of Polish-Yiddish novelists I. M. Weissenberg, Oyzer Warshawski, M. Bursztyn, and Shimon Horonczyk, whose legacy lived on without them, not to speak of those, like Israel Rabon, Yehoshue Perle, and Peretz Opoczynski, who continued to write under Nazi domination. At a cultural program for young people held in the Warsaw ghetto to honor the memory of I. M. Weissenberg (1881–1938), the writer was eulogized by the educator Abraham Lewin as the Yiddish Gorky.[14] As the last chapter of Yiddish social realism on Polish soil, ghetto writings enjoy no special status. But while ghetto writings are continuous with the dominant literary modes that directly preceded them, postwar Yiddish prose moves away from the dense social reality of the Nazi ghettos toward a metahistorical perspective as it addresses itself to an audience that cannot be expected to know where the General Government ended and Wartheland began; or even, for that matter, how Trawniki differed from Treblinka.[15]

The Function of Time

In his best reportages, Opoczynski provided both a microcosmic view of the ghetto's social organism and a chronological overview of how this part-for-the-whole (be it the courtyard, the mail delivery, the gang of smugglers) was transformed over a long stretch of time. That ability to *recapitulate* the changes that occurred over two, three, and four years of Nazi occupation, and to measure the pace of change, was precisely the task that Ringelblum had set for his collaborative effort. "What a quantum leap from the pre-Deportation shop to that which came after!" he wrote in his retrospective essay. "The same is true of smuggling, and of social and cultural life; even the clothes Jews wore were different in the different periods. O[yneg] S[habes] therefore tried to grasp an event at the moment it happened, since each day was like decades in an earlier time" (p. 391). Few, if any, were the postwar writers who could conjure up these differences after the fact. During the war, however, ghetto chroniclers took careful note of every significant change, each a potential sign of salvation or apocalypse.

The sense of *duration* is likewise an aspect of time that is virtually irretrievable after the war. As Marian Turski points out, we do not need ghetto diaries to provide us with data on food rations. We can get this data elsewhere. But nowhere else do we get such an individuated sense of time, of the day-to-day response to deprivation and starvation.[16] Turski speaks of Lodz. In the Warsaw ghetto he might have cited Leyb Goldin (1906–1942) and his semifictional "Chronicle of a Single Day," the entire plot of which is this: Before the Daily Bowl of Soup, During the Soup, and After the Soup. Acknowledging that he is not the first writer to render the malleable and evanescent quality of time, with Thomas Mann's *The Magic Mountain* as the towering precedent, Goldin's narrator protests his own predicament:[17]

> The war has been going on for a full two years, and you've eaten
> nothing but soup for some four months, and those few months are
> thousands and thousands of times longer for you than the whole of the
> previous twenty months—no, longer than your whole life until now.
> (p. 427)

Everything in this remarkable piece of psychological fiction hinges on the bowl of soup that "Arke" is to receive at twenty minutes to one.

To provide the full flavor of that bowl of soup, Goldin draws numerous analogies between time present and time past. Pre-ghetto time was so rich with possibilities: it was a time of love and great literature; of struggling for the betterment of the masses; even of suicide, which, in retrospect, seems like such a luxury, whereas at the center of ghetto time there lies only the horribly uneven split between Arke the Intellectual and his stomach.

> Who's talking to you in this way? You are two people, Arke. It's a lie.
> A pose. Don't be so conceited. That kind of a split was all right at one
> time when one was full. *Then* one could say, "Two people are battling
> in me," and one would make a dramatic, martyred face.
> Yet, this kind of thing can be found quite often in literature. But
> today? Don't talk nonsense—it's you and your stomach. It's your

stomach and you. It's 90 percent your stomach and a little bit you.
(p. 425)

Even allowing that the recent past was a time of personal suffering, it still could not compare with today. Because "all sicknesses are *human*, and some even make a human being of the patient. Make him nobler. While hunger is a bestial, a wild, a rawly primitive—yes, a bestial thing." Goldin's narrator is an intellectual (like Peretz, whose name is invoked in the epigraph), because only such a one can anatomize a single day's worth of hunger and arrive at a new measurement of time.

Time can be measured either as continuum or break. When, at some point, the function of time is neither to recapitulate nor to render the unbearable duration but to *signal the moment of truth*, analogies break down and a new awareness is born.

Toward the end of his chronicle, after consuming not one but two bowls of soup, Goldin's narrator compares the ghetto to a zoo. "Each day the profiles of our children, of our wives, acquire the mourning look of foxes, dingoes, kangaroos. Our howls are like the cry of jackals." "But we are not animals," he is forced to admit. "We operate on our infants. It may be pointless or even criminal. But animals do not operate on their young!" (p. 434). Thus a mitigating truth could still be wrested from the zoo-like existence of the ghetto early on in the Nazi occupation.

But even this is not the last word—because Arke's internal monologue is cyclical: it ends where it began, with the same bits and snippets of apocalyptic news from the official news service (probably the *Gazeta Żydowska*, published in Cracow), and with the constant, gnawing hunger. The date is only August 1941, and the apocalypse is yet to come.

Wartime writings show us (almost uniquely) how the time of terror took on flesh and blood.[18] Each month reveals a new and terrible truth; each date carries some portentous meaning—provided one knows how to tell Holocaust time. (A significant number of wartime poems and prose works carry specific dates.) After the Great Deportation—the first major caesura in the life of the Warsaw ghetto—Opoczynski could not possibly have written his upbeat portrait of ghetto smugglers; or if he did, he certainly would not have credited them with sustaining the lives of so many ghetto Jews.

Only in diaries and in the works of those writers who continued to hold a pen in their hands can we glimpse the exact moment when the Truth was revealed to them: that the German plan was to erase the name of Jew from the world of the living. This is *bifurcated time,* time cut in half, time-before and time-after; the basic demarcation of time in the literature of the Holocaust.

For some it happens sooner; for others, later. The moment of truth was different in each ghetto and for each individual. For diarist Chaim Kaplan the moment of truth came with the final liquidation of the Lublin ghetto in March 1942. If "Jewish Lublin, a city of sages and authors, a center of Torah and piety" could be "completely and utterly destroyed," then it would surely happen, sooner or later, to Warsaw (entry for April 17, 1942). Diarist Abraham Lewin signaled the bifurcation of time by switching from Yiddish to Hebrew the moment the Deportation began. For the novelist Yehoshue Perle, the destruction of Warsaw's Jewish proletariat, with the active collaboration of the Jewish police, marked the end of all hope and all self-delusion.

The sum of these individual "moments of truth" add up to a new archetype of destruction.

The Function of Moral Criticism

It began erev Tisha b'Av and ended on Yom Kippur: *di oyszidlung,* the Great Deportation. First the Germans demanded that six thousand Jews be delivered to the Umschlagplatz each day, then ten thousand a day. Adam Czerniakow, head of the Judenrat, took his own life rather than sign away the lives of the children—the children, the only hope of regeneration. Dr. Janusz Korczak went to his death leading all the children of his orphanage behind him. At the end of July, the Heḥalutz Youth Movement organized the first combat unit. At the end of August most of the ghetto shops were closed down, thus dooming the dream that productivity would guarantee survival. The first couriers sent by the Bund and the Zionists returned from Treblinka and confirmed the rumors about the final destination of the cattle cars. At the same time, Israel Lichtenstein and a few assistants buried the first part of the Oyneg Shabes Archive in the basement of the soup kitchen for children at 68 Nowolipki Street.

The work of the Oyneg Shabes was temporarily interrupted, as some three hundred thousand of Warsaw's Jews were shipped off to their death in Treblinka. The only task that remained for the surviving members of the Oyneg Shabes staff was to chronicle the Great Deportation. "Only a very few comrades kept pen in hand during those tragic days and continued to write about what was happening in Warsaw," Ringelblum recalls. Nevertheless,

we began to reconstruct the period of the Deportation and to collect
material on the slaughterhouse of European Jewry—Treblinka. On the
basis of reports made by those who returned from various camps in
the province, we tried to form a picture of the experiences of Jews in
the provincial cities during the time of the deportation. At the moment
of writing, the work is proceeding full force. If we only get some
breathing space, we will be able to ensure that no important fact about
Jewish life in wartime shall remain hidden from the world. (p. 389).

Among the first to take pen in hand to describe *Geyrush Varshe*, the
Expulsion of Jewish Warsaw, was Yehoshue Perle (1888–1944). He began
writing his chronicle in the very midst of the daily roundups, in the brief
respite from August 27 to September 5, 1942, and completed it three weeks
later, having changed the title to *Khurbm Varshe*, indicating that the destruction was as great as that of the Jerusalem Temple.[19]

Even as Perle tries to give things a name, to define the terminology of
mass murder (*iberzidlung*, Umschlagplatz, *aktsye*, shops, numbers), and to
place events in chronological order, beginning with the execution of fifty-
four ghetto Jews back in mid-April, he admits to the limits of his own moral
imagination:

> Of Hitler, of this antediluvian beast, it is possible to believe anything.
> The sadistic methods that he employs surpass all human understanding.
> No criminal, no matter how great, would ever come up with such
> bloodthirsty, sophisticated means. . . . (p. 103)

> They [the Jewish Police] dragged their tortured victims up from
> underground and down from the sky; from all the cellars, from all the
> holes, from all the chimneys. They performed their duty with such zeal,
> with such self-sacrifice [*mesires-nefesh*] that it is simply impossible to
> comprehend what kind of wild dybbuk these youngsters were possessed
> by. (p. 125)

The mind latches on to countervailing acts of "true" self-sacrifice, such
as the orderly procession of Janusz Korczak and his children, which Perle
describes in vivid detail, but these only strengthen the chronicler's final
indictment, his sense of utter self-betrayal.

This, more than any single work of the Oyneg Shabes Archive published
after the war, shocked the surviving Yiddish world and provoked an extremely aggressive polemic on the part of the historian Ber Mark.[20] It was
bad enough that Mark sullied the good name of one of interwar Poland's

most popular novelists. Worse yet, he ascribed the following denunciation to Perle's own hand:

> 3 mol hundert toyznt mentshn hobn nisht gehat dem mut tsu zogn 'neyn.' Yeder eyner hot gevolt rateven nor zikh. Afile an eygenem tatn hot men makriv geven, an eygene mame, an eygn vayb un eygene kinder.

> Three times 100,000 people lacked the courage to say: NO. Each one of them was out to save his own skin. Each one was ready to sacrifice even his own father, his own mother, his own wife and children. (p. 140)

Today there can no longer be any doubt that Yehoshue Perle actually penned this terrible indictment of his own people, not only because Mark answered his critics by producing facsimiles of the manuscript, but also because today we understand the authentic core of writings from the Holocaust much better than we did forty to fifty years ago.

Perhaps nothing distinguishes more clearly the authentic core of Holocaust writing from that which came later than the degree of moral criticism. Most of the anger prior to the Liberation is directed inward. This may be because, as Turski reminds us, extreme conditions polarize behavior: debasement on the one hand, saintliness on the other. Or it may be, as Ruth R. Wisse has repeatedly written, that the more Jews come under attack from without, the more they turn that aggression inward. Ringelblum, moreover, specifically instructed his staff to write *as if the war were already over*, not to fear retribution from those in power because the indictment would not be read until everyone in question was either living in freedom or already dead.[21] Hence, the profound antipathy of Oyneg Shabes writers for the Judenrat. Hence, before calling down a heavenly fire to destroy the entire German nation in the final canto of his *Song of the Murdered Jewish People*, Yitskhak Katzenelson excoriates their Jewish lackeys—the police— who disgraced the Star of David and the name of Jew (Canto III).

So scathing are these documents that their postwar publication is often marred by censorship or is placed under a ban. Katzenelson's *Vittel Diary*, which names the names of his political opponents, the Bundists Boruch Shefner, Shloyme Mendelson, and even the Yiddish lyric poet Itzik Manger, all of whom were living in safety outside the war zone, was not published in full until 1988. In 1987, Gerer Hasidim in Brooklyn bought up and burned copies of the English translation of Shimon Huberband's *Kiddush Hashem: Jewish Religious and Cultural Life in Poland during the Holocaust* because Huberband, a trusted member of the Oyneg

Shabes, documents the moral laxity of young Gerer Hasidim in the Warsaw ghetto. After the war, the tendency is for all the Jewish victims to be viewed as martyrs. Henceforth what is probed is the moral behavior of the murderers, their willing collaborators, the bystanders, and the survivors.[22]

"Number 4580" (written in December 1942) is Perle's exposé of how the ghetto turns the survivor of the Great Deportation into a faceless, history-less number.[23] All human activities and aspirations, all dreams and ethical conflicts are here reduced to a cipher, absolutely devoid of content. "The number is the former 'I.' This number is my former name."

> And who's to blame?
> Amalek, may his name and memory be blotted out, gave the order;
> and the head of the kehillah, whose learning and wisdom are known
> throughout the Jewish Diaspora, carried it out—to the letter. (p. 452)

Although the narrator has been stripped of his own name, he is still possessed of sufficient learning to invoke the most culturally specific curse in the Jewish repertory: calling for the name of Israel's arch-enemy Amalek (i.e., the Germans) to be blotted out. As for the unnamed *rosh-hakool* (the unfortunate Marek Lichtenbaum, forced by the Germans to take over after Czerniakow's suicide), *toyre un khokhme* (Torah and [Jewish] wisdom) are his domain, which stretches *bekhol tfutses Yisroel*, o'er all of Israel's dispersions, and whatever Amalek decrees, that is what this exalted Jewish leader *hot mekayem geven*, carried out as if it came from the Lord on high.

The moral counterweight to Perle's invective is the unsparing criticism of the narrator himself, whose number was "chosen" at the expense of all those other numbers, chosen to be murdered. "Of 3 times 100,000 Jewish souls it was granted that some 30,000 ciphers of the Chosen People be left." A *por un draysik toyznt ato-bekhartonudike numern*, more properly translated as "some 30,000 chosen-peoplish numbers," signifies the complicity of Number 4580 in the profanation of what was once a central article of Jewish faith.

Perle turned from writing a chronicle of destruction to an autobiographical sketch narrated in a superidiomatic and satiric style, the better to interpret the meaning of the unassimilable facts. For him, as for the other professional writers who worked alongside Ringelblum, the meaning of the present reality was best arrived at through analogies—however painful and bitter—to the received traditions, both sacred and secular. Once before, in Jewish letters, a lively and lovable soul named Motl, son of Peyse the Cantor, had been left an orphan, and his tragicomic slogan, familiar to every reader of Yiddish, was "I'm alright, I'm an orphan!" Playing on that famous line, Perle's nameless narrator signs off with "I'm alright, I'm a number!" The distance between Sholem Aleichem's orphan from Kasrilevke and the Holocaust survivor is the covenantal measure of history.

The Function of the Covenant

Such unsparing moral criticism obviously betrays the religious, moral, and political values that writers continued to uphold in the face of all that negated them. The Jewish intellectuals who were asked by the staff of the Oyneg Shabes Archive to comment on the spiritual state of the ghetto made their own position clear by focusing on those aspects of ghetto life they found most repellant: rampant assimilationism (Hillel Zeitlin), and delusionary faith in Jewish autonomy (Dr. Israel Milejkowski). Because the brutal and ultimately genocidal reality challenged their own belief system beyond anything they had ever before experienced, writers, artists, and thinkers naturally fell back on forms of self-expression and symbol systems inherited from their immediate past. While Simkhe-Bumen Shayevitsh moved from writing prose to poetry in the Lodz ghetto, he remained thoroughly wedded to the modern literary enterprise, indeed hoping that his epic poems would someday occupy a space between Rav Ashi and Sholem Asch. While the Yiddish philologist Zelig Kalmanovitsh became an observant Jew in the Vilna ghetto and began keeping a diary in Hebrew, his ghetto addresses were a direct outgrowth of his prescient prewar essays on the fate of the Jewish people. Kalmanovitsh also produced major critical essays on Peretz and Aḥad Haᶜam. Meanwhile, in the Warsaw ghetto, Rabbi Kalonymus Kalman Shapira continued to deliver weekly sermons that probed the meaning of suffering, faith, and evil in the highly mediated language of Scripture, Talmud, the liturgy, and the Zohar.[24]

This is not to say that Orthodox Jews could only deliver sermons or swap miracle tales between late afternoon and evening prayers. We now know that the surviving *Scrolls of Auschwitz* were all authored by pious Polish Jews, one of whom was even a former *dayyan* (rabbi's assistant who decided on ritual matters and other disputes). Nor is this to say that secular Jews were incapable of enlisting religious terminology in their attempt to record, commemorate, or mourn the catastrophe. Quite the opposite is true.[25]

"Yizkor, 1943," a central document in the literature of Jewish catastrophe, was authored by Rokhl Auerbach (1903–1976), a Yiddish-Polish journalist, one-time companion of Itzik Manger, and friend of the Polish avant-garde. The liturgical title notwithstanding, it begins with an analogy between nature and nation:[26]

> I saw a flood once in the mountains. Wooden huts, torn from their foundations were carried above the raging waters. One could still see lighted lamps in them; men and women; children in their cradles were tied to their ceiling beams. Other huts were empty inside, but one could see a tangle of arms waving from the roof, like branches blowing in the wind waving desperately toward heaven, toward the river banks for help. At a distance, one could see mouths gaping, but one could not hear the cries because the roar of the waters drowned out everything.
>
> And that's how the Jewish masses flowed to their destruction at the time of the deportations. Sinking as helplessly into the deluge of destruction.
>
> And if, for even one of the days of my life, I should forget how I saw you then, my people, desperate and confused, delivered over to extinction, may all knowledge of me be forgotten and my name be cursed like that of those traitors who are unworthy to share your pain.

The "heavens" are deaf to the cries of the drowning flood victims, and to the sole survivor the historical deluge seems to have struck with the blind force of some natural law. Yet the words of Psalm 137, "If I forget thee, O Jerusalem," echo from her solemn oath. There is but one oblique note of moral criticism directed inward, toward "those traitors" (the Jewish police?) who are unworthy to share the pain of the murdered people. As for the people, they are invoked group by group—the children, the young men, the pious Jews in black gaberdines; the artisans, workers, wagon drivers, porters; the merchants and philanthropists; the mothers and fathers, grandfathers and grandmothers; the mad folk, the peddlers, and the beggars. Group by group she recalls their living, breathing presence in the ghetto, on the eve of their destruction.

> Ah, the ways of Warsaw—the black soil of Jewish Warsaw.
>
> My heart weeps even for the pettiest thief on Krochmalna Street; even for the worst of the knife wielders of narrow Mila, because even they were killed for being Jewish. Anointed and purified in the brotherhood of death.
>
> Ah, where are you, petty thieves of Warsaw; you illegal street vendors and sellers of rotten apples. And you, the more harmful folk—members of the great gangs who held their own courts; who supported their own

synagogues in the Days of Awe; who conducted festive funerals and who gave alms like the most prosperous burghers. (p. 462)

Each description is as detailed as this, true to the lingo of the Warsaw street, like the slang word *khesedlekh*, which in this context does not mean "good deeds," much less "little Hasidim," as I and the translator Leonard Wolf originally thought, but "barrowmen" or "illegal street vendors," a term specific to Warsaw that appears in no Yiddish dictionary.

Only someone who was flesh of the people's flesh yet thoroughly trained in analytic observation could have produced—fourteen months after the events described—a chronicle of destruction that combined reportage and liturgy, the documentary sweep of Lamentations and the individual pathos of Psalms. Only someone standing on the other side of the ghetto wall could possess such total recall.

Writing in November 1943, Auerbach already understood that in order to mourn, the martyrdom of the masses had to be kept separate from the resistance of the few. Nowhere does she mention the Warsaw ghetto uprising that occurred in April. This decision to portray the spiritual dimension of the Jewish response to catastrophe as continuous with the acts of armed resistance but distinct from them is consistent with her master metaphor of the flood. As flood victims, the Jews of Warsaw were blameless. They, the Jewish multitude, had been like a force of nature. "There was no power on earth, no calamity that could interfere with their quarrelsome presence in that Jewish street. Until there came that Day of Curses—a day that was entirely night." The Destruction occurred beyond the realm of historical causality. The Uprising occurred within.

Postscript 1

The Oyneg Shabes Archive literally had the last word. The last underground publication to appear within the ghetto walls was *Wiadomości*, a Polish-language news bulletin issued by the Archive for January 9–15, 1943. In April 1942, still addressing itself to the ghetto population, the Archive had published *Mitteylungen*, in Yiddish. Now that the End was in sight, the truth about the Nazi genocide had to reach the Aryan Side, or further away still—the Polish Government in Exile.[27]

But the Oyneg Shabes Archive spoke with more than one voice, in more than one language, and for more than one audience. The singular greatness of its staff is that they went far beyond their fact-finding mandate. Had they remained but a disciplined cadre of party faithful, slavishly literal, condemned to telling the whole truth and nothing but the truth, so help them Ringelblum, the Archive would have remained just that: disparate documents hidden inside a time capsule from another planet. Because in the aftermath of the Great Deportation each surviving chronicler was forced to become a threnodist, an interpreter, a theologian, and a poet, a new synthesis had to be found.

Where then does one seek the truth about the destruction of European Jewry? Does one find it in the documentary truth of eyewitness accounts, or in the subjective truth of the witness-as-threnodist?

One truth clearly reinforces the other. The metahistorical reading of the Holocaust lifts the survivor-witness above the data and the strictures of chronology. But scholarly rigor, scientific observation, scrupulous attention to detail ground one's personal pain in the bedrock of a sociohistorical reality. It is surely a miracle that Ringelblum was able to "ensure that no important fact about Jewish life in wartime would remain hidden from the world." It is no smaller miracle that a tiny group of writers achieved a synthesis between documentary truth and covenantal truth even as the war against the Jews raged on and on and on.

Postscript 2

One of the two milk canisters unearthed on the grounds of the former Warsaw ghetto on December 1, 1950, contained the second part of the Oyneg Shabes Archive and is now on permanent loan to the United States Holocaust Memorial Museum in Washington, D.C. It is worth the price of admission. But no one would ever know it. It looks like a primitive relic, surrounded by scraps of paper in incomprehensible languages. Even if the Museum were equipped to bring those scraps to life—which it is not—the canister and its contents are a dead letter. They are dead in comparison to the far more arresting artifacts that surround it: half of a wooden barrack from Birkenau, a cattle car, film footage of naked Jews being led to the gas chambers, video testimonies of survivors.

The milk canister might just as well have dropped from another planet, the inhabitants of which have all perished. It bears mute witness that Hitler won his war against the Jews of Europe. The canister is open. But the literary-historical canon it protected from destruction still remains closed.

4 The Shtetl in Jewish Collective Memory

Every shtetl in Poland, every Jewish alleyway, had its own character. Jews from the Lublin area spoke in a different way and even, it seemed, looked different from Jews from Kalisz or Siedlce. The Jewish towns by the Vistula were very different from those in Volhynia. In Wąwolnica, near Lublin, the Scroll of Esther was read on the day *after* Purim because of a tradition that the site had been surrounded by a wall even in the time of Joshua. In Tyszowce, the Messiah son of Joseph had lived and was martyred.

—Isaac Bashevis Singer, 1943

What am I doing here? I ask myself. People shout, wave their arms about, making shushing noises. It is an unseemly sight, the Jews as I do not like to see them: undisciplined, petty, disputatious, disunited.

—Theo Richmond, 1995

The shtetl, or Jewish market town of Eastern Europe, is arguably the greatest single invention of Yiddish literature. What the Western is to American popular culture, the shtetl novella is to the Yiddish imagination. Its symbolic landscape is etched into the Yiddish psyche. Main Street is dominated by the marketplace and is occupied solely by Jews. Instead of the saloon, there is the *besmedresh* (the house of study); instead of the church, the *shul*. The *kohol-shtibl*, where the Jewish notables meet, replaces the sheriff's office. And of course there is the train depot, either nearby or somewhat removed, through which unwelcome news and travelers arrive in town.

Unlike the Hollywood scriptwriters, directors, and studio bosses, who invented the Wild West out of whole celluloid, those who fashioned the literary image of the shtetl were themselves but one step removed from the crowded, poverty-stricken, Yiddish-speaking market towns of Russia, Poland, and Galicia. But when first they introduced the shtetl into literature, they did so as if they were on the outside looking in. From the outside—itself an imagined community of tolerant, educated, and productive citizens—the shtetl represented the stagnant feudal economy (Aksenfeld), the crippled education of the young (Linetzky), the collective folly (Isaac

Meir Dik), the crisis in moral values (Abramovitsh).[1] For German-Jewish writers, the shtetl was the last vestige of the medieval "ghetto."

Tourists in their own home, these expatriate writers signaled their estrangement by disassembling the shtetl into its constituent parts. Seemingly unique to the shtetl was the communal bathhouse. For Sholem-Yankev Abramovitsh it represented both the obscene intimacy so "typical" of Jewish life, and the Jewish penchant for political debate.[2] Only then did our tour move on to the *besmedresh*, usually mistranslated as "synagogue." Here, "*same untern oyvn*, right before the tiled stove, where all things reach their final destination," is where Abramovitsh's most memorable native son, Benjamin of Tuneyadevke, received his entire education in worldly affairs: "family secrets, business deals, Turkish and Austrian politics, the wealth of Rothschild, the latest mail delivery with news of evil decrees or a discovery of a tribe of lost Jews. . . . "[3] One would hardly guess, judging from the pages of nineteenth-century Yiddish and Hebrew fiction, that the studyhouse was built for the sake of daily prayer and study. As for the main synagogue, left high and dry when the various hasidic sects established alternative houses of worship, the only ones who made a point of stopping there were *real* tourists, native sons and daughters paying a brief visit home.

Among the first to revisit the fictional shtetl from the vantage point of the New World was the Yiddish-English-Russian writer Abraham Cahan (1860–1951). What he found was a fragmented landscape, "like things seen in a cyclorama," with the strongest sensory images emanating precisely from the shtetl's outer boundaries: its natural surroundings and the Jewish cemetery.[4]

Asriel Stroon, a retired businessman, decides to return to his town of Pravly in order to procure a "proper" bridegroom for his appropriately named daughter, Flora. Arriving at the outskirts of town, he is immediately transported by "a whiff of May aroma" and by the scent of flowers for which he lacks the names in "his poor mother tongue" (namely, Yiddish). Though usually not prone to introspection, Asriel is "seized with doubt as to his own identity," caught up as he is in a flood of memory. To add to his confusion, the shtetl has barely changed. The moment of disengagement—and estrangement—comes in the wake of the Sabbath prayers, just when one would expect the opposite.

> When Asriel issued forth from the synagogue he found Pravly completely changed. It was as if, while he was praying and battling, the little town had undergone a trivializing process. All the poetry of thirty-five years' separation had fled from it, leaving a heap of beggarly

squalor. He felt as though he had never been away from the place, and were tired to death of it, and at the same time his heart was contracted with homesickness for America. The only interest the town now had for him was that of a medium to be filled with the rays of his financial triumph. "I'll show them who they are and who Asriel is," he comforted himself. (p. 111)

By story's end, both Asriel's scheme of importing the shtetl and his hard-won American dream are ground to dust. A crushed man, he decides to live out his last remaining years in the Land of Israel. Fortunately for Cahan's readers, the story's focus has long since shifted away from old Asriel's romance with the shtetl to the young bridegroom's romance with America.

In the pages of Yiddish and Hebrew fiction, meanwhile, many were the prodigal sons who tried in vain to rescue something of value from the shtetl. Some returned, after the pogroms of 1881–1882, in sackcloth and ashes. Others tried to cover their tracks by reappearing incognito, as "travelers disguised," Dan Miron's master metaphor for the entire course of nine-teenth-century Yiddish literature.[5] Still others came back on fact-finding missions, armed with ideological verities for social reform. Travel itself became the master metaphor for the internal exile of the modern Jew.[6] Whatever the personal motive or historical exigency, one rule pertained: the more estranged these Jews became, the more they were drawn back to the shtetl; even, as we shall see, to a shtetl they never knew.

Jews were obviously not the only people in modern times to have experienced a loss of their homeland. Nor were Jewish rebels, revolutionaries, and just plain immigrants the only ones to discover that "you can't go home again." What distinguished the Jews from other uprooted peoples, however, was the symbolic shorthand that they developed, a modern "semiotics of exile" that allowed them to read their individual experience in the light of historical archetypes. At the creative heart of their cultural code lay the evolving image of the shtetl: as the ghetto-existence best left behind; as the Jewish body politic under siege; as the idealized *Heimat,* the local Old Country homeland, arrested in time; as paradise lost; and finally, as the staging ground for Jewish mass martyrdom. Because the Jews are a ferociously literate people, and because they mastered various means of memorial production, one image-cluster did not seamlessly blend into another; they clashed and coexisted in highbrow and popular culture alike, on opposite sides of the barricades, and on both sides of the Atlantic. If our itinerary begins with the artful fashioning of a high-literary image of the shtetl, it is because writers and poets were major players during this formative period of nation building. At the end of the road, the shtetl would emerge not only as one of the greatest inventions of the Jewish literary imagination but also as a key to modern Jewish self-understanding.

Between Fiction and Fact

Two very different perspectives converged on the shtetl: the one static and synoptic, the other dynamic and deconstructive. Neither owed much to the "real" past. So far as the shtetl itself was concerned, it existed on a timeless plain at the nexus of the Jews and their God.[7] Like Jerusalem, the shtetl defined itself as a *kehillah kedoshah*, a covenantal community. As such, it maintained the essential institutions of *shul* (synagogue), *besmedresh* (studyhouse), *shtiblekh* (hasidic houses of prayer), *khadorim* (elementary schools), *mikve* (ritual bath), and *besoylem* (sanctified burial ground). These secured the bond between Jews and God, just as the various voluntary societies and professional guilds called *khevres* organized the social interaction among the Jews themselves. Critics were quick to point out that power was concentrated in the hands of the male burghers, who elected the Jewish community council called the *kahal*.[8] They shed no tears for the abolition of the kahal by Tsar Nicholas I in 1844. Whether the shtetl of memory was located at the nexus of Jews-and-God or of Jews-and-other-Jews, it lay outside of time and geopolitical space. The shtetl was seen, for better or worse, as a kind of Greek city-state: independent, self-regulating, and oblivious of the contemporary world.

Herein lies the central paradox of the shtetl as an exilic community, for this mini-kingdom of the Jews did not belong to them; it belonged to the Polish nobility. This Jewish collective presence, the product of two millennia of talent for self-government, was structurally, inherently, powerless.

Jews originally settled the towns of Poland and the Ukraine upon the invitation of one or another Polish squire (called *porits* in Yiddish) or came under his personal protection. The historian Murray Rosman titled his pioneering study of "Magnate-Jewish Relations in the Polish Commonwealth during the 18th Century" *The Lord's Jews* in order to signify not the Lord of Abraham, Isaac, and Jacob, but the all-powerful Polish nobleman. Historians distinguish between "royal towns," belonging to the crown, and "private towns," belonging to the nobleman's estate, which included all the surrounding villages, organized into a *klucz*, or *shlisl* (literally a "key"). Yes, each private town was a world unto itself, as the historian Gershon Hundert rediscovered when he examined the rich archival materials in Polish, Latin, Hebrew, and Yiddish on the town of Opatów.[9] But in these pri-

vate towns, writes Hundert of the eighteenth century, "municipal autonomy was a fiction."

> Even in towns where the form of elections to municipal office was
> retained, those elected wielded no real power. The towns, like the
> villages in the countryside, were the property of the magnate-aristocrats.
> The authority of the kahal, therefore, was subject to that of the town
> owner. He saw the Jews' institutions as part of the administrative
> network of his estate, whose purpose was to serve his interests.
> (pp. 135–36)

Historically, then, the shtetl represented a typically medieval experiment
in Jewish-magnate relations, its rise and fall directly calibrated to the
changing fortunes of the powers-that-be.

When the shtetl entered into literature, between 1831 and 1863, the dates
of the two failed Polish uprisings against the tsar, it was just as the Polish
nobility was being stripped of its powers. Thus the porits, for all that he
once loomed so large on the shtetl landscape and saw to it that nothing
much in that landscape ever changed, himself became transported to the
land of legend, either as the benign ruler, such as Graf Potocki, or as the
sadistic and dissolute nobleman who signaled the collapse of all moral
authority.[10] The porits, much like the Roman emperor before him, came
to be seen as merely a pawn in the divine scheme of things.

The role of the peasants was similarly bifurcated. When the market
economy was still viable, the Ukrainian- Belorussian- and Polish-speaking
peasants were the Jews' main source of livelihood. On market days the
peasantry from the surrounding villages descended upon the shtetl with
their open wagons loaded with livestock and produce. These they sold to
the Jews in return for goods and services. By nightfall, the peasants were
gone, including those who drank away their earnings in the local Jewish
tavern. In fact, there were Gentiles who resided permanently within the
town proper, but they mostly lived on the outskirts, and owned plots of
land, which embodied their ongoing link to an agrarian lifestyle. (This is
true even in present-day Poland.) Although the spire of the Roman Catholic kośchół dominated the shtetl skyline, often rivaled by the onion-shaped
dome of the Eastern Orthodox tserkov, the gentile majority made its presence felt only on market days, Sundays, or religious festivals. The surest
sign of trouble was if the peasants reappeared en masse and off schedule.
Then the only one who could save the Jews was the Russian constable or
sheriff, and that only for a price.

This ethnic mosaic was also reflected in Jewish linguistic practice. The Jews spoke Yiddish but prayed and studied in the Holy Tongue, Hebrew. When they negotiated with the outside world, they did so either in High Goyish or Low Goyish. High Goyish was the language of *nachalstvo*, of officialdom: in the old days, before the Partitions, in Polish; since then, and especially since the Insurrection of 1863, in Russian. Low Goyish was the language spoken by the peasants and the local priest: Ukrainian in the south, Belorussian in the north.[11]

So while the all-powerful porits was eventually eclipsed by the all-corrupt Russian bureaucracy, the fate of the actual, historical shtetl hung in the balance along the nexus of Jewish-gentile relations. There *was* no safety in numbers, as past historical experience had dictated; and the Goyim, seemingly so backward, would gradually inherit the spoils. Only the Jews who fled could see just how bad things were. As recompense for the loss of their homes, the survivors and expatriates either demonized the Goyim or erased them from the landscape, to conjure up a place more perfect and durable than ever existed. Out of its very destruction and long before its end had come, the shtetl was reborn as myth.

The Shtetl as Protagonist

The usual hero of modern literature is a prodigal son or daughter facing off against organized religion, bourgeois society, and the whole of the burdensome past. Modern Jewish literature is no exception, and among it many virtues, the shtetl offered the Jewish writer a perfect fictional backdrop in which and against which to enact one's independence, critical distance, and alienation from the world of the "little Jews." Here is Sholem Aleichem's heroine Rachel the Beautiful all festively attired as she steps out of a raucous wedding into the humdrum shtetl marketplace. What does she experience? Her first moment of angst and romantic awakening (*Stempenyu*, 1888). Here is young Shloyme, the son of Reb Khayim, so isolated in the Lithuanian shtetl of his birth that his only true friends are the artisans, who literally and figuratively occupy the margins of respectable society. Is it any wonder that Shloyme will one day grow up to be the great artist Sholem-Yankev Abramovitsh (*Of Bygone Days*, 1899)? And here is the young man in Hayyim Nahman Bialik's poem standing "On the Threshold of the House of Prayer." Is he about to enter in order to study a tractate of the Talmud or to join a quorum of male Jews in the afternoon prayer? No. He remains staring at its "smoke-covered walls" and "beams blackened with soot"—the projection of his own inner barrenness (1894).[12]

But alongside the inevitable process of breakdown and alienation and during the roughly one hundred years between the literary invention of the shtetl and its final destruction, Jewish writers managed an artistic feat of more far-reaching consequences: they turned the shtetl collective itself into a living, speaking, and highly reactive, character.

Some of the techniques employed were the stock-in-trade of every satirist. Inventing a fictional geography, for instance, was a time-honored method of changing the names to protect the guilty. The -evke and -sk suffixes immediately identified the place names as Ukrainian or generically Slavic. Seeing as how the secular writers were all propagating the centrifugal movement of Jewry away from the old breeding grounds, anything too Slavic-sounding smacked of the feudal outback.

Hebrew writers, equally intent upon breaking loose, were faced with a problem of linguistic decorum. Heeding an etiquette that did not allow for the presence of "foreign"-sounding words, Hebrew writers compensated by finding biblical place names that did double duty. When translating his novels into Hebrew, Abramovitsh turned Tuneyadevke into Betalon, Idletown, from the Hebrew root b-t-l (empty), and Kaptsansk became Kabzeel, creatively derived from the Hebrew word for "beggar" but actually appearing in a list of place names in the Book of Joshua, chapter 15.[13]

Sholem Aleichem, Abramovitsh's disciple, made the reader's task more difficult by mixing and matching invented, comical, place names like Kasrilevke, Zlodeyevke, and Kozodoyevke, with pseudohistorical place names like Khmielnitsk, Mazepevke, and Gontoyarsk, and with real place names like Yampele (Yampol) and Strishtsh (Stavishche). It didn't take a folk-etymologist to parse "Zlodeyevke" as Roguesville and "Kozodoyevke" as Goatsburg, but "Kasrilevke" was something of a tease. While the author insisted that it came from the preexisting word "Kasrilik," a happy pauper, the more discerning reader could identify the Hebrew keter, or crown, preserved in the spelling. By imbedding the names of Chmielnicki, Mazepa, and Gonta, moreover, Sholem Aleichem meant to suggest an unbroken legacy of enmity and blood.[14] Alas, by the mid-twentieth century, with the destruction of this world and access to this literature limited to translations, only professors of Yiddish (and their students) would know the difference.

If the name just about summed up who they were, the depiction of the shtetl populace as a species of animals delivered the final verdict: the foolish, cackling geese of Isaac Meir Dik's town of Heres, or the ubiquitous goats of Abramovitsh's Kapstansk and Tuneyadevke.[15] They were a herdlike people, these shtetl-folk, who lived so terribly close together, and who perforce dreamed together as well. As they do, most brilliantly, at the close of Book One of Abramovitsh's *The Wishing Ring* (1888). Almost naked they lie, the "whole" shtetl population, men, women, and children, outdoors on a parodic midsummer's night, dreaming a single, implausible dream—of miraculous wealth.[16]

When judged by West European standards of culture and civility, the verdict on the shtetl was unanimous: the sooner this small, homogeneous, insular, and linguistically distinct provincial backwater deconstructed, the better for all concerned. Yet how compelling was this collective as a subject of fiction! How memorable its group behavior! How comical its visceral responses! And how adaptable its monolithic image to the shifting political landscape. For no sooner did the intellectuals' faith in imminent reform begin to wane, in the last decades of the nineteenth century, than the same shtetl monolith was resurrected for opposite ends.

Shtetl poverty remains unchanged, but in Sholem Aleichem's Kasrilevke (introduced in 1901), it is the sign of a classless society, devoid of real conflict. The houses are just as cramped and crumble as before, only now they do so under divine sanction.[17]

> Se shteyt in posek *"losheves yestoro,"* iz der pshat: di velt iz bashafn
> gevorn af yishev, *af tsu zitsn,* nisht af tsu kukn. Vos far a kukn?

> It says in Scripture [Isa. 45:18] "He formed it for habitation," which
> means just that, it was meant to be dwelt in, *to be sat in,* not looked at.
> Who asked you to look at it?

So much for urban planning. But never fear. This overcrowded slum can be likened unto a sunflower, chock full of seeds, or to a noodle board scattered with *farfl,* and the shtetl entire exists in a state of perfect ecological balance with nature. There is, thank God, a cemetery on the outskirts of town, which is both the repository of its living past and its only plot of arable land. Here the Jewish goats freely graze, thus providing Jewish children with badly needed milk. "How fair are your tents, O Jacob!" the narrator ends on a rhapsodic note, "your dwellings, O Israel!" (Num. 24:5).[18]

The cemetery was added to the original panorama of "The Town of the Little People," probably in the early years of World War I, when the actual, historical shtetl was under siege. Sholem Aleichem was then an exile in New York City and in failing health. At least as far back as Karl Emil Franzos's story "Nameless Graves" (1873), the cemetery became a requisite part of the shtetl's symbolic—and sentimental—landscape, a monument to life-in-death, the seat of its myth and its most arcane customs.[19]

Sholem Aleichem's shift in perspective from the crooked streets and marketplace of Kasrilevke to its crowded cemetery, from the tragicomic present to the mock-mythic past, is enormously suggestive. Something analogous happened to his great contemporary and rival, I. L. Peretz. In 1890, armed with the ideological verities of Polish Positivism, one of the major tenets of which was critical self-analysis in the cause of social reform, Peretz set out on a fact-finding mission underwritten by the wealthy industrialist Jan Bloch. Peretz's "Impressions of a Journey through the Tomaszow Region" was a stark panorama of the shtetl's social and economic collapse, in which nothing sustains the close and fruitful interaction of Jews-and-other-Jews. The gentrified traveler discovers dead Jewish towns at every turn of the road.[20]

Polish literary culture then offered Peretz an alternative perspective, that of neoromanticism. Instead of focusing relentlessly on the internal decay of Polish Jewry in the present, instead of demythologizing the shtetl and all that it stood for, Peretz returned to the preindustrial past, to a shtetl life where each beggar might be Elijah the Prophet in disguise and where the Hasidim danced under the open sky. It was a polarized, legendary landscape in which the spirit battled it out with the flesh, the mystical soul struggled against the rational soul, and the Jew faced off against his age-old enemy, the Gentile.[21] So it was that in 1904, Peretz added one more episode to his earlier "Impressions," an encounter with a Polish wagon driver and a Jewish traveling companion. Together they embark on a journey across a vanished pond, which embodies the legendary past of Polish Jewry and underscores the cultural abyss between the Poles and the Jews.

The shtetl was dead. Long live the shtetl! Now that there was no going back, the shtetl came to represent a useful myth of origins: "In the beginning was the shtetl, home and haven for all." Ukrainians had their Wild East of Hetmen and Cossacks; Poles had their valiant kings and noblemen of the old republic, and the Jews now had a collective hero in the shtetl of old. Within this mythic landscape the Jews of Eastern Europe were even given a choice: between a shtetl that recycled its own materials, however decaying (Sholem Aleichem), and a shtetl that restored its lost glory, however far removed in the past (Peretz). Whether or not the shtetl would ever rise from the ashes *in the present* now depended on the third, and heretofore unexplored, nexus: that of Jewish-gentile relations.

The Shtetl through the Eyes of the Other

Every decade now brought about a profound ideological shift. The Revolution of 1905 with its heightened messianic hopes and its devastating repercussions was just such a catalytic event.[22] Two Polish-Yiddish writers who came of age at this time signaled the new political reality by transforming the shtetl landscape. They did so, as in the case of Sholem Aleichem and Peretz, for opposite ends.

Sholem Asch, who, from first to last would be the chief architect of Yiddish popular taste and would eventually enjoy a larger following among gentile than among Jewish readers, signaled his ecumenical direction in a novella titled *The Shtetl*.[23] Published on the eve of the revolution, in 1904, this fictional portrait of Kuzmir/Kazimierz Dolny in the mid-nineteenth century was as close to an earthly paradise as Jews were ever likely to inhabit. The prayers that emanated from its synagogue and the prayers that echoed from the Catholic church ascended to a single God. Its only resident Goyim were the contented servants of the equally contented Jewish *balebos* (householder).[24]

Far more programmatic was Asch's "Kola Street," written about two years later, which told the story of the shtetl in crisis. Never before had a writer situated the shtetl so firmly within the Polish landscape. In a lush descriptive passage of the kind that would later win him a prize from the Polish government, Asch located the shtetl within a triangular area that derived its uniqueness from what at first appeared to be an utter lack of individuality.[25]

> This triangular area, which includes Kutno, Zychlin, Gostynin, Gombin, and a number of smaller towns, has none of the mysterious charm of its neighbor, the province of Kujawy, so rich in legends about the souls of the dead that haunt back lanes, wander in the fields, and lure people into the swamps; nor is it as rich in color and in sound as its other neighbor, the Duchy of Lowicz, which gave birth to the greatest Polish composer and creator of the mazurka, Chopin. Flat and monotonous are its fields, and the peasant who cultivates them is as plain as the potatoes they yield.

So, too, the Jew native to this region, who partakes "more of the flavor of wheat and of apples than of the synagogue and the ritual bath." And so, while other towns can boast of their rabbis and Judaic scholars, what makes this town unique is Kola Street, wherein live the horse traders and tough Jews. They are the salt of the Polish earth, and they know how to fight. Reb Israel Zychliner is the Godfather, a man both pious and fearless. Notte, the hot-blooded son, loves his horse and his pigeons even more than he loves the Polish *shiksa*, Josephine. It is Notte who provokes the local Goyim to stage a pogrom; it is Josephine who helps him break out of jail and enter the fray; and it is the slaughter of Notte's beloved pigeons that helps restore the moral order at story's end. As befits a shtetl so firmly rooted in a natural landscape, most of the action takes place outdoors and moves in and out of specific Jewish streets.

Sholem Asch's ecumenicism, his emphasis on the cyclical, almost mystical forces of regeneration emanating from within the shtetl's very soil, were immediately challenged by I. M. Weissenberg, who introduced class warfare into shtetl fiction.[26] In Weissenberg's nameless shtetl, probably modeled on his native Zelechow, there is no variegated landscape à la Asch, no eternal past à la Sholem Aleichem, no sense of history whatsoever. Instead, there are plenty of Christian Poles, who come to town either as Marxist agitators from Warsaw or as devout Catholic peasants asserting their claim to a Poland without Jews.

Weissenberg begins and ends his anatomy of shtetl violence in the *besmedresh*. The anonymous "young men" who hang out at the back lose their first confrontation with the shtetl oligarchy, but they return at the end to unseat the rabbi. The tea shop, never before depicted in shtetl fiction, becomes the new center of gravity. At first it is just a hangout for young workers. But soon enough, every worker and artisan ends up there as a sign of allegiance to the Movement. Eventually, it becomes the shtetl's court of appeals. By then, most of the action has shifted to the great outdoors, outside the town limits, the scene of mass rallies. Just when it appears that the Jewish "proletariat" has seized control, the Christians reclaim the outdoors with a procession of their own. The procession is the first reminder that the whole revolution is taking place in a glass of water; that "there, beyond the shtetl, lay such a vast multitude, and here everything was so small, so puny, held together by just a dab of spit." Itchele the bootmaker, whose insight this is, goes on to imagine the worst-case scenario:

> It occurred to him that if the thousands out there suddenly decided to have a bit of fun—just a simple bit of peasant fun—if each of them took from the houses of the Jews no more than a couple of rotting floor boards apiece and carried them off under his arm, nothing would remain of the shtetl but an empty plot of land. (p. 55)

As for the marketplace, the only space that properly belongs to the Jews, it is won and lost, won and lost again. In their final debacle, the revolutionaries are hauled away under armed guard.

Adopting the perspective of the Other, Asch and Weissenberg arrive at opposite conclusions. The shtetl, according to Asch, occupies a layered landscape. The passions of one group dovetail with the passions of another, and when they occasionally flare up into violence, shtetl society possesses the means to restore order. Asch remythologizes the shtetl by turning it into a mutually reliant Holy Community of Christians and Jews. Weissenberg revisits the shtetl and finds nothing to salvage in the present, much less in the past. He radically flattens all perspectives. Yes, the moral order is restored, but by outside intervention. Once visited from the outside, the Holy Community shatters into fragments, and the Jewish body politic is revealed to be helpless before the potentially deadly alliance of Christian Jew-hatred and Polish patriotism. The denuded shtetl possesses no resources from which to rebuild a more secure future.

The decision to focus on the fate of the shtetl, as opposed to the large urban centers of Warsaw, Lodz, Bialystok, Lemberg, Kiev, and Vienna, where the majority of East European Jews then lived, was based on the decision that less was more. What commended the shtetl was precisely its smallness, its remove from the main line of fire, and most importantly, its symbolic landscape, perfected over three generations. With the stroke of a pen a writer could locate the story's thematic core. The *besmedresh* or hasidic *shtibl* stood for the shtetl's claim to sanctity. If the main synagogue were gutted or burned, it signified nothing less than the Destruction of the Temple. The bathhouse or *kool-shtibl* (kahal chamber) were the Jewish parliament and represented the shtetl's claim to self-sufficiency. The marketplace was the main arena of commerce and ethnic strife. In the home, where the servant girl or *Shabes-goy* spoke Low Goyish and Yiddish, they stood for peaceful coexistence. And the cemetery was the seat of the community's deep past. Here, then, was a symbolic landscape so stable and internally coherent that it could register and absorb whatever tremors that history had in store.

The place: the sleepy Ukrainian shtetl of Sloveshne. The time: *Khadoshim un teg*, months, days, and hours in the summer of 1919 when the Ukrainians are about to slaughter the local Jews.[27] To demonstrate how deep are the roots of that violence, the young novelist Itsik Kipnis interrupts the killing with a public trial that for all its mundane setting appears timeless and archetypal.

> It was a strange trial. It was a day that was neither a working day nor a holiday. A little like a fair in the center of the mareketplace, and yet no business was conducted. The priest and the rabbi stood at the center of the crowd. The rabbi was bloodstained, but he neither wept nor groaned. He did not wince, but it was clear from the way that he sweated that his strength had been sapped. There was no trial here of equal strengths where, at some point, one could call a halt and an authority would say, "Right. That's right. Right. That's right."

The priest spoke first. "We have to persuade the people to restrain themselves. To stop its turbulence; or the Jews will have to be careful (about what?). The Jews will have to (what?) . . . " The priest spoke guardedly, ambiguously. He was still in his right mind and knew that power was not with the church now. In church he could speak quite differently. Here, he had to be a bit careful.

Not only is local time out of kilter — neither a working day nor a holiday — but historical time, too. The forced debate between the priest and the rabbi might be a scene out of the hoary Middle Ages. The argument against the Jews, however, is only just beginning.

Now it was Stodot's turn to talk. The name Stodot may not mean anything to those who are not acquainted with that bumpy-featured murderous bastard with the gray, protruding eyes. A huge man in his forties. . . . Jews, he said, were foreigners; they were harmful. Jewish cattle devoured the pastures. Jews cut down whole forests in order to make brooms. Jewish geese spoiled the wheat fields, so that the community was put to the trouble of rounding up Jewish livestock every year. And, if Stodot was in charge of the roundup, any Jewish woman who owned a cow had a hard time of it. Now it was Stodot who spoke. And, as far as Jews were concerned, there were things that he loved to say loud and clear. And he was saying them.

"And Jews have always been like this. They even sent noodles to the Germans during the war. Now we don't want them to be communists."[28]

Stodot and company make good their threat. It is only the Red Army's eleventh-hour intervention that stops the slaughter and Soviet might that avenges the deed measure for measure.

By depicting, within the shtetl's symbolic landscape, violence such as even the bloodstained earth of the Ukraine had never witnessed — Kipnis cut it down to size. At the same time, the story of the narrator's love for Buzi, his newly-wedded wife, and the studied simplicity of his narrative resonates with another poignant chronicle of abiding shtetl love, Sholem Aleichem's "Song of Songs." Given the strictures of official Soviet policy, which branded the shtetl a hotbed of bourgeois nationalism, Kipnis went as far as a Soviet Yiddish writer could go to erect a memorial for the shtetl.[29] Alternatively, by introducing a riotous Jewish commune into the shtetl's symbolic landscape and describing the result in a pastiche of modern and biblical Hebrew, Hayyim Hazaz read the Bolshevik Revolution as a sign of the apocalypse. Then he got the hell out of there himself.[30]

Bracketed by two revolutions, one a dry run, the other all too real, the image of the shtetl was completely unbound. So long as writers believed in a brave new world, the image of the shtetl as a small, homogeneous, and self-sufficient community could still be very inviting. ("The Jew native to this region partakes more of the flavor of wheat and of apples than of the synagogue and the ritual bath.") But once the political horizons began to contract and to split, the very same image underscored how powerless the Jews had become. ("Here everything was so small, so puny, held together by just a dab of spit.") The presence or absence of Goyim likewise became more fraught with meaning. In Kasrilevke, the presence of one hostile Goy (Yeremi the postmaster, Makar Kholodny the local antisemite) suggested that the shtetl could still roll with the punches. The presence of many organized Goyim was something else again. By naming their names, exposing the politics of each, distinguishing between the good, the bad, and the morally ambiguous, Kipnis was engaged in an act of purgation, which suggested that a new society would be erected on the ruins of the old. Not so in Weissenberg's and Hazaz's revolutionary shtetlekh, where the Goyim were a faceless mob that did not distinguish between capitalist and worker, parasite and progressive.

The Apotheosis of the Polish Shtetl

Between the two world wars, Poland became the last frontier of the shtetl, both living and dead. Galicia was reunited with the Polish heartland after a separation of one hundred and fifty years. So too was a swatch of the northeastern "borderlands," including the multiethnic city of Vilna. Inside the Polish shtetl, Jews were becoming an embattled minority. This alone was not reason enough, however, for them to resurface as a subject worthy of literature. The return to the shtetl was motivated by a full-blown ideology, which itself was divided along nationalistic lines. Founded in 1926, the Jewish Society for Exploring the Countryside—*landkentenish* in Yiddish and *krajoznawstwo* in Polish—brought together two disparate ideological strands: the old Enlightenment ideal of being close to nature and the new nationalism that laid exclusive claim to the land and its historic landmarks. Because Jewish membership in the Polish Nature Society was severely restricted and because the Poles made no effort to preserve Jewish landmarks, Jewish historians, ethnographers, novelists, poets and other committed intellectuals formed their own society and issued their own publications.[31] Among the various "Excursions" that Dr. I. Lejpuner reported on—to Palestine, Egypt, and Italy—the most exotic by far was to the Polish shtetl of "Jen . . . ". Here he was astonished to witness the carnivalesque atmosphere attending the installation of a new Torah scroll. Who could have guessed that such exotic rites were still being performed — and in full view of the Christian population![32] In the 1930s, the novelist Michal Bursztyn became the Society's major spokesman (both in Yiddish and in Polish). Studying and touring the historic Polish shtetlekh, he argued, would bring urban Jews back to nature, would close the gap between the intellectuals and the folk, would counteract the geographical fragmentation of the Jews, and would even offer a secular alternative to the old religious faith.[33]

Despite the upbeat program that looked ahead to a permanent Jewish presence in the Polish Republic, the literary monuments these committed writers erected to Polish-Jewish life were emblems of loss. Rokhl Korn's volume of short stories, *Erd* (Earth, 1936), was an exquisitely poignant record of loss shared by Jews, Polish and Ukrainian peasants, and German colonists in the immediate aftermath of World War I.[34] Because her focus was on the earth, however, on the soil they had tilled that never was really theirs, the shtetl did not figure here at all. It was left to Bursztyn to write a jeremiad for the old and new shtetl way of life. Two of his three novels, *Iber di khurves fun Ployne* (Over the ruins of Ployne, 1931) and *Bay di taykhn fun Mazovye* (By the rivers of Mazowsze, 1937), refracted the recent events in Poland through the prism of the shtetl. The more real and pervasive the presence of Poles and Polish culture in these novels, the more the physical and spiritual horizons of the shtetl population were seen to contract. In the face of economic boycotts, social discrimination, and pogroms, the immediate task was simply to record the struggle itself.[35]

The rescue operation was left in the hands of those who left Poland altogether. For two of the proudest sons of Polish Jewry — S. Y. Agnon and Isaac Bashevis Singer — the shtetl would live on as the touchstone of some higher truth or reality. Upon his return to Palestine in 1924, Agnon began to write a series of novels that follow a loose chronology. He began with an epic and encyclopedic novel, set in early nineteenth-century Galicia, about the travels of an extremely learned, pious, and impecunious Hasid named Reb Yudl. Here, in *Hakhnasat kalah* (*The Bridal Canopy*, 1931), the shtetl is Canterbury, a dazzlingly rich backdrop for a gallery of disparate, traditional types. It is Agnon's most elusive, allusive, and Jewish work, the first to be translated into English and the last to be understood.[36] In *Sippur pashut* (*A Simple Story*, 1935) the shtetl is Middlemarch, a traditional town in a time of intense change. In *Oreah nata lalun* (*A Guest for the Night*, 1938–1939), the shtetl is the Magic Mountain, where the permanent spectre of death casts its pallor over all social and theological discourse.

Nowhere is the shtetl's symbolic landscape exploited more brilliantly than in Agnon's novels. Tsirl Hurwitz's "shipshape shop" dominates the Szybusz marketplace in *A Simple Story* as Tsirl herself dominates the lives of all her menfolk. Both the Little and Great Synagogues, meanwhile, are relegated to the sidelines. But in *A Guest for the Night*, describing the aftermath of World War I, the marketplace is empty, and the protagonist spends most of his time in the Old House of Study, to which he alone has the key.[37] "The whole town is weary and sad," says the sojourner about a month into his stay (p. 42). He notes that the town's two Jewish wagoners stand all day long in the marketplace, clapping their hands to warm themselves a little. And as for the peasants, "From the ninety villages that surround the town, not a man comes to buy anything in the shops. . . . Each farmer sells his crops himself and has no need of a middleman" (p. 43). Instead, what is salvaged from the poverty-stricken shtetl is nothing less than the Jewish God. The shtetl-to-Jerusalem axis is hereby restored in the most literal way imaginable: the narrator takes the key back with him to his new home in Jerusalem.

For Singer, rousing himself out of a seven-year-long depression in *his* new home, America, the lost shtetl became the cherished home of his imagination. Chiding his now-murdered colleagues for their putative neglect, he declared:[38]

> Every shtetl in Poland, every Jewish alleyway, had its own character.
> Jews from the Lublin area spoke in a different way and even, it seemed,
> looked different from Jews from Kalisz or Siedlce. The Jewish towns by
> the Vistula were very different from those in Volhynia. In Wąwolnica,
> near Lublin, the Scroll of Esther was read on the day *after* Purim
> because of a tradition that the site had been surrounded by a wall even
> in the time of Joshua. In Tyszowce, the Messiah son of Joseph had lived
> and was martyred.

Like Bursztyn, Singer saw the shtetl as a unique repository of layered folkways and national distinctiveness. The return to a reimagined shtetl therefore entailed "reviving Old Yiddish," peopling his stories with "old wives who spoke the language of the medieval women's prayer book," and exploiting the superidiomatic "argot for musicians and . . . for thieves." But unlike his murdered colleagues, Singer also saw the shtetl as the ideal fictional setting for the playing out of Jewish religious passions. Wherever messianic hope had flourished, there Satan could not be far behind. If ever the Jews needed chastisement for whoring after strange gods, the time was, Singer believed, after the Stalinist purges and in the midst of the Nazi genocide.

The Shtetl as Covenantal Landscape

And America, home to the largest number of former shtetl Jews, was the place to do it. For this to happen, the East European Jewish immigrants had first to experience a series of profound breaks with their immediate past. During World War I and the Ukrainian Civil War they were forced to stand by and watch as the heartland was destroyed. "When the shocking news of the Pogrom reached us here," writes a spokesman for the First Felshteener Benevolent Association,

> we, and especially our women, were prostrated with grief. The sudden realization that we had lost so many of our relatives, so abruptly by such a cruel death, that never again would we see them—mother, father, sister, brother—filled us with great distress.
>
> What were we to do? The dead were beyond all aid. It was the living who called for our help. We immediately set out to do all we could for those survivors who had miraculously escaped from a sudden, violent and cruel death. We formed a relief committee to collect funds.[39]

So complete was the break with the Old Home, that of the six hundred Jews who were slaughtered in Felshtin by Petlura's Ukrainian nationalists on February 18 and June 6, 1919, fewer than half would eventually be listed in the *Felshtin Memorial Book*.

Then, in 1924, America closed its gates to mass immigration. No more would the ranks of the landsmanshaftn, of the Jewish labor movement, of Yiddish readers and theatergoers, of Yiddish writers and journalists, not to speak of one's own family, be constantly replenished from the East. The Polish and Lithuanian shtetl became instead a major recipient of organized philanthropy, a dirt-cheap place in which to film Yiddish musicals on location, with the local populace thrown in as extras, and a popular tourist site. Hundreds could now follow the path that only Cahan's retired businessman, Asriel Stroon, had been able to travel before. The place of the shtetl in the self-understanding of millions of American Jews now became fixed for all time. The shtetl was reclaimed as the place of common origin (even when it wasn't), the source of a collective folk identity rooted in a particular historical past and, most importantly, as the locus of a new, secular, covenant.[40]

A new covenant was needed precisely because the old one was no longer viable. The vast majority of American Jews had ceased to obey the myriad do's and don'ts of Jewish law. What's more, the absence of suffering from

Fig. 4.1. Notte Kozlovsky, "The Slaughter" [of Jewish Felshtin], from *Felshtin zamlbukh: tsum ondenk fun di felshtiner kdoyshim*, ed. J. Baum (New York: First Felsteener Benevolent Association, 1937).

persecution made the New World completely different from the Old. For the first time in living memory, Jews were living—in H. Leivick's memorable phrase—"without an axe." The idealized image of the shtetl, according to the cultural anthropologist Ewa Morawska, is what entered the breach.[41]

There is no more graphic illustration of Morawska's thesis than *Felshtin: Anthology in Memory of the Felshtiner Martyrs* (1937), one of the first memorial volumes to a lost shtetl produced on North American soil. Felshtin and Proskurov led the way because their Jewish communities were among the first to be destroyed—during the Ukrainian Civil War (see fig. 4.1). This proves, if further proof is needed, that in modern times, the dynamic of inner-Jewish renewal is always predicated on the awareness of loss. The moment the past is finally laid to rest is the very moment that it reasserts its claim upon the living.

Easier said than done. So great was the divide between the Old World and the New that the task of memorial demanded such means as were still beyond those of the vicarious survivors. Year in, year out, the members of the First Felsteener Benevolent Association gathered on New York's Lower East Side to commemorate the martyrs. This spontaneous gesture grew directly out of the received norms of group behavior. Assembling a memorial book was something else again.

For starters, the concept of a map was utterly foreign to the shtetl's conceptual universe. Mendele the Book Peddler had already known this, trapped as he was within a make-believe world of satiric place names. And so the Felshtiner commissioned a "bird's-eye view" of their beloved town from the popular illustrator of Yiddish children's books, Notte Kozlovsky (fig. 4.2). The sun is always shining on this quaint little town, flanked on its south side by a millstream, on the west by an onion-domed Eastern Orthodox church, and in the east by a huge Catholic church, whose spire casts a long shadow.

When it came time to document the history of its town and its most prominent sites, however, the editorial board came up short. There was no information to be had on the main shul, situated in the heart of the Jewish quarter. None even about the two tallest buildings in town that towered over the marketplace and were now owned by Jews—or had been, until the pogrom. The profusely apologetic editor of the memorial book and its chief contributor, Jonah Baum, documented his futile efforts to glean archival material: from elderly Jews who still remained in Felshtin, from the young professional archivist Ezekiel Lifschutz, and from the YIVO Institute in Vilna. As if to compensate, Kozlovsky was asked to illustrate a number of dramatic and sentimental memoirs (which gives the volume an un-

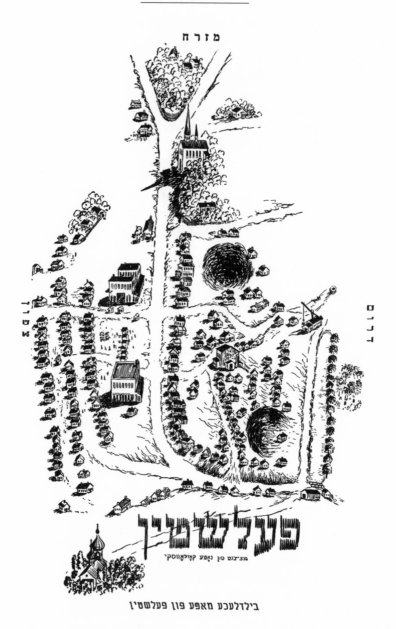

מזרח

מערב

דרום

פעלשטין

געצ״בנט פון נאטע קאזלאווסקי

בילדלעכע מאפע פון פעלשטין

Fig. 4.2. Notte Kozlovsky, "Bird's-Eye View of Felshtin," from *Felshtin zamlbukh: tsum ondenk fun di felshtiner kdoyshim*, ed. J. Baum (New York: First Felsteener Benevolent Association, 1937).

intentionally juvenile appearance, for all its massive size), and to provide two more versions of the shtetl entire: one a ghoulish image of Felshtin in the shape of a skull (fig. 4.3), and another that depicts the town—churches and all—descending like a cloud until it comes to rest within the Manhattan skyline (fig. 4.4). The message could not be clearer. Taken together, the maps lay out the narrative history of the shtetl according to a familiar, archetypal pattern: from obscure birth, to full flowering, to suffering and mass martyrdom, to rebirth in the Promised Land.

The Felshtin memorial book was the second of many. For the most profound break was still to come. In the shtetl's last chapter, the surviving sons and daughters of the European catastrophe became the scribes of a new, collective scripture. Together, in the face of their common loss, they found a form of recovery commensurate with the loss.

At long last, the Jews of the shtetl assumed full responsibility for recording its history. They did so piecemeal, town by town, with little professional help, and from the geographical remove of North and South America, Israel, and France. There are by now some twelve hundred such *yizkor* books, and they have become the memory bank of East European Jewry. This grassroots phenomenon is unique. Although the yizkor books await their own historian, it is possible to draw some tentative conclusions.[42]

1. The yizkor books represent a valiant group effort to shape the disparate and conflicting memories of former shtetl inhabitants and the pieces of the symbolic shtetl landscape into a lasting, coherent, memorial.

2. The primary function of these communal histories is to work through the collective trauma of the Holocaust. The crowded pages of yizkor books are therefore dedicated to the memory of the Jewish life that was destroyed.

3. After a brief chapter that outlines what little is known about Jewish life in the town prior to the twentieth century, the yizkor book hits its stride with vignettes about the coexistence of tradition and modernity on the crowded shtetl streets: rabbis, scholars, philanthropists, merchants, and madmen, rubbing shoulders with political activists, youth groups, amateur actors, soccer players, cyclists, modern women, and local boys who made good.

4. Within that idealized group portrait, there is an occasional Polish nobleman to liven things up. Otherwise, the Gentiles are depicted as an undifferentiated mass of peasants who appear and disappear on market day. Jewish-gentile relations are recalled in the context of strikes, pogroms, anti-Jewish boycotts, murders, and the Holocaust.

5. Every yizkor book includes detailed eyewitness accounts of the beat-

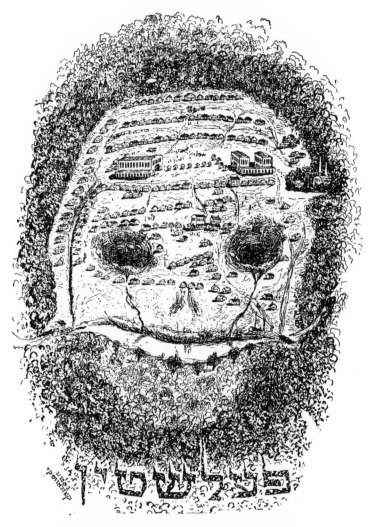

פעלשטין האָט אויסגעזעהן ווי אַ שאַרבען

Fig. 4.3. Notte Kozlovsky, "Felshtin Looked Like a Skull," from
Felshtin zamlbukh: tsum ondenk fun di felshtiner kdoyshim, ed. J. Baum
(New York: First Felsteener Benevolent Association, 1937). The lime pits
that doubled as the town dump define the eyes.

Fig. 4.4. Notte Kozlovsky, "The Felshtin Association," from *Felshtin zamlbukh: tsum ondenk fun di felshtiner kdoyshim*, ed. J. Baum (New York: First Felsteener Benevolent Association, 1937).

ings, hangings, shootings, ghettoization, and total annihilation of the Jews. They name names. They are almost too harrowing to read.

In more ways than one, these memorial books are a species of fiction. They borrow unconsciously from literary sources, even as they interpolate bona fide works of prose, poetry, and professional memoir. The *landslayt* are justifiably proud of their native sons and daughters who became published authors, and they comb through their writings for suitable material. In this way, paradoxically, a literature that tried to emancipate itself from the shtetl was reabsorbed back into it.

The evolution of the shtetl into a covenantal landscape reaches its logical conclusion in the yizkor books. The literary image of the shtetl, as we have seen, was deliberately fashioned *from the very outset* to incorporate the shtetl's demise into its physical landscape, its mythic structure, and its ideological message. The writers—who were the prophets and rabbis of the Jewish immigrant masses—had been pronouncing the shtetl's last rites for a hundred years. The immigrant experience now confirmed from below what the writers had been pronouncing from above at least since the days of Sholem Aleichem and Peretz: The shtetl is dead. Long live the shtetl!

The memorial books, by never allocating more than a third of their space to documenting the destruction of the town at the hands of the Germans and their willing collaborators, make each volume into a testament of life-in-death. As tradition and modernity once rubbed shoulders on the shtetl streets, so are grainy images of the lost home juxtaposed with photos of well-dressed shtetl sons and daughters in their far-flung promised lands. Whenever and wherever they reconvene for a group photo, they reassert the final, stirring words of the Partisans' Hymn: "*Mir zaynen do*, we are here!"

Two Polish towns have come to embody the struggle for the resurrected soul of the shtetl: Konin and Brańsk. And they are as different as any two towns can be. The British-born author Theo Richmond pieced together the history and life of Jewish Konin by learning Yiddish, memorizing the *Konin Memorial Book*, interviewing and corresponding with informants living on three continents, and finally, making the pilgrimage to Konin proper. In *Konin: A Quest*, he reenacts the arduous journey and shows how difficult it is to flesh out the censored memories, reconcile partisan perspectives, and negotiate among warring personalities.[43] Richmond is never more honest than when he attends a memorial meeting of the Ladies' and Men's Society of Konin, Inc., on the Lower East Side of Manhattan. Seeing them as a group, in all their contentiousness, our second-generation Koniner reasserts his British abhorrence for "undisciplined" and "petty" behavior (p. 151). Here Richmond also reveals a profound truth: that it is often easier to love the dead Jews than the living.

Richmond's last stop, Konin proper, is the least satisfying, because he is rushed through it by an over-eager guide and because—and this is a moment of truth—Konin is *Judenrein*. Richmond underscores the screaming silence of present-day Konin by saving for last the most terrible text in the most terrible tongue: a Polish "Protokol" of the Konin killing fields. Nothing has prepared the reader for the unmediated horror of this document, taken straight out of the memorial book. Yet for all that, there are still two more chapters to go. Death will have no dominion over this resurrected town of Polish Jews.

In *Shtetl* (1994), the documentary filmmaker Marian Marzynski takes the opposite route.[44] Marzynski begins in present-day Brańsk, and Polish is his lingua franca. Here, the full weight of the Holocaust is brought to bear both upon the town itself and upon the following cast of characters: Nathan Kaplan, an American Jew who wants to touch his parents' and grandparents' shtetl just once before he dies; Jack (alias Yankele) Rubin, a robust survivor who is lured into going back; a sensitive young Pole named Zbyszek Romaniuk, who makes the excavation of Brańsk's Jewish past into his abiding passion; and Marian Marzynski, a survivor of a different hell, who is using the shtetl to settle a very old score. The film makes but a perfunctory nod to the shtetl's prewar past. For several hours, the viewer watches Marzynski and Company crisscross the globe as they debate one single point: How and why the Poles betrayed their Jewish neighbors. After all is said and done, the shtetl emerges as a place no one in his right mind would ever want to die in, much less live in.

From the Holy Community to the Yizkor Book; from Kola Street to Konin; from the Dead Town to the town of the vengeful dead. There are manifold signs that the shtetl will continue to excite the imagination and to jog the memories of those who never lived there. Recently, the shtetl has made a surprising comeback within American-Jewish writing. The town of Proszowice is the setting of Melvin Jules Bukiet's irreverent bildungsroman, *Stories of an Imaginary Childhood* (1992), and the more improbable town of "Shluftchev (i.e, Sleepyville), Galicia" in Rebecca Goldstein's *Mazel* (1995) is home to a feminist family that loves nothing better than to sit around and sing. The main communal activity described by Steve Stern in his shtetl-by-the-Mississippi is dreaming; hence the title, *A Plague of Dreamers* (1994). But unlike Abramovitsh's and Sholem Aleichem's shtetl folk, who dream in concert, Stern's almost-American offspring each dreams his and her individual dreams.[45] The only recent novelist who renders the shtetl as a self-regulating, culturally autonomous, and historically vulnerable Jewish community is Allen Hoffman.[46] He does so, in the long-standing tradition of shtetl fiction, by centering the plot on the house of study. The place is Krimsk, a border town somewhere in the Polish part of the Pale of Settlement. The year is 1903, in the aftermath of the infamous Kishinev pogrom. The day is Tisha b'Av, and the whole male Jewish population of town is assembled in the Krimsker Rebbe's *besmedresh* to recite the Dirges and the Book of Lamentations while sitting on overturned benches. Like Jerusalem, Krimsk is under siege, as much from the inside as from the outside. But all is not doom and gloom, for it is a shtetl rendered by means of magic realism and drenched in Jewish knowledge. According to the jacket copy, Hoffman has set out to reclaim the shtetl as a covenantal community, this being "the first in a series of novels following the people of Krimsk and their descendants in America, Russia, Poland, and Israel." Krimsk, in other words, is a "small world" that contains within itself the seeds of its own redemption.

5 Rabbis, Rebels, and the Lost Art of the Law

"The revolution—we will say yes to her, but will we say no to the Sabbath?"
—Isaac Babel, 1924

"Please! Listen to yourself! My God, who was the man? Rabbi Isaac Kornfeld! Talk of honor! Wasn't he a teacher? Wasn't he a scholar?"
  "He was a pagan."
—Cynthia Ozick, 1966

They were an obvious target, universally revered. In the folk imagination, rabbis writ small were the butt of countless jokes. Writ large, they embodied the model of the sacred life. The greatest among them were referred to solely by their code names. Since the advent of printing, Rashi's eleventh-century commentary in its own special typeface turned the Hebrew Bible into a lucid and contemporary text. His "true" historical identity as Rabbi Solomon ben Isaac was replaced by his acronym, an intimate in every Jewish household. Israel Zychlinski, for example, dealt in cattle, and was certainly no scholar, but "Reb Israel loved Rashi with all his heart, looking upon him as a near relative, a member of the family of all Jews."[1] In more learned homes, one turned to the great and imperious "Rambam" (Maimonides), to the erudite "Maharsha" (Rabbi Samuel Eliezer Edels, 1555–1631), or to the "saintly Shelo," whose acronym derived from his major tome, *Shnei luḥot habrit [The Two Tablets of the Covenant]*), and not from his "real" name, Rabbi Isaiah Horowitz (ca. 1565–1630). These great men also lived on as the heroes of legend, notably, the Ari, or "Lion," Rabbi Isaac Luria of Safed (1534–1572), whose mystical exploits spread far and wide. Sometimes, their fanciful likenesses hung from the walls.

Even without recourse to these mnemonics, which turned the whole of the Exile into an unbroken chain of great rabbinic figures, those who observed the Jews from up close shared a similar construction. Dispersed among the nations, the Jews bore the signs of the covenant upon their foreheads and on the doorposts of their segregated houses; and in lieu of temporal rulers, they were guided by scholars noted for their piety and full-length beards. What distinguished the Jews, for better or worse, was the somber or comical or bedraggled or regal figure that their rabbis cut in the world. In Poland today, you can find rabbis carved out of wood, in all shapes and sizes. There are gaunt ones, stained a deep brown, from Lodz, and grotesque ones, in gaudy colors, from Nowy Sądz. In the Old Town of Warsaw, rebuilt from the ruins, a talented young sculptor hawks his large figurines of a rabbi with deep-set eyes. He is sculpted carrying a book half the size of his body.

However revered by the folk, the traditional *mara d'atra*, the rabbi as halachic authority, was increasingly under siege: from Hasidism, which sought to replace him with the charismatic zaddik; from the Haskalah, which sought to replace him either with the government-appointed Rabbiner or with the didactic writer passing himself off as a preacher and teacher in Israel; and, most subversive of all, from within the ranks of the rabbinic elite itself, the so-called Misnagdim, or "Opponents," who sought to replace him with the Rosh Yeshiva, the head of the talmudic academies newly established throughout White Russia.[2] What the folk said only in jest—"*ikh her im vi dem rov*, I wouldn't listen to so-and-so any more than I would to the rabbi"—became the rallying cry all across Jewish Eastern Europe. A campaign to delegitimate the rabbinic leadership was being waged on all fronts.

In Jewish linguistic practice, each side encamped under a different flag. Any male Jew in standard Yiddish parlance was addressed as "Reb yid, Mr. Jew." Children and boys called their teacher *rebe* (plural: *rebes*). *Rebe* (plural: *rebeim*) was the hasidic leader, also known as "der guter yid, the good Jew," or the zaddik. The most radical sect of Hasidim were the followers of Nahman ben Simha of Braslav, who never chose another zaddik in his stead. One of the ways in which they kept his presence alive was by referring to him as *Reb* Nahman, a term of endearment. Modern disciples who "correct" this to *Rav* Nahman are making a big mistake, because they are blurring the essential distinction between the charismatic leader, who derived his authority directly from God, as it were, and the rabbi, who received his title by mastering God's Law. A rabbi—always addressed in the third person as *der rov* (plural: *rabonim*), with a definite article—was the one (along with his qualified assistant, the *dayyan*) to adjudicate all matters of Jewish law. Finally, there was a new class of government-appointed rabbis who, because their title was imported from the West, went by the German name of *Rabbiner*. It was an assignment for which only maskilic cadets need apply.

The latter, while few in number, waged the battle for the hearts and minds of the literate Jewish population with the arsenal of the newest available weaponry. For if the *am hasefer*, the People of Scripture, were ever to become the People of the Secular Book, the critical objective was to neutralize the whole class of men who controlled the writing and explication of great Jewish books. As the Maskilim began to seize alternative means of cultural production—novels, newspapers, pamphlets, and plays—they discovered a remarkably effective way of beating the intellectual and spiritual leaders on their own turf. Turn them into fictional characters, then burlesque them, upstage them, and efface them. Divide and conquer, driving a wedge between the "good" class of rabbis and the "bad," the rabbis of yesteryear and today. Better yet—coopt them, turning the rabbi into a mouthpiece for a new subversive Torah. The first generation of secular Jewish writers had their tactical goal laid out for them: nothing less than constructing a Jewish future with an enlightened officer leading the charge.

Rabbis, Rebels, and Rebeim in Crisis

It was easy enough for the Maskilim, vocal advocates of educational reform, to make short shrift of all the rebes-as-in-teachers, with whom they were in direct competition. A sorry lot, underpaid and underqualified. Or so it would seem, judging from the myriad autobiographies and novels-of-education by Jewish males, all of whom, from Linetzky's *Polish Lad* (1867) to Henry Roth's David Schearl in *Call It Sleep* (1934), suffered terribly at the hands of sadistic and ignorant rebes.[3]

Because the same Maskilim viewed the rebeim as the root of all evil, ruthlessly exploiting their credulous flock, entering into unholy alliances with the local Polish squire, seducing men away from their wives and families for months on end, the hasidic leaders became a permanent fixture of Yiddish and Hebrew satire, where they were portrayed as corpulent, malevolent, Asiatic, as charlatans.[4] So far, so bad.

The campaign against the rabbinate was of an entirely different order. Moderate Maskilim, like the Yiddish popularizer Isaac Meir Dik, used a divide-and-conquer strategy. Just as he lampooned the rebeim and rebes of his own time, he raided the Ashkenazic past for heroic exploits, peopling his thirty-two-page chapbooks with real and invented episodes in the life of Rabbi Yom Tov Lipmann Heller (1579–1654), Rabbi David Halevi (the TaZ; 1586–1667), and Reb Shmelke of Nikolsburg (1726–1778).[5] If only Russian Jewry could produce an enlightened rabbinate as had existed before the rise of Hasidism!

The more radical Russian Maskilim engaged in a frontal attack. The Hebrew poet and essayist Judah Leib Gordon (1830–1892) was the great exemplar. His mock epic poem, "The Tip of the Yud" (1875), in particular, which exposed the ignorance and obscurantism of the Russian rabbis and their heartless attitude to the plight of Jewish women, won him instant renown as a leading exponent of religious reform. Gordon paid with a prison sentence and temporary exile.[6]

Who would fill the power vacuum, in fiction if not in fact, once the education of the young was no longer entrusted to the old class of Bible and Talmud instructors, once the wonder-working rebbes were laughed off the stage of history, and once the present-day rabbinate was cut down to size? The most brilliant tactic, adapted for the field of literary battle by Sholem Yankev Abramovitsh, was to upstage the rabbi with someone far more clever, critical, and above all, autonomous, than any rabbi could possibly be. Earlier in the nineteenth century, this figure had appeared in the guise of The Spectator Unto the House of Israel.[7] This was acceptable in Hebrew letters, where bombast was the order of the day. The lowly field of Yiddish required someone more modest, and therefore, potentially more subversive.

And so it is that Abramovitsh's inaugural Yiddish work, *The Parasite* (*Dos kleyne mentshele*, 1864), opens with Reb Mendele the Book Peddler driving into Glupsk (or Foolstown) with his horse and book-laden buggy, whereupon he is urgently called away to the home of the rabbi. The local Croesus has just dropped dead and has left instructions that his last will and testament be entrusted to none other than Reb Mendele. From this moment on, Mendele, by playing the straight man and never overstaying his welcome, will steal this and every other show. Over the course of his peripatetic career, Mendele will embody a bold new counternorm, which replaces culture with nature, stasis with movement, the credulous collective with the critical individual.[8]

In Abramovitsh's voluminous writings, all of them set in the cities and towns of Jewish Eastern Europe, rabbis make but a cameo appearance. For all the ethnographic and historical sweep of his celebrated memoir, *Of Bygone Days*, Abramovitsh's reimagined White Russian shtetl has no rabbis or even Talmud scholars. Besides mother and father, both portrayed in soft hues, those who loom largest in Shloyme's spiritual landscape are shtetl artisans, who occupy the margins of respectable society. Father, who collects the tax for kosher meat, is the only man in town to interact with the Polish count. When father dies, the shtetl's security dies with him. Later, Shloyme will go off to study—and to starve—in the Slutsk yeshiva. Meanwhile, those gratuitous barbs at the expense of the hasidic rebeim, which had betrayed Abramovitsh's allegiance to the Haskalah, were systematically expunged from the definitive edition of his *Collected Works*. It did not behoove a "classical" writer to beat a dead horse.[9]

The Maskilim who entered the fray had every reason to expect logistical support from headquarters. Why else would the tsar have established two rabbinical seminaries, one in Vilna, the other in Zhitomir, if not to train a Jewish officer corps that would help vanquish the foe? One such cadet was Solomon Rabinovitsh, whose first posting as Rabbiner was in the godforsaken town of Luben. It was also his last. Ignored and rebuffed by the Jews of the shtetl, Rabinovitsh deserted the ranks of the rabbinic reformers and resurfaced as a writer with a new nom-de-guerre: Sholem Aleichem. His inaugural sketch under that assumed name made it clear that satire and ironic self-effacement were the better part of valor. Throughout "The Elections" for government-appointed Rabbiner, the candidate never gets a word in edgewise.[10]

In Sholem Aleichem's mature fiction, there is similarly no historical role for rabbis to play. All of Sholem Aleichem's main actors are salt of the earth: Tevye the Dairyman, Menakhem-Mendl the schlemiel, Shimen-Elye Shma-Koleynu, Shimele Soroker, Motl the orphaned son of Peyse the cantor. At best, Reb Yuzifl the rabbi of Kasrilevke can offer up psalms in times of distress ("The Great Panic of the Little People," 1904), or the rabbi of Krushnik may himself be offered up on the gallows as a silent prayer ("Tales of 1001 Nights," 1914).[11]

Through this fusion of the tragic and the comic, Sholem Aleichem reinvigorated the folk conception of the rabbi-as-schlemiel, the one who ends up with egg on his face precisely because he is the guardian of public morals. A brilliant variation on this theme is Hayyim Nahman Bialik's Reb Lippe, himself a close cousin of one Reb Zaynvl, whose foibles were once described in the pages of a Yiddish newspaper. There, through a comic turn of events, a rabbi desecrated the Sabbath in full public view, bearing out the benign moral of the story: Everything depends on luck. Here, in "The Short Friday" (1925), Bialik's rabbi is guilty of slavish adherence to routine and to time. What happens to a man who never allows the Aggadah, the imagination, to inform his strict observance of the Halachah? His fate is left subversively hanging in the Sabbath afternoon air.[12]

What is this? Rabbis desecrating the Sabbath, even if only by mistake? Rabbis upstaged by mere itinerant book peddlers? Dairymen who can play with Scripture more inventively than professional "men of the cloth"? And *where* is all this happening? In the very country where the greatest prose masters—Dostoevsky, Tolstoy, and Leskov—have brought religious passion into the foreground of secular culture! Where is the Jewish Alyosha Karamazov? The Grand Inquisitor? Ivan Ilych's epiphany before death? The equivalent gallery of Leskov's Old Believers?

The equivalent Jewish drama was being played out in the confessions of young Hebrew intellectuals. Theirs was a wrenching tale of loss of faith, of young men "banished from their father's table," as Alan Mintz titled his excellent book on the subject. Where once Jewish poets and chroniclers lamented the *ḥurban beit hamikdash*, the destruction of the Temple in Jerusalem, they now lamented the *ḥurban beit hamidrash*, the loss of traditional faith as centered in the old House of Study. Suddenly, in a literary movement fueled by optimism and hope for imminent reform, all was generational breakdown, apostasy, sexual impotence, despair. Where the attack on the old order had been predicated on the victory of a new, secular, leadership, the battlefield was now littered with corpses. Where once there was a Spectator Over the House of Israel, there was now a lone Wanderer in the Ways of Life.[13]

Many were the new paths these young men—and now, women—would follow: nihilism, populism, socialism, Zionism, aestheticism. Some writers, like Berdyczewski, Bergelson, and Brenner (the last, a disciple of Dostoevsky), would make the *talush*, or uprooted intellectual, the hero of a new age, who was caught dangling among a myriad of possibilities. Their psychologically realistic novels and novellas rank among the masterpieces of Jewish literary modernism.[14]

But there was another direction taken that cuts to the very core of our inquiry about the dynamic of loss and retrieval in modern Jewish culture. Once rebellion became the sine qua non of authenticity, and once there was no escape from the recognition of the multiple losses that had occurred, the dynamic of cultural retrieval kicked in. For the young, second-generation rebels of Jewish Eastern Europe, the only usable past was a rebellious past. Rabbis, for the time being, were unsalvageable, both because they were the sworn guardians of an ultraconservative Tradition and because the rebellion against them was still in full swing. If the model for a sacred person were to be found, it would have to be found somewhere else—in the severed past and beyond the pale of strict halachic observance. This is how the hasidic rebbe was reborn as a rebel.

It began, modestly enough, in 1900, with a rebe-as-in-teacher narrating a story in honor of the festival of Simhat Torah. With breathless adulation, he tells of one Reb Noah, who broke away from the yeshiva of the Brisker Rov because he found the misnagdic Torah too "cold" and forbidding. Escaping to the more spiritual pastures of Hasidism, Reb Noah eventually "revealed himself" as a rebbe in the town of Biala. At the story's climax, the credulous narrator finds himself standing "Between Two Mountains," between the dry, uncompromising rule of the Law, and the spontaneous communion with nature and song that Hasidism offers. Were this any other day of the Jewish calendar, there might still have been a contest. On Simhat

Torah, when even the most strictly observant Jews are enjoined to sing and dance in honor of the Torah, there is little question that the lovable Reb Noah has the upper hand over the imperious Brisker Rov. What's more, the face-off between them occurs in Biala, on Reb Noah's own turf. Yet, so meager were I. L. Peretz's artistic resources at this point in time that the contest ends in a draw.[15]

Peretz's next attempts were exponentially more ambitious. Influenced by Nietzsche and parallel trends in Polish culture, Peretz began to celebrate the visionary leaders who transcended historical exigency. In Hasidism, which he knew mainly from books and articles in the Polish-Jewish press, Peretz found exactly the forms and plots that he needed. Early Hasidism, as opposed to its later, dynastic rule, served Peretz as the breeding ground for a true spiritual leader who could hasten the millennium by severing the bonds of historical determinism. That is how Peretz came upon the first "modern" Yiddish storyteller, Reb Nahman of Braslav, whose enigmatic tales and dreams became a vehicle for Peretz's own hopes and fears.[16] The later, dynastic struggle within the hasidic movement gave Peretz the dramatic means to plot the metahistorical crisis of modern Jewry. The more he betrayed Hasidism in the name of modern values, the easier it was for him to rescue what little he deemed salvageable.

When the curtain rises on Peretz's drama *The Golden Chain*, we come upon the rebbe in his moment of crisis.[17] The meticulous stage design does not as yet give anything away, other than that the rebbe holds court in a former nobleman's mansion, in which the statues have had their noses cut off to avert the sin of idolatry. Nor has the audience yet learned the rule of thumb of a modern Yiddish play, novel, or poem: the more overtly "religious" its setting, the more secular its concerns. Since the messianic theme in particular, as Khone Shmeruk has cogently argued, arose not from an ongoing debate with past traditions but precisely from the crisis of Jewish modernity, it follows that the figure who stood for that crisis could not be some fabulously successful miracle worker busily negotiating this world and the next, but rather, the zaddik at odds with his surroundings, captured in a moment of personal, religious, and existential turmoil.[18]

Reb Shloyme desires nothing less than the abrogation of Time. Calling for a race of spiritual giants, Reb Shloyme's ecstatic vision of *shabes-yontefdike yidn*, who would force God's hand by ushering in the messianic Sabbath, is doomed from the start. Each of his successors will likewise attempt a reversal of the natural order and will face defeat within his own hasidic court, but for sheer poetic force, none will match Reb Shloyme's defiance of history itself. Shloyme's offspring, with weaker lines to speak and less transcendental ambitions, are that much worse off, coming as they do after the last great hurrah of Jewish self-liberation. *Their* struggle is more closely confined to the historical arena, while Peretz invented Reb Shloyme out of whole cloth, just as he did the image of an unbroken chain going back to the Besht. In form and content, Peretz's drama owes much more to Polish Romanticism than it does to Polish Hasidism.[19]

The Lost Art of the Law

Peretz reemployed a divide-and-conquer strategy in order to sepa-rate the usable past from the dead present. Peretz's rabbis, great talmudists, and rebeim flourish in the Poland of yesteryear, in a mock-legendary world of miracles, and languish in the Poland of today.[20] By weighting down the few survivors with so much ideological freight, however, he robbed them of their essential humanity. The harsh verdict handed down by Chaim Grade some half-century later is an indictment of Peretz and his legacy. "Our only spiritual leaders," Grade lamented in the preface to *The Agunah* (1961),

> have either been characterized in a completely negative way, under the general, pejorative, label of "clergy"; or they have been described only in terms of externals (the beards, the kaftans and the gestures) but not separated into different types, as though following a formula that "all rabbis have one face"; or they have been removed from their bodies and appearances altogether in order to present them as symbols of good deeds or personifications of pure ideas; or they have become legendary heroes; or theatrical figures, decorative and pathetic.[21]

Grade's words cannot be dismissed merely as an advertisement for himself and for the novels he would produce during the two decades to come. They point to a blind spot within secular Jewish culture as a whole.

In fashioning their own artistic medium, modern writers made a signifi-cant contribution to the Jewish mnemonic arts by refashioning a model of the sacred person (the zaddik), of sacred space (the shtetl), and, eventually, of awesome time (the Holocaust). The quintessential Jewish art—that of the law—was accorded no role at all. From Heine on, Jewish poets and neoromantics waxed eloquent about the Sabbath, when even the lowliest Jew was transformed into a prince.[22] But the Sabbath is nothing if not a legal construct, fenced in by centuries of rabbinic legislation. The defini-tion of one's private domain is the *eyruv*, the wire or string that delineates the outer boundaries where carrying is permitted on the Sabbath. The most intimate contact between Jews and Gentiles occurred on the Sabbath in the institution of the *shabes-goy*, the Gentile who performed such forbidden yet essential tasks as remove the candlesticks from the table, or extinguish the oven. The foods that set the Sabbath apart from the rest of the week—the braided chalas and the heavy, meat-laden stew called *tsholnt*—met the strict halachic requirements. Without rabbinic law and those who enforced it, there was no time to read, relax, feast, or fantasize.

From the perspective of those who rebelled against it, the law was an art neither in form nor in content. Formally, the talmudic *sugyah* and the medieval codes of law were unassimilable within the Hellenistic scheme of epic, lyric, satire, and melodrama. The best that could be done in the modern Hellenistic age was to "rescue" the lore from the body of the law and repackage it as narrative and folklore. This is what Bialik and Ravnitzky did in *Sefer haʾaggadah*.[23] In a separate essay on "Halachah and Aggadah," Bialik allowed that Jewish law was alive to the poetry of nature, but in a form so cramped and chaotic that it would require a poet-magician to transform it into true epic.[24] The same was true even for Hasidism, for all its much-vaunted celebration of spontaneity, story, and song. So much attention is lavished on hasidic tales and songs precisely because they are the only forms of hasidic self-expression that are accessible to Western sensibilities. "Real" hasidic teaching is embedded in a dense and associative fabric that nowadays requires for decoding an advanced degree in Bible, Midrash, medieval Bible commentary, and Zohar.

Studied selectively, Hasidism was so much more "betrayable," which is to say, usable, than the Halachah. The law is the law, the thing itself, seemingly immutable. Compare that with the mystical credo of God's immanence in all things, and the mystical style that borders on stream of consciousness. The latter make it relatively easy to read one's own belief system back into the Jewish past. In this century alone, Hasidism has been reappropriated in the name of Romanticism, Socialism, Orientalism, Symbolism, Ecumenicism, Freudianism, Communitarianism, Existentialism, and then some. For a time, from 1907 to 1913, the debate over the essence of Hasidism became a critical exercise in values clarification among members of the Hebrew intelligentsia. For acculturated German Jews, the Buber-*mayses* replaced the Bible.[25]

At the risk of breaking my neat chronology, let me introduce a passage from *Khayim Gravitser* (1922), a novel about the beginnings of the Lubavitsh branch of Hasidism in White Russia. Until now, we have barely seen or heard from the hero, whose name is shrouded in legend even in his lifetime. No sooner is Gravitser offered a rabbinical post recently vacated, however, than he has this to say:[26]

"So I gather that you idiots of the town council want to make Khayim Gravitser into a fine rabbi? Don't you know, first off, that Khayim Gravitser downs 100 proof vodka all the time, is a perpetual wanderer who throws himself this way and that and gives no quarter either to himself or to others—is this a fit for a fine rabbi? Second, a rabbi gets all kinds of creatures brought before him to decide whether they're kosher, but another time the whole of Khayim Gravitser needs to be brought before the real rabbi to decide whether he, Gravitser, is kosher. Third, a fine rabbi cannot be reminding all the fools that they are really and truly fools, heaven forbid. So if you made Khayim Gravitser into a fine rabbi, who would be the one to remind you? But most important"—and at this point he jumped up and spoke with anger—"how did you maniacs get it into your head to choose a rabbi without asking the rebbe's permission? Ask Lubavitsh—that's where we all draw all our sustenance from!" Pointing to a package of manuscripts that lay on the table, he said, "Just take a look at what Isaac-Monish brought yesterday when he arrived on foot from Lubavitsh. When you study them your mind can burst—what miraculous times we've been privileged to live in! So who will explain these holy teachings to you? You depend on a lucky break, that Isaac-Monish the pauper will do it, that Khayim Gravitser the drunk will do it. The rebbe will send us a rabbi who will arouse and quench our thirst from that holy source that flows in front of our very eyes and never runs dry. Gevald! You idiots! You certainly hit on the right person to kiss up to. Town idiots!"

Who needs to be a rabbi when radical self-confrontation is the route to holiness? What is the Law at a time of new revelation? What authority does a rabbi have over new states of consciousness? Clearly, when Dr. Fishl Schneourson raided the teachings of his illustrious forebear, he did so not in order to sing the praises of Rabbi Schneor Zalman of Lyadi (1745–1812), the first Lubavitsher Rebbe, but to tell "the true story of the Fallen One," Khayim Gravitser. A "true," hard-drinking Hasid was a rebel by any other name.

Young Rebel Takes All

The stage was now set for S. Ansky to map out a brilliant strategy for Jewish renewal: if the young did not rebel against the past, it would be lost forever.

Ansky was ideally suited for the task because, as a hasid of I. L. Peretz, he undertook the most systematic search to date for a positive hero and heroine in all walks of traditional Jewish life. The operative principle of Ansky's stylized folktales, written between 1903 and 1910, was *mesires-nefesh farn klal-yisroel*, self-sacrifice for the sake of the Jewish collective. Exemplars of such sacrifice he discovered among all classes and all ideological strands of Jewry. Next, Ansky turned back to his own adolescent rebellion and recast the young and totally self-sacrificing Maskilim of the 1870s and 1880s as folk heroes. Finally, in his crowning work, *Between Two Worlds, or The Dybbuk* (1914–1917), he brought all these strands together. Ansky satisfied the audience's hunger to glimpse the beauty of a lost civilization by providing a rich tapestry of hasidic life and lore. Most thrilling for the youthful audience, however, was to see *itself* mirrored in the shtetl past. For the star-crossed lovers Khonon and Leah, alone and in the face of all odds, challenged the moral and metaphysical order by sacrificing their own earthly pleasures and desires. Together, Reb Azrielke, the zaddik, and Reb Shimshon, the Rabbi of Miropolye, could not counteract the irrational power of young love. Only the love that had sundered the worlds could bring them back together—but at the price of a future that was tragically dead-ended.[27]

Something similar happens to young Mordecai, the intellectual hero of Joseph Opatoshu's *In poylishe velder* (*In Polish Woods*, 1921), the first bona fide historical novel in Yiddish.[28] By choosing as his initial setting a forest far removed from organized Jewish life, Opatoshu made the contest amongst competing cultural forces that much more dramatic. Mordecai's life is a crash course in the history of Polish Jewry; a Jewry, he is to learn, that sprang directly from the verdant Polish forests with their birdsong and beech trees, each inscribed with the names of the Jewish Founding Fathers; with their half-pagan, half-Christian fisherfolk; with their Jewish military heroes and heretics, mystics and rebels, scholars and saints. Reaching out behind him to the preceding generations, Mordecai "felt in him a surge of power to continue spinning the thread" (Y 38; E 37). As in Peretz, the generational "golden chain" is forged out of great rebellious spirits. As in Ansky, the tapestry of the living past is spread as wide as possible. Mordecai's curriculum now includes the legend of Napoleon, the cobbler's apprentice who rose to be emperor; the saga of Berek Joselewicz, martyred to the cause of Polish independence; the story of Yosl Shtral, the last "light-beam" of the Haskalah; the glorious exploits of Shlomo Molkho—"Elijah the Prophet, who came to tell the world that the Messiah was seated before the gates of Rome, preaching God's word, declaring that the Tiber would inundate the sinful city, and that Clement the Seventh was abandoning his palace in terror, was running away . . . " (Y 258; E 299). Young and ever so malleable, Mordecai is also on the run—from one century to another—as he tries to keep the precious thread of Jewish continuity from snapping.

The crucible of Jewish continuity is the Polish shtetl of Kotsk (Kock), the goal of Mordecai's pilgrimage and the place of his longest sojourn. The reason is obvious. Menakhem-Mendl, the Rebbe of Kotsk (1787–1859), is the consummate Jewish rebel, having spent thirteen years of his life in self-imposed isolation. Unfortunately, Mordecai's timing is disastrously off, since the rebbe has emerged from isolation just long enough to blaspheme against God. The more reclusive, the more the zaddik is now beset by the lamed, the crazed, and the impoverished. Mordecai's first encounter with one of Polish Jewry's greatest religious personalities is most inauspicious:

> The rabbi, a diminutive gray figure, with a beard so heavy that it
> obscured his face altogether, was at the window, his fists clenched, and
> was shouting to the crowd:
> "You oxen, you! Out of my sight! I'm no physician! I had hoped to be
> a doctor of souls, but you've turned me into a horse doctor. What do
> you want now?" (Y 155; E 179)

Things do not improve once he is granted an audience with the rebbe. Mordecai discovers a misanthrope motivated solely by self-interest, a man preoccupied with death and the afterlife.

Kotsk is in its death throes, as is the rebbe himself. Not even the saintly and Christ-like figure of Reb Itche, who routinely brings solace to all the infirm, whether Jewish or gentile, and who throws himself at the Kotsker's feet to demonstrate his fealty before the unruly crowd, will ultimately keep our impressionable hero loyal to Kotsk. Militating against the decision to stay is Mordecai's growing attraction to the worldly and unhappily married Felice, followed by the grotesque sight of the community fighting over who will wash the zaddik's corpse. Kotsk, itself in terminal crisis, offers no solace for a young Jew caught up in the maelstrom of historical forces and se-duced by the greater riches that lie in store for him in the salons of Poland and beyond.[29]

Opatoshu's novel, and the trilogy of which it was to form a part, did much to make the history of Jewish rebellion into a covenantal narrative, but it did little to reinstate the Jewish religious leadership as the guardians of that covenant. The desperate need to believe in a living Jewish past, rooted in a mythic, preindustrial landscape and answering the call of uni-versal redemption, could be met only by expunging the arcane halachic particulars of rabbinic Judaism and the extreme particularism of East European Jewish pietism.

The rebellion of the young, be they the idealistic Leah, Khonon, or Mordecai, presupposes a secular humanistic world order in which individual action counts for something and where the betterment of life on earth is a laudable goal. The Miropolyer zaddik and the Kotsker Rebbe were of sufficient stature to make the contest worthwhile. Not so in I. J. Singer's novel *Yoshe Kalb* (1932), where the zaddik of Nyesheve is finally bested by the pathological young Nachum-Yoshe.[30] A venal ignoramus, ironically named Reb Melekh (King), Singer's patriarch sets the plot in motion by marrying off his youngest daughter in order to make room for his own remarriage. In a grotesque replay of Peretz's "Between Two Mountains," Singer has the misnagdic Rabbi of Rachmanivke meet his hasidic counterpart in Carlsbad:

> The Rabbi of Rachmanivke found his prospective relative insufferable. He was ashamed of him, ashamed of his wild voice and his wilder gestures, ashamed of the noisy way he sucked his cigar and spat on the floor, ashamed of his shapeless, unbuttoned satin *capote*, his unkempt beard and ear-locks, his indelicate language, and his whole vast body, covered with hair and reeking of sweat, cigar smoke, leather, food and drink (Y 13; E 10).

Not since the feisty days of the Galician Haskalah were Jewish readers treated to a zaddik more earthbound than the Rebbe Reb Melekh.

Or a zaddik more corrupt. The moral bankruptcy and social disparity of the hasidic court, whose royal family take the European spas at the expense of their vassals, make Nyesheve resemble nothing so much as a New Testament version of Herod's Temple. For Singer, the Hasidim are the Temple Priests incarnate. To bring about the destruction of this rotting Temple, there appears the ascetic and perpetually seeking figure of the rebbe's son-in-law, Nachum-Yoshe. He is a rebel without a cause. Like his namesake, Yoshke Pandre, the Yiddish folk-Jesus, the hero is an equivocal sinner condemned to wander in perpetual silence. Yoshe Kalb has the same initials as Jesus Christ.[31]

The Rebbe as Christian Saint

The identification of Hasidism with Christianity was bound to happen sooner or later. There were simply too many similarities between the

Gospels and *Shivhei haBesht* to have gone unnoticed. The "real" Baʿal Shem Tov may have been a prominent rabbi, just as the historical Jesus was a rabbinic Jew, but in legend, the Besht was of lowly origin, like the carpenter's son from Nazareth. In one unauthorized version, the Besht was conceived through immaculate conception.[32] The legendary lives of Jesus and the Baʿal Shem Tov were similarly taken up with going from one place to another, gathering disciples, healing the sick, doing miracles, preaching, and teaching. Although the Besht and all the zaddikim in his wake slept with their wives—there is no celibacy among the hasidic masters, as I. J. Singer graphically demonstrated—the Besht, like Jesus, would leave sacred relics behind. When the young Simon Dubnov went in search of the historical Baʿal Shem Tov, he was inspired to do so by reading Ernst Renan's *History of Christianity.* Like Renan, Dubnov separated the nature-loving spiritualist from the earth-bound institutions that he spawned; the teacher from his disciples; the man from the miracles.[33]

Ideologically, too, the two movements seemed to share common ground. Hasidism originally defined itself in opposition to rabbinic (= Pharisaic) authority. There was a strong messianic tendency in both faiths. And in legend at least, Hasidism was kind to women. All of these points of communality were enormously attractive to Peretz's chief disciple, Sholem Asch (1880–1957). Asch introduced a sentimental cult of Jewish motherhood bordering on Mariology; he led a vigorous campaign to ban the "barbaric" practice of circumcision; and he sought to drive a permanent wedge between Jewish law and ethics.[34] To close the hasidic-Christian circle, Asch wrote the first full-scale biography of a Jewish saint.

The road to sainthood is transgression, a path already tried by Yoshe Kalb. The more obscure his origins, the more certain it is that the Jewish saint will break down the barriers of time and space, rich and poor, Gentile and Jew. *Der tilim-yid* (1933), translated into German as *Der Trost des Volkes,* and from there into English as *Salvation,* is based on the obscure figure of Yechiel of Gostynin, a disciple of the Kotsker Rebbe.[35] Like Mordecai, our young seeker makes the pilgrimage to Kotsk. Like Nachum-Yoshe, he is reviled as a sinner. Like Khonon, he defies the limitations of the body in order to redeem the soul. *The Psalm Jew* is an encyclopedic work. Here, Sholem Asch revisits the entire course of Jewish spirituality in order to map out a new, syncretistic theology of mercy and compassion. Psalms eclipse every other book in the Torah. The Aggadah takes over completely from the Halachah. And all the great spiritual movements that Jews have ever spawned—Christianity, Pietism, Sabbatianism, and Hasidism—are appropriated to a single end: the fashioning of an ecumenical zaddik.

In the course of his eventful, miraculous life, Yechiel's single-minded pursuit of mercy puts him at odds with the stern justice of his father, of the Fruma Kuppa, a local woman who specializes in hellfire sermons, and, most significantly, with the Kotsker Rebbe. While yet a boy, Yechiel turns his back on the study of Talmud and is promptly demoted to the ranks of the semi-literate Reciters of Psalms. At the same time, Yechiel is consistently drawn to the downtrodden (beginning with his own mother), to Christians (beginning with his innocent attempt to convert them to the true faith in the very midst of a Corpus Christi procession), and to heretics (beginning with the Pitch Jew, a follower of Shabbetai Zvi). From the latter, the young adult learns to reconcile within himself the attributes of justice and mercy, to transmute the sin of sexuality, and to discover the messianic potential in every generation. On an unconscious level, Yechiel reenacts the life and crucifixion of Jesus.

At his most godlike, Yechiel acts as the spiritual catalyst in the birth of a girl to a childless couple. This not only comes close to superseding the Christian Nativity but also constitutes an act of hubris for which he, the girl, and her parents must endure great suffering. Yechiel has himself become a rebbe by this time, with many miracles to his name. The last is to engage in a cosmic struggle that pits justice against mercy. What tips the scales of heaven is the girl's decision to convert to Christianity so that she may marry outside the faith. To prevent this from happening, Yechiel, after intense spiritual turmoil, prays for her to die. Then, to fully expiate his own sin of complicity, in the Christian logic of this Polish-Yiddish narrative, Yechiel, too, must die.[36]

Yechiel—the rebbe of the poor and downtrodden—emerges as the apotheosis of a true Christianity and of Hasidism—as representing the highest ideals of European humanism. Taking *devekut*, for example, the central hasidic doctrine of merging one's individual identity with that of God, Yechiel adapts it for his own ends by fusing his identity with the divine attribute of mercy. This puts Yechiel on a collision course with the Kotsker Rebbe, who insists upon the primacy of law and divine justice. Yechiel emerges unscathed, with the Kotsker forced to acknowledge the validity of the young man's rebellious path. However, for Yechiel to alleviate the suffering of others, the Kotsker informs him, he must pay with his own suffering. By novel's end, the Psalm Jew comes to understand that it is not only *his* destiny but that of the entire People Israel to bear the sins of humanity.[37]

The Return of the Rabbi

That a hasidic rebbe, thus far represented as a mere mouthpiece (Peretz) or foil to the rebellion of the young (Ansky, Opatoshu, I. J. Singer), became a full-blown character with a complex psychological profile, represents a significant cultural development. No other single work of the Jewish literary imagination did more to reinstate the zaddik as the model of the sacred person than *The Psalm Jew*. But the one and only rabbi whom Asch would ever elevate to comparable status was Rabbi Yeshua ben Joseph of Nazareth, the hero of his historical novel, *The Nazarene* (1939). With true religious zeal, both the Yiddish establishment and its rank-and-file rejected Asch's attempt to rehabilitate the rabbinate in the name of Christianity.[38]

In all fairness, it must be said that Asch's radical ecumenicism was fueled by a sense of historical crisis. German Jewry was under siege when *The Psalm Jew* was written, and by the time it was finished, the only German-speaking country that would publish the translation was Switzerland. Ansky, too, had argued in 1913, before the board of the Jewish Ethnographic Expedition, that hasidic tales and legends were the best possible means of acquainting non-Jews with the aesthetic and ethical dimensions of Jewish culture.[39] As he witnessed the plunder, expulsion, and murder of hasidic Jewry in the World War, which brought his expedition to a crashing halt, Ansky conceived *The Dybbuk*. This richest of hasidic tapestries was woven while the hasidic heartland itself was being ripped to shreds. *The Dybbuk*, written simultaneously in Yiddish and in Russian, was slated to premier in Stanislawski's Moscow Art Theater. Thus the romance of Hasidism, which had begun as an internal Jewish rescue operation, was rapidly being transformed into an ecumenical act of triage. If the Jewish body politic could not be saved, Jewish writers hoped at least to save its soul.

Such a one was the Odessa-born writer Isaac Babel, who first encountered hasidic Jewry in 1920, riding with the *Red Cavalry* through Poland. Casting about this apocalyptic landscape for something, anything, to salvage, he found a veritable gallery of heretics, rebels, and anarchists: Pan Apolek, the sacrilegious painter of a new Christian iconography; Makhno, the brilliant strategist of guerilla warfare; and "the passionate edifice of Hasidism," embodied by Reb Motale Bratslavsky, his follower, Gedali, and his son, Ilya. Politically and militarily, Makhno was doomed. Artistically, Pan Apolek's credo was appropriated by Lyutov, the painter-in-words. And the spiritual fervor of Ilya was sacrificed to the Bolshevik cause. This may not seem like much, but against the backdrop of the most relentless campaign ever waged against rabbis, rebbes, and priests, a campaign that was joined by latter-day Maskilim now armed with absolute power, Babel's kaddish for Polish Hasidism was an act of considerable courage.

In Poland itself, after the crushing defeat of the Bolshevik campaign, the real-life counterparts of Ilya Bratslavsky began to swell the ranks of the newly established Warsaw Yiddish Writers' Club. Communism and Zionism beckoned, as did every other radical solution under the sun. This was not a time in which rabbinism was likely to enjoy a comeback among the young generation of Jewish writers and artists, especially since Polish Orthodoxy did not roll over and play dead. Rather, it entered into a new and energetic phase of political activity.[40] The logic of modernity dictated that the rabbinate was not yet dead enough to be revived. The logic of art dictated that the best way to address the universal heresy of the present was through the localized heresy of the past. If not today, then in the Polish shtetl of old there had existed a last line of defense, erected not by the zaddik as poet-dreamer, and not by the zaddik as humanist saint, but by the rabbi as stern upholder of the Law.

Rabbi Benish Ashkenazi, his body and soul intact in the wake of the Ukrainian massacres, returns with other of his kinsmen to help rebuild the devastated town of Goray (Polish Goraj). The year is 1665. But the rabbi's house is divided against itself, a portent of things to come. What's more, the convoluted rhetoric of the law, as Ruth Wisse has shown in her analysis of *Satan in Goray*, is no match for the rhetoric of evil. When Rabbi Benish succumbs to the powers of darkness and abandons his flock, the town and all of Polish Jewry are torn apart by the messianic heresy of Shabbetai Zvi. Henceforth, Satan reigns supreme.[41] Only the artificial imposition of the old moral order can save these Jews from self-destructing. In the novel, this happens through an old-fashioned storybook ending. In the dramatized version that was never staged, Isaac Bashevis Singer brings Rabbi Benish himself back from retirement to do the job.[42] Either way, the Halachah is here represented—perhaps for the first time in the secular Jewish imagination—as the last line of defense in the fight against idolatry.

To revise the secular humanistic foundations of modern Jewish culture—and of modern culture as a whole—required that the law, not merely the mystical lore, be given a voice within the new Torah of literature. Yiddish literature led the way because its ideological foundations were destroyed at the root, along with its writers and readers. *Satan in Goray* faced off against the demonic-messianic allure of Stalin. Reversing the whole direction of Jewish secular faith, which had heretofore been predicated on the inevitable movement from a dim past to a bright future, the American-Yiddish poet Jacob Glatstein called on his fellow intellectuals to "slam shut the gate" on the "big stinking world" and return, voluntarily

Tsum din, tsum tifn meyn, tsum khoyv, tsum gerekht,
Velt, ikh shpan mit freyd tsum shtiln getolekht.

To Law, to deep meaning, to duty, to right,
World, I stride with joy to the quiet ghetto-light.

The time was April 1938, seven months before the Kristallnacht.[43] Yiddish culture underwent *tsimtsum*, a cosmic contraction, in the wake of the Nazi and Soviet apocalypse.

The internal revision begun before the war was completed by two former Polish-Jewish renegades who made it to the shores of America—I. B. Singer and Chaim Grade. Both writers signaled the change by liberating the rabbis from the tyranny of the past and situating them in the modern metropolis. To be sure, this could only happen when the Jewish urban centers of Warsaw and Vilna had already been destroyed.

In My Father's Court (1956) begins with a genealogy of the rabbinical court, from Moses, the Men of the Great Assembly, and the Sanhedrin, all the way to the penurious Rabbi Pinchas Menachem Singer of 10 (and later 12) Krochmalna Street in Warsaw.[44] The Beth Din, according to his son the chronicler, was much more than the longest lasting institution among the Jews; it became the crucible of Jewish particularity as well, for "the Beth Din could exist only among a people with a deep faith and humility, and it reached its apex among the Jews when they were completely bereft of worldly power and influence. The weapon of the judge was the handkerchief the litigants touched to signify their acceptance of the judgment." Within this sphere of justice and morality, the individual traits of each rabbi came to the fore. "The Beth Din not only differed in every generation, but every Rabbi who participated in it colored it with his character and personality" (preface). Embodying the dual principles of cultural continuity and individualism, the Beth Din, he foretells, "will be reinstated and evolve into a universal institution," based on the concept "that there can be no justice without godliness." Through these disparate episodes from his father's court, Singer gives full voice to his conservative-restorative impulse.

Despite this high-minded rhetoric, the Beth Din does not emerge as the towering memorial to Jewish faith and humility. How can it, if the Beth Din, much like the hasidic court in Peretz's scheme, is only as strong as its family members? Each episode tells of an ineffectual father at war with his sons, or an ineffectual husband at odds with his wife. While Rabbi Pinchas remains firm in his faith, if often puzzled by the depths of human depravity, his eldest son Israel Joshua is off exploring the temporal world and its pleasures while his middle son Itsikl seeks refuge on the balcony, there to ponder the great philosophical enigmas of life. Batsheva, more the man than her husband, heads some of the litigants off in the kitchen. As a cross-section of Polish Jewry troops in and out of Rabbi Pinchas Singer's tenement apartment, the vignettes add up to little more than an "experimental" vehicle for Bashevis Singer's own autobiography.

The closed and airless study of Rabbi Pinchas Singer stands for the closed world of Polish Orthodoxy. Challenging this self-serving portrayal, and questioning the validity of all prior portraits of Jewish spiritual leaders in literature, Chaim Grade (1910–1982) began writing a series of novels and novellas about the lost worlds of Lithuanian Orthodoxy. It was the ongoing struggle between "the studyhouse and the street" that was to bring those worlds back to life. "Since I spent my youth in the study house and in Lithuanian yeshivas," he wrote in the preface to the first of these novels,

> I came to know well scholars and their human temptations, their frame
> of mind and way of thinking, their social circumstances and family life,
> and the ones of great faith for whom the world to come was a tangible
> thing, often truer than the world of their daily lives. I also came to know
> the neighbors on our poor street and their relationships to the students
> in the house of study—sometimes full of courtesy and love, and
> sometimes at war with the students of the Torah and even with the
> Torah itself.[45]

Remarkably, the Vilna streets depicted in *The Agunah* are, if anything, more claustrophobic than Pinchas Singer's Beth Din. Outside their borders are an old-age home, an insane asylum, and a forest, where the heroine will go to her voluntary death. Inside, there is only more suffering. The heroine, exactly as in *Satan in Goray*, is an orphan caught between two powerful and contrasting male figures. In the contest between them, she is destroyed, and her death acts to purge the "street" of its baseless hatred.

The two adversaries are both rabbis. One, Reb Levi Hurwitz, is the embodiment of *mides-hadin,* the full severity of the Law, and the other, Reb David Zelver—of *mides-harakhmim* (compassion). As an agunah, a grass widow whose husband is missing in action, the heroine, in turn, embodies one of the most intractable problems of Jewish law. Unless there is reliable testimony of her husband's death, Merl is forbidden to remarry. It is the Torah itself that stands on the dock. "Do you think," Reb Levi asks Merl, "that the entire tumult in town stems from your living with a man illegally? These things are a daily occurrence and the rabbis don't say a word. No one consults us and no one obeys us. Your affair has stirred up the entire town *because a rabbi permitted something that is forbidden.*"[46] Although Grade's sympathies lie clearly with Reb David, the novel does not adjudicate who and what is to blame for the tragedy: the violation of the law or its zealous preservation. Unlike the ending of Singer's novel, where the Law descends from on high to put an end to the chaos, the death of the innocent in Grade's retelling expiates the collective sin and allows for redemption. Life is vouchsafed the living despite the fact that the Torah is no longer a Tree of Life. Grade's is a parable for a post-Holocaust age.[47]

Grade also makes good on his promise, giving flesh and human feeling to these once-faceless rabbis. More than that, he shows how even for men with the purest of motives, the instinctual and egotistical drives come first, the halachic rationale—second. No matter that a literature that once embraced the world entire now occupies a few impoverished city blocks. It can still lay claim to the universal drama of id versus superego.

After serving as jacks-of-all-literary-trades, the rabbinic elite of Eastern Europe finally came into their own as the shakers and makers of a meaningful Jewish past. In a sense, because of the Holocaust, every novel set in prewar Vilna or Warsaw or Lodz can be read as a historical novel, recreating a life that the Germans consigned to oblivion. Grade's achievement, then, is as symbolic as it is real. Beginning with *The Agunah* and culminating in his monumental *Tsemakh Atlas* (translated as *The Yeshiva*, 1967–1977), Grade placed the rabbis and their law squarely within the world-as-we-know-it. The rabbis and rogues who peopled *Satan in Goray* were still living in the shtetl, after all, and behaved more like characters in a romance than a novel, while I. B. Singer's tales of the Warsaw Beth Din were just that: disparate episodes arranged in a very loose chronology. The rabbi regained full human stature when and only when he negotiated both city and town, the study house and the street, the courtroom and the bedroom.

Grade's fiction signaled the closing of three circles:

(1) By turning them into fictional characters, the Maskilim had tried to displace the established religious leadership with a secular alternative. The second generation of modern Jewish writers then drove a wedge between the rabbi and the rebbe and portrayed the latter as a rebel: either a lone visionary wandering in the wilderness, or an angry scholar facing off against an apathetic, selfish "street." By the third generation, each alternative was turned into a lasting memorial. The American-Yiddish poet Menahem Boraisha produced an epic about *Der geyer* (*The Wanderer*, 1933–1942), and Abraham Joshua Heschel, scion of two hasidic dynasties, placed the Kotsker Rebbe's *Struggle for Truth* on a par with the existentialism of Kier-

kegaard.[48] It seemed as if the romance of Hasidism would never play itself out.

Grade, the Litvak, restored the rabbi and Rosh Yeshiva to primacy of place, and by fleshing them out with superabundant social, linguistic, and psychological detail, gave added weight to their adversarial proceedings. Through the rabbi as activist and adversary, Jewish law reemerged as the counterculture of the Jews. As a secular writer of fiction, Grade could not hope to restore the lost art of the law. But in the wake of the Great Destruction, he determined to rescue some of its lost artists.

(2) Formally, the only thing rescuable from two thousand years of legal disputation and Torah study was the rhetoric of disputation itself, the syntax of debate, the freedom of "two Jews talking," or of one Jew arguing with God. In works of Hebrew fiction, this was strictly a male prerogative. In Yiddish, even women got into the act. Sholem Aleichem's Yente brings a meat pot before the rabbi, which gives her license to talk, to talk about talking, and almost to blaspheme—at which point the rabbi faints dead away.[49] All this was but a dry run compared to Grade's masterpiece, "My Quarrel with Hersh Rasseyner." Here, returning in his imagination to the fiercely combative *muser-shmuesn* of the Navaredok yeshiva, and paying a belated debt to Alyosha Karamazov and the Grand Inquisitor, Grade vivified the religious passions of the Lithuanian Mussar movement. Here, the two sides of Grade's own soul engaged in immortal combat.[50]

(3) Insofar as the rabbi functioned in Grade's work as adjudicator of God's Law, he was beholden to a set of values that not only lay outside the text but outside of the system of literature as a whole. Peretz, Asch, & Co. had skirted the law by charting instead the religious leader's search for personal salvation; hence, the plot-of-rebellion. Grade understood, as the Maskilim had known from the very beginning, that the Halachah could not be reconciled with secular humanism. Secular heroes, Jewish or otherwise, were only happy when facing off against the past, against society, or against the Other. The real existential quest of the Jew *qua* Jew lay somewhere else: in trying to reconcile the mundane details of everyday life with a code of law designed for a nation of priests.

Pagan Rabbis: A Postscript

By the late 1930s a native-born generation of religiously committed intellectuals went on the offensive against the rampant secularism and radical socialist tendencies of the American-Jewish street. Owing nothing to the Hebrew and Yiddish writers who came before them, they reinvented the literary image of the rabbi by returning to the invention of rabbinic

Judaism itself: the first and second centuries C.E. In 1936, the Judaic scholar Louis Finkelstein rehabilitated Rabbi Akiba (ca. 50–135) as a *Scholar, Saint and Martyr*. The appendix to this popular biography made it clear that Akiba was also to be ranked (alongside the other leading Pharisees) as a working-class hero.[51] Three years later, Rabbi Milton Steinberg wrote a philosophically nuanced novel about the paragon of rabbinic heretics, Elisha ben Abuyah.[52]

The rabbi as rebel and loner: check. The hasidic rebbe locked in battle with his rebellious son (in Chaim Potok's *The Chosen*): check. And a new category: the rabbi as problem solver. The enormously popular detective novel *Friday the Rabbi Slept Late*, and its numerous sequels by Harry Kemelman, owe as little to the Yiddish tradition as does the American rabbi who has increasingly become a facilitator, counselor, therapist, social activist, and most recently—a woman.

Thus, it is with a woman writer that our story appropriately ends. Isaac Kornfeld, the one who stands indicted in the title of Cynthia Ozick's "The Pagan Rabbi," is another in a long line of rabbinic-hasidic rebels.[53] Ozick, like Steinberg, exposes the philosophical rift that underlies the rebellion of someone sworn to uphold the precepts of rabbinic Judaism. Whosoever worships nature, and fornicates with trees, has written himself out of the fold and deserves to die. What is strikingly new is that the verdict is delivered by Isaac Kornfeld's stern and unsentimental wife, a survivor of the Holocaust. Sheindel, born near the electrified fence of the concentration camp, was married behind a fence of dancing women and, alone in this story, upholds the "fences" of the Law.

Time will tell whether the rabbis and rebbes of Yiddish memory will join their wooden effigies to become souvenirs of a tragic past. Were they, instead, to assume an adversarial role in the present, they might help to renegotiate the exorbitant price that the Jews have paid for their conquest of modernity.

6 The Golden Peacock: The Art of Song

Vot ken you makh? Es iz Amerike! Amerike un bol'she nitshevo.

What can you do? It's America!
America, and nothing more.

—Aaron Lebedeff, ca. 1929

The late Rabbi Wolfe Kelman used to kibitz that if deep sea divers were to be sent down into the mid-Atlantic, halfway between Hamburg and New York, they would discover a million pairs of *tefillin* that were thrown overboard during the great ocean crossings from 1881–1924. If such a place indeed existed, where millions of male Jews, raised in traditional homes, had cast off the onerous burden of Jewish religious life so as to arrive unencumbered in America, I would call it the Jewish Bermuda Triangle.

What cultural baggage did make it through the internal migration from shtetl to city and the external migration from Old World to New?[1] They traveled light, and followed no one in particular, save for the short-lived Am Olam movement, which succeeded in settling a few hundred communarians in Louisiana, South Dakota, and Oregon. To be sure, they brought their languages—Yiddish, Hebrew-Aramaic, German, Polish, Russian, Ukrainian—as they brought their urban skills, their talent for self-help, and their dreams for a better life. But what of their cultural baggage? Was there anything in the culture of Jewish Eastern Europe that could be put to good use once they arrived on these shores?

What traveled best was a specific repertory of Yiddish songs. We know this from handwritten songbooks that once belonged to East European immigrants and that were handed down to their children and grandchildren; and we know this from a weekly column in the *Forverts (Jewish Daily Forward)* conducted since 1970 by the husband-and-wife team of Chana and Joseph Mlotek. Asked to identify anonymous song texts and to submit any songs or fragments they could remember, the elderly readers of the *Forverts* revealed the amazing resilience of Yiddish song culture both in the old country and the new. Bit by bit, the compilers, one Polish-born, one American-born, became the repository of a living song archive, which

Lyrically

Fig. 6.1. "Di goldene pave," from *Mir trogn a gezang! Favorite Yiddish Songs of Our Generation*, ed. Eleanor Gordon Mlotek. 2nd rev. ed. (New York: Workmen's Circle Education Department, 1977), p. 107.

they, in turn, began to disseminate both in print and on cassette recordings. In the 1990s, with the fall of communism, the lost tribes of Soviet Jewry also joined the collective rescue effort.[2]

The Yiddish Song in Its Traditional Settings

The decisive factor in the dissemination of these songs was not so much their content as their manner of performance.[3] Whether a song was sung solo or in chorus, in private or in public, by men or by women, were factors that determined its longevity and adaptability. Hasidic songs proved extraordinarily resilient, I would argue, not only because distinct groups of Hasidim, like the Braslaver, Lubavitsher, and Bobover, preserved their musical traditions, but also because these were the only choral and public songs that existed in Yiddish tradition outside the liturgy. They survived precisely because they were repeatedly sung by *groups* of male Hasidim. And this was equally true of the raucous *tishlider* ("table songs") set to Napoleonic or other military marches; the *freylekhs*, lively tunes that accompanied the men as they danced; and of the haunting *dveykes-niggunim*, wordless contemplative songs whose *yam-bam-bams* were repeated over and over again like mantras. There were a few notable exceptions — zaddikim who sang solo, and even one, Reb Levi Yitskhok of Berdichev, who composed his own songs in Yiddish — but the hasidic ambience was nothing if not communal.[4]

Outside the charmed circle of particular zaddikim, the public performance of Yiddish songs was strictly limited to weddings and to specific festivals like Purim — and sanctioned only for men. Women were forbidden by the strict application of Jewish law from making their voices heard in public; they sang, if at all, in the presence of other women, or within the tight family circle.[5]

Perhaps not coincidentally, the private and intimate song idiom of Jewish women was overwhelmingly Slavic, from their lullabies to their plaintive love songs. Such, for example, was the song about the Golden Peacock, who lost a golden feather of hers in shame, carrying the sad tidings of a newly wedded bride to her father and mother back home. This song had its Ukrainian parallel for both the music and the lyrics.[6]

Es kumt tsu flien di goldene pave
fun a fremdn land.
Hot zi farloyrn dem gildenem feder
mit a groysn shand.

(The golden peacock came flying / from a distant land. / Carrying her sad greetings / she lost her golden feather in shame.)

In Yiddish folksong, love and marriage do not go together like a horse and carriage. Like their Slavic counterparts, these lyric songs speak of thwarted love, separation, unrequited longing, and always with the same *abcb* rhyme scheme and in a minor key.[7]

Not so the songs performed at an actual wedding by the *badkhn* or *marshalik*—the Jewish wedding bard. On those few occasions when men and women actually mixed, it was the wedding bard who presided, making sure that whatever else transpired, expressions of romantic love did not come into play.[8]

The wedding ceremony itself was inviolable. Even musicians did not play while the marriage took place. Before the ceremony, when there were guests to invite, a bride to accompany on her way to the ritual bath, and gifts to exchange between bride and groom, the badkhn's repertory was governed by centuries' worth of oral tradition. Here the rhymes were as thoroughly predictable as the klezmer tunes that accompanied each stage of the festivities: "The bride must be careful to observe the laws of *nide* (ritual purity)," he warned; "otherwise she will die, God forbid, without reciting *vide* (the confession of sins)." "*Khosn-kale*, the bride and groom," invariably rhymed with "*mazl-tov aykh ale, ale*, congratulations to you all, [to you] all."[9]

It was after the ceremony, at the wedding feast, that his manifold talents came into play, as riddler, mime artist, magician, and chaste moralist. He performed on a chair or table, chanting or singing his improvised rhymes about the bride, groom, in-laws, and guests; moved the assembled to tears by reminding them of their child-bearing responsibilities and their mortality; described the latest pogrom, fire, or technological advance, then switched abruptly to satire and mime. With a showy display of learned phrases and alphabetical acrostics, the badkhn flattered the piety of his audience, just as his use of High German and Russian words was a compliment to their (and his) worldliness. In between the dances, also governed by tradition, the more accomplished (and high-priced) badkhn performed a one-man play, such as the ever-popular "Jerusalemite" or "Jew from the Holy Land," the trickster tale that Sholem Aleichem adapted in one of his holiday stories, or "From Cradle to Grave," the title of which said it all.[10] When the badkhn put on straw sandals, unbuttoned his gaberdine, and pretended to be a Ukrainian or Polish peasant, it brought the house down.[11]

Because he presided over both ends of the wedding, the badkhn was the master of zany juxtapositions. Folk art routinely combined high and low, pathos and parody, and the badkhn was the consummate folk artist.[12] He took the wedding party through its paces, preserved the traditional rhymes, and injected as much levity, blasphemy, and contemporaneity as he could get away with. No one paid him to be simple, straight-laced, and artless.[13]

If the combination of Hebrew and Yiddish, morality and buffoonery, learning and vulgarity, words and gesture, were the hallmark of the badkhn, who performed for the bride only once in her lifetime (in theory, at least), how much more so was this true on the one-day-a-year carnival of Purim. The manifold prohibitions against (1) wearing masks; (2) men dressing up as women; (3) attending the theater or circus; and (4) general rowdiness—these went back to early rabbinic times and were reinforced throughout the nineteenth century. Yet all were obeyed in the breach on Purim.[14] On Purim, sadness turned to joy, destruction gave way to salvation, and the perpetual underdogs—the Jews—had their moment under the sun (alas but a metaphor, because in early spring the shtetl streets were still covered with mud). The celebration of Purim was marked by heavy drinking, until the men no longer knew the difference between the good guys and the bad; by the exchange of food gifts called *shalekhmones*; by much feasting; and by the performance of the last real folk plays on European soil. No Bayreuth festival was needed to revive the *Purim-shpil* because Yiddish-speaking Jews continued performing plays on Purim from the seventeenth century onward.

By the late nineteenth century, the repertory had expanded far beyond the Scroll of Esther to include The Sacrifice of Isaac, The Selling of Joseph, David and Goliath, King Solomon's Judgment, Solomon and Ashmedai, and a variety of nonbiblical subjects.[15]

> Enter the CLOWN (dressed in red from head to toe, with a yellow stripe running down his trousers. Wears a dunce cap on his head):
>
> > Alyom payats, ikh bin payats,
> > a kashe broyt, a veytsn broyt,
> > un khap arayn, tralalalala . . .
>
> > Hello the Clown, I am the Clown,
> > a bread of rye, a bread of wheat
> > and grab a bite, tralalalala,
> > hello the Clown.

Listen to a tale full of wonders,
the adventure of Joseph and his brothers;
listen to a tale full of splendor,
a marvelous tale you will always remember.[16]

Did any of this survive the breakup of the shtetl? If Abraham Cahan is to be believed, the wedding bard was still a requisite, if greatly diminished, part of "A Ghetto Wedding" on the Lower East Side, as late as 1898.[17] Even within the boundaries of Eastern Europe, moreover, the badkhn's solo performance made the transition from folk to popular culture, from shtetl to city, from wedding to weekday.

The New Class of Popular Entertainers

The first modest sign of change was the rise of a new class of folksingers, only one step removed from the *badkhonim* of tradition, who cast the stodgy folk repertory into a contemporary mold. They are fondly known as the Brody Singers, after the name of their founder, Berl Broder-Margulies (ca. 1817–1868). The appearance on the scene of a native talent, unencumbered by Jewish learning, pedigree, or ideology, who spread the good cheer beyond weddings and Purim to the rest of the calendar year, was something entirely new.[18] The year 1857 has gone down in Yiddish literary history as the date Berl Broder gave up his job in the pig bristle business and took up entertaining at inns with two former synagogue choirboys as members of his troupe. The original repertory was sad, the melodies too, and consisted of individual monologues of a poor shepherd, night watchman, shingler, drayman, money lender, wanderer, cantor, matchmaker, Hebrew school teacher, preacher, or water carrier. Once the routine caught on, each monologue-in-song was performed in appropriate costume, followed by a little dance. "I, poor so-and-so" became the universally popular signature of the Brody Singers.

In "The Song of Berl Broder" the folksinger disarms his (live) audience with his openness, coy modesty, and absence of malice.[19]

Ikh, Broder Berl,
ikh shray tsu ale mentshn:
Hert oys verter vi perl
mit kheyn zol mir got bentshn!

(I, Brody Berl, / I cry to everybody: / Listen to words like pearls / and may God bless me with popularity!)

"Berl of Brod," in the song's refrain, rhymes with *"loyb dir, du ziser got,* praise to you, sweet God," a perfect joining of publicity and piety.

But as the song progresses, we learn that, like the shepherd all alone with his flock night and day, like the shingler on his precarious perch, "Berl Broder" is a lone and lonely toiler. Within this closed circle of personal sorrow, the folksinger tells each story in the language and with the realia peculiar to his work. The power of Yiddish to render individual, mundane experience is here being heard for the first time.

There was still something chaste and maggidic about the first Brody Singers, for all that they performed in big cities (like Warsaw and Bucharest) in front of an all-male clientele. The hard-drinking, erudite, and brilliantly parodic Velvl Zbarzher-Ehrenkrantz (1826–1883) changed that for all time to come.[20] As a loyal son of the Galician Haskalah and a veteran of its Kulturkampf, he turned to folksinging after the Hasidim blackballed him from the teaching profession.[21] He was the first to use song to beat the Hasidim at their own game and to cover all his bases by singing in both Hebrew and Yiddish. If the Hasidim brought mystical longing into popular song, and the professional *badkhonim* brought topical morality, then Velvl Zbarzher can be credited as both "the father of Yiddish bohemian poets in Eastern Europe," and the one who made parody into a national Jewish sport.[22]

Zbarzher's claim to fame were the hundred-odd songs he published in four volumes of his *Makel noʿam* (*The Staff of Beauty*, 1869–1878). At least twenty of them were still being sung on the eve of World War II, some, presumably, to Zbarzher's original melodies.[23] The most famous was the antihasidic "Dos gute kepl," universally remembered as "Kum aher, du filozof," in which a credulous Hasid challenges a freethinker ("philosopher") to a debate. What are all the new-fangled technological advances, claims the Hasid, like the telegraph and steamboat, when compared to the supernatural powers of the Rebbe!

> Kum aher, du filozof,
> mit dayn ketsishn moykhl,
> kum aher tsum rebns tish
> un lern zikh do seykhl.
>
> A damfshif hostu oysgetrakht
> un nemst dermit zikh iber,
> der rebe shpreyt zayn tikhl oys
> un shpant dem yam ariber.
>
> (Come here, my philosopher, / with your catty brains; / come and learn
> real wisdom / at the rebbe's side. // A steamboat you've invented / and

Moderate tempo

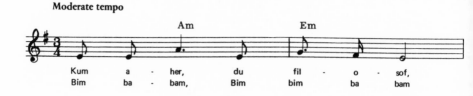

Am — Em

Kum a - her, du fil - o - sof,
Bim ba - bam, Bim bim ba bam

D7 — G

Mit dayn ke - tsi - shn moy - khl, Oy,
Bim ba - bim ba bim - bam

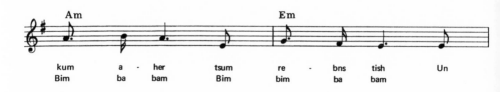

Am — Em

kum a - her tsum re - bns tish Un
Bim ba bam Bim bim ba bam

C — Em

le - rn zikh do sey - khl.
Bim ba bim ba bim - bam.

Fig. 6.2. Velvl Zbarzher, "Der filozof," from *Mir trogn a gezang! Favorite Yiddish Songs of Our Generation*, ed. Eleanor Gordon Mlotek. 2nd rev. ed. (New York: Workmen's Circle Education Department, 1977), p. 125.

think it's so very grand. / The rebbe spreads his handkerchief / and crosses sea and land.)

This parody, in turn, later inspired numerous others aimed at Zionists, Bundists, and anti-Bolsheviks.[24]

Velvl Zbarzher also perfected the art of Yiddish lament, both comical and serious. His impact was such that the lyrical side of his muse survived almost as well as the satiric.

Biter iz mir azoy vi gal,
vi gift fun di shlangen,—
klogt un veynt di nakhtigal
ven zi vert gefangen.
Ikh vel di velt shoyn nisht genisn,
biter iz mir un zoyer,
m'vet dokh mikh bald farshlisn
in a fester moyer.

("How I am bitter as if filled with bile, / or with the poison of a snake," / laments and cries the nightingale / when captive she is taken. / "No more will I enjoy this world, / woe and bitter is me; / soon I will be bolted in / within firm masonry.")

From her captivity, the nightingale contemplates the shortsightedness of humankind, never satisfied with its lot, and decries her captors, who mistake her weeping for song. Were humans to understand the implications of her plight—that the body is but a cage for the singing soul—they would take her lament to heart. As indeed was the case with Jewish pickpockets and thieves doing time in Polish prisons, who later adapted Zbarzher's allegory to the punishing reality of their cell. It would take another generation, however, for Zbarzher himself to be rehabilitated—by the Yiddish troubadour, Itzik Manger.[25]

The personal fate of this first generation of folksingers was not too happy either: they died in obscurity far away from home. Berl Broder died somewhere near Bucharest. Zbarzher was buried in Constantinople, but Malkele the Beautiful, his second wife, erected a handsome tombstone. Vilna-born Mikhl Gordon (1823–1890), the most militant and for a time most popular Yiddish singer-and-songwriter, died alone in Kiev, with none but the members of the Burial Society attending his funeral.[26] Denied the status and highbrow recognition of their fellow poets who wrote

Fig. 6.3. Velvl Zbarzher, "Der nakhtigal," from *Yidishe ganovim-lider mit melodyes*, ed. Shmuel Lehman (Warsaw, 1928), p. 7.

in Hebrew, the Yiddish folksingers reaped a different reward: their songs have survived in Jewish folk memory until this very day.[27]

Among the most resilient were Mikhl Gordon's satiric and sentimental songs that touched on matrimony and motherhood. Gordon was the first to write songs for a solo female voice.[28] In one justly famous song, the speaker is a super-pious wife lamenting her wayward husband. Proof positive of his deviance is that he returns home without his beard. "*Gevald!*" she screams at the end of each stanza, "*di bord zol mir vern,* I want your beard back again!" After her pleas for its return prove futile, she resorts to divination—

> Gor nit lang hob ikh gezen in kholem
> dayn gantse berdele olehasholem. . . .
>
> (I found in a dream not long ago / your beard entire, God rest her soul. . . .)

Satisfied that she knows its whereabouts, she resolves to bury the sacred relic in the cemetery and erect a memorial to her husband's lost piety.

Other of his songs portray the darker side of a bad marriage. Love, Gordon explained in a footnote to one of his songs, was an unknown concept in Jewish Eastern Europe. All the evils of Jewish family life follow from that.[29]

Like Velvl Zbarzher, Gordon directed his sharpest arrows at the bull's-eye of Jewish backwardness—the Hasidim. Of these songs, "The Borscht" and "The Booze" lived on among the folk quite apart from their antihasidic provenance—thanks to their ebullient celebration of the good life, their witty rhymes, their parodic use of Jewish myth, and their dance rhythms.

> Beshas der shadkhn iz gekumen tsu mayn zeydn,
> dem tatn mit der mamen a shidekh reydn,
> hot men geredt un geredt un s'iz gevorn nisht,
> biz vanen di mashke hot zikh arayngemisht.
> Tsulib der mashke iz der shidekh geshlosn,
> der tate iz gevorn der mames khosn, yam-ba-bam-ba-bam. . . .
>
> (When the matchmaker came to my grandfather / to arrange a match between my mom and dad, / they talked and talked and nothing came of it / until a glass of whiskey was brought into the room. / It's because of the booze that the match was made / and dad became my mother's groom.)

Fig. 6.4. Mikhl Gordon, "Di mashke," from *Perl fun yidishn lid: Favorite Folk, Art, and Theatre Songs,* ed. Eleanor Gordon Mlotek and Joseph Mlotek (New York: Education Department of the Workmen's Circle, 1988), p. 164.

The solo singer, a drunk "little Hasid," begins with the prenatal meeting of his grandparents, and then reviews the role that whiskey played at all the key moments of his life: the courtship of his parents, his circumcision feast, bar mitzvah, and wedding. Speaking of weddings, he is reminded of Adam and Eve and their primordial sin, also brought about by a weakness for drink. But never fear,

> Tsu tkhies-hameysim bin ikh vider do
> un trink bald mashke in der ershter sho.
>
> (When the resurrection comes I'll be there, you bet, / and have a drink the very first chance I get.)

Yes, when the Messiah came, the whiskey would flow like water.[30] For the mock-message to travel unhindered, later singers simply removed its topical references to the tax on whiskey and its gratuitous barbs about the zaddikim. In its modernized and folklorized version, "Di mashke" became the perfect *tishlid* for my mother to sing with her fellow students in Vilna and for the Kapelye Klezmer Band to perform on the streets of Manhattan.[31]

It was now time to take the show on the road. Given that Yiddish topical and heretical songs traveled so well, the secular folksingers began to dream of conquering the New World. The first to do so was the Vilna-born badkhn Elyokum Zunser (1836–1913), who started as a local celebrity in Kovno, went professional and in 1861 moved back to Vilna, where he fell in with a circle of learned Maskilim, and with the coming of the trains that very same year began to travel to ever more lucrative weddings.[32] (He performed, among others, at the first wedding of my grandmother, Fradl Matz.) Like other Vilna Maskilim, he saw America as the great opportunity for starting Jewish life all over again on emancipated, productive ground. In the wake of the pogroms of 1881–1882, Zunser began passionately to advocate a return to Zion.

From then on, the Yiddish folksinger was the voice of utopian change. Though adhering to the same rhyme schemes and rhythms and using the same kind of melodies as before, Zunser's ideas turned to more radical solutions. *In sokhe / ligt di mazl-brokhe*, began his most popular song, "In the hook plow / lies the blessing." The Slavic *sokhe* made a perfect rhyme with the doubly beneficent Hebrew compound of *mazl-brokhe* (good-fortune-and-blessing), thus linking heaven and earth, peasant and Jew with one fell swoop. Zunser had played on this rhyme before, but never to espouse the agrarian ideal of "true" productive labor in the newly founded colonies on Palestinian soil.[33]

> In sokhe ligt di mazl-brokhe,
> der varer glik fun lebn,
> keyn zakh mir nit felt!
> Es kumt der frimorgn,
> ikh darf nit layen, borgn,
> der moyakh darf nit zorgn
> af tog-hoystoes, gelt.
> S'iz ongegreyt af vinter
> a zasik a gezinter,
> ikh zey un shnayd gants munter—
> fray in gotes velt . . .

(In the plow / there is good fortune, / true happiness of life, / what more do I need! / Comes the morrow, / no need to borrow / or worry myself sick / about making it through the day. / For the winter there's enough stored away / my granary bin is full to the brim / I sow and reap to my heart's content / free under God's tent.)

Failing that pioneering route, which was open only to the young and chosen few, there was the American Zion, where all Jews could prove their worth. Encouraged by the New York branch of the Lovers of Zion, Zunser set sail for America in 1889.

Behind his back, the medium of Yiddish song had already been transformed, from hymn and homily to professional entertainment. Its new and permanent venue was *The Yiddish Stage*, an eight-hundred-page extravaganza published in New York City to celebrate the twentieth anniversary of the Yiddish theater and republished many times since.[34] Theater songs, arranged by operetta title, took up four-fifths of the densely printed volume. Credit for folklorized versions of the Old World repertory, like Velvl Zbarzher's "Come Here, My Philosopher," now went to the actor who performed them, like somebody named "Friedman." "Worker- and Folk-Songs, and Poems for Declamation" made up the rest, including a paltry five songs by Zunser. There was not a single bona fide, anonymous "folk-song" in the bunch; not one. What the folk was singing, in America at least, were the songs of Abraham Goldfaden, the father of the Yiddish theater. Founded in Romania in 1877 and exported to the New World five years later, the Yiddish theater was already being celebrated by the "largest Yiddish publication in America."

Moderate tempo

Fig. 6.5. Elyokum Zunser, "Di sokhe," from *Mir trogn a gezang! Favorite Yiddish Songs of Our Generation*, ed. Eleanor Gordon Mlotek. 2nd rev. ed. (New York: Workmen's Circle Education Department, 1977), p. 97.

Goldfaden and the Yiddish Musical Stage

A professional Yiddish theater was obviously an idea whose time had come. Folk theater was losing ground to such urban forms of entertainment as the one-night stand of the Brody Singers. The wonder of it all is that it took Abraham Goldfaden (né Goldenfodem, 1840–1908) so long to make the historic leap from the Purim-shpil and cabaret to a permanent ensemble of male and female actors who played an original repertory of Yiddish operettas. Here, in any event, was the right man for the job.

Like Velvl Zbarzher-Ehrenkrantz before him, Goldfaden originally doubled as a Hebrew and Yiddish poet—and soon discovered the difference. *Tsitsim ufraḥim* (*Buds and Flowers*, 1865), his inaugural Hebrew volume, was not reissued for another century, while *Dos yidele* (*The Little Jew*, 1867) went through more than twelve editions and some of its songs are still popular today. He also discovered, the hard way, at Shimen Mark's Pomul Verde—the Green Tree—in Jassy, Romania, that what the simple folk wanted was not allegorical poems declaimed in top hat and tails, but sight gags and satire and song. Goldfaden was hooted off the stage.[35] Though remaining an engagé poet throughout his career, Goldfaden quickly learned the ways of Yiddish popular culture. Bringing Hebrew and Yiddish, Purim play and melodrama, cantorial and opera music together, Goldfaden charted the future course of Yiddish song.

Simply and dramatically, Goldfaden put male and female solos together and pioneered the Yiddish duet. Where only the Song of Disputation existed before—between the Moldavian and Polish Jews (Zbarzher) or the Village and Urban Jew (Zunser)—the Yiddish theater featured duets as sung by a male and (real-live) female singer. Once the taboo of hearing a woman's voice was finally broken, it was open season for love songs and (mild) displays of eroticism on stage: between Mirele the Orphan and Marcus the Maskil or between the biblical lovers Shulamith and Absalom. Indeed, there was no more exalted setting for love than the biblical landscape. Singing melodies adapted from Italian, French, and German operas and speaking a high literary Yiddish, his biblical lovers swore eternal fealty, taking a well and a weasel as their witnesses. The audience, unperturbed by the echoes of Verdi's lovers in *La Traviata*, then went away humming "The Oath" of Shulamith and Absalom.[36]

The secret of success was not to flaunt the theater's "modernity" but to maintain strong links to the audience's musical, theatrical, and ideological habits. Goldfaden's most popular numbers followed the melody types already familiar to the audience, especially the Phrygian mode that pervaded the Sabbath and holiday prayers.[37] To bring the Bible closer to home, his most exalted biblical melodramas, like *Shulamith or the Daughter of Jerusalem* (1880), included a farcical Purim-shpil character named Tsingitang, who parodied the high-flown aspirations and arias of the romantic leads. In Act III, Joab the Gideonite's boasting song (set to a Ukrainian melody) came straight from the *Goliath Play* of old. As on Purim, anachronism was the order of the day. Here was Absalom singing a solo in Act I, Scene 3, about his longing for the Temple in Jerusalem. Suddenly this Judean warrior (scion of the Maccabees) breaks into a lullaby about Yidele, the "little Jew" under whose cradle there stands "a pure white goat," at the end of which he has a clairvoyant vision of Yidele's future career as a capitalist banker made rich by building railroads throughout the realm!

> Es vet kumen a tsayt fun ayznbanen,
> zey veln farfleytsn a halbe velt;
> ayzerne vegn vestu oysshpanen
> un vest in dem oykh fardinen fil gelt.
>
> Un az du vest vern raykh, Yidele,
> zolstu zikh dermonen in dem lidele;
> rozhinkes mit mandlen!
> Dos vet zayn dayn baruf—
> Yidele vet alts handlen,
> shlof, zhe, Yidele, shlof.
>
> (There will come a time when railroads / will cover half the globe; / building these roads made of iron / you will earn great wealth. // But even when you're rich, Yidele, / remember mama's lullaby / trading in raisins and almonds— / that will still be Yidele's calling. / So sleep now, Yidele, sleep.)

The audience loved it and made "Raisins and Almonds" a synonym for the Yiddish folksong as a whole.[38]

However belabored the programmatic messages of Goldfaden's operettas, they were definitely a force for the new. As performed on a stage and set within a dramatic tale of villainy and virtue, they actualized secular forms of life that were rooted within a universal Jewish idiom. Celebrating a birthday (rather than commemorating a *yortsayt*, the anniversary of someone's death) did not become real until Jewish audiences heard the choir sing a rousing "On Your Birthday" to cheer up poor orphaned Mirele in the opening scene of *The Witch*. (Let us recall that our own "Happy Birthday to You" was not handed down from Mount Sinai. It was composed

Fig. 6.6. Abraham Goldfaden, "Rozhinkes mit mandlen," from *Mir trogn a gezang! Favorite Yiddish Songs of Our Generation,* ed. Eleanor Gordon Mlotek. 2nd rev. ed. (New York: Workmen's Circle Education Department, 1977), p. 5.

by another Jewish genius of the popular stage, Irving Berlin, for the 1940 film *Dumbo*.)

If Yiddish musical theater was a force for the new—inspiring synagogue choirboys and young ladies from good homes to choose a life on the stage, their pious parents to issue bans on attending the theater, and the tsarist government to close down the whole shebang in 1883—it was just as surely the crucible of a new, urban, folk culture in the making.

New World Settings

Whether or not they threw their *tefillin* overboard, Jewish immigrants arriving on these shores discovered a whole satellite industry surrounding the Yiddish theater: special publications dedicated to the Yiddish stage, sheet music, and somewhat later, gramophone records. Because they didn't know that their favorite songs were already available on the mass market, or because they could not yet afford the price of *The Yiddish Stage*, many immigrants copied out their own song books. This mine of information on the repertory of Jewish immigrants on the move from shtetl to city and from Europe to the Americas has hardly been touched, though such handwritten heirlooms are surely in the possession of people reading these very lines. From the three such song books that I have had occasion to study, and from the little bit of research done in the former Soviet Union, one thing is overwhelmingly clear: the song lyrics that Jewish immigrants, male and female, committed to writing were not venerable and anonymous but recent and of known authorship.[39] Like co-eds going off to college with their cassettes and CDs, Jews leaving the Old World for the New took the newest sounds along with them because they and only they captured the pace and wrenching price of change.

To survive that perilous crossing, Yiddish songs now needed to have institutional backing. Old-style *badkhonim* like Zunser cut a rather pathetic figure on New York's Lower East Side, if Hutchins Hapgood's *Spirit of the Ghetto* is reliable testimony.[40] When Hapgood met him, circa 1900, Zunser was working as a printer in Rutgers Square. For the benefit of his Anglo-Saxon visitor he could still chant his "dirges," swaying back and forth, with a melancholy "common to all Jewish poets." Not so for another former badkhn from Minsk, Shloyme Shmulewitz (1868–1943), alias Samuel Small, who quickly learned the ropes and eventually wrote over five hundred songs for the American Yiddish stage.

Like his famous *landsman*, Shmulewitz had already published some of his songs before coming to America. He too called them "folksongs," capitalizing on the new fashion. But while the aged Zunser was already relegated by Hapgood to the sorrowful gallery of ghetto dreamers, Shmulewitz was able to pick up on his old partnership with Shomer, whose name was synonymous with Yiddish Vaudeville. And Shmulewitz knew how to peddle his goods. In his 1913 collection of *Lider*, Shmulewitz provided the names and addresses of the stores on New York's Lower East Side where the sheet music and gramophone recording of the given song could be purchased.[41]

These (now old) recordings of his songs—written, composed, and performed by Shmulewitz himself—reveal his debt to the recitative style of the old wedding jesters. But Shmulewitz was nothing if not persistent. After composing many "letter" songs he finally struck gold with "A brivele der mamen" (A letter to Mama) because, as Mark Slobin points out, it tapped into the deep Oedipal struggle in the lives of so many immigrants.[42]

A brivele der mamen
zolstu nit farzamen,
shrayb geshvind, libes kind,
shenk ir di nekhome.
Di mame vet dayn brivele lezn
un zi vet genezn,
heylst ir shmarts, ir biter harts,
derkvikst ir di neshome.

(Don't put off writing / a little letter to Mama; / write it soon, my child, / for it will bring her solace. / The moment your Mama will read it / she will be comforted; / so ease her pain, her bitter heart, / and refresh her soul.)

Second Avenue, with no ideology save that of the marketplace, was cruel to Shmulewitz. By the end of World War I, he was washed up as a professional songwriter and was forced to take his show on the road. And here, on the road, he finally blew his folksy cover. It happened in my hometown of Montreal, where a benefit performance was organized by the local Labor Zionists, eager to honor a true folk poet. Part one of the program went smoothly enough, but in the second, fifty-year-old Shmulewitz came on stage with his skimpily clad daughter Dorothy and together they performed one-act skits of questionable propriety. The intellectuals walked out in a huff, while the unwashed masses could not believe their good fortune.[43]

What the intellectuals wanted was enlightenment, and the preferred "handmaiden of enlightenment" was Socialism in her varied garb.[44] Most

Fig. 6.7. S. Shmulewitz, "A brivele der mamen," from *Mir trogn a gezang!*
Favorite Yiddish Songs of Our Generation, ed. Eleanor Gordon Mlotek. 2nd rev.
ed. (New York: Workmen's Circle Education Department, 1977), p. 145.

effective as a vehicle of socialist agitation were the *protest- manifest- un agitatsye-gezangen*, i.e., the repertory of social protest songs, which used a highbrow Germanic style. Morris Winchevsky (1856–1932), Morris Rosenfeld (1862–1923), David Edelstadt (1866–1892), and Yoysef Bovshover (1873–1915) sought a more refined and cosmopolitan diction to express the plight of the workingman and the dream of global revolution.[45] Edelstadt's *in letstn kamf fun blut un shmarts*, his vision of the Armageddon that would precede the final victory of the proletariat, was a perfect rhyme for *un vel bagaystern zayn harts*, i.e, that even from the grave his freedom song would inspire the hearts of the faithful.[46] This *shturemlid*, or "song of storm," was likewise coupled in rhyme with *krist un yid*, "Christian and Jew," for the hymn's ecumenical imagery was its utopian message.[47]

> And in my grave too I will hear
> My song of storm that rose and flew,
> And I will shed again a tear
> For the enslaved Christian and Jew.
>
> And when I hear the swords that ring
> In the last fight of blood and pain—
> From the grave, I'll to my people sing
> And will inspire their hearts again!

Written in a diction far removed from everyday speech, these protest songs became an authentic expression of the folk. More than that. They became the new liturgy for hundreds of thousands of Jews who only yesterday had ceased to pray.

Though they were distinctly a product of the New World, the socialist songwriters were a throwback to the Maskilim of old. They were all of them didactic poets for whom song was essentially a vehicle to improve the lot of the Jews, and for whom Yiddish (initially, at least) was a lowly language useful in reaching the masses. They stooped to conquer.

At the opposite end of the spectrum were the tiny group of Yiddish aesthetes known as *Di Yunge*, the Youngsters, who were no less intent upon breaking with the past. "Those—Without Tradition," is how H. Leivick (1888–1962) characterized the members of his circle.[48] As someone already "stuffed to the gills with Shloyme Nogid's fish, with Tevye the Dairyman's blintzes, with the tra-la-la's emanating from deep in the woods," the modern, urban Jew looked to Yiddish literature for a more individualized palate.[49] If the whole neoromantic menu offered up by Sholem Asch, Sholem Aleichem, and Zalman Schneour was so much sugar-and-spice-and-every-

Solemnly

O gu - te fraynd, ven ikh vel

shtar - bn, Trogt tsu mayn key - ver un - dzer

fon, Di fray - e fon, mit roy - te far - bn, Ba - shpritst mit

blut fun ar - bets - man. Di fray - e man.

Fig. 6.8. David Edelstadt, "Mayn tsavoe," from *Mir trogn a gezang! Favorite Yiddish Songs of Our Generation,* ed. Eleanor Gordon Mlotek. 2nd rev. ed. (New York: Workmen's Circle Education Department, 1977), p. 93.

thing-nice, the social protest poetry of and for the masses was too coarse a meal to even contemplate. The "rhyme department" of the various political parties, as Zishe Landau put it so memorably, hardly qualified as poetry at all![50]

Their crusade for the still small voice of Yiddish poetry emanated not from the sweatshops and crowded tenements of the Lower East Side, not from the colorful and chaotic stage of Second Avenue, but from Goodman and Levine's and other literary cafés, which they came to cherish as their "houses of study."[51] Within that unlikely temple of art, these very young men (still bachelors for the most part), and even fewer women, reinvented Yiddish poetry along the lines of Verlaine and Sologub.

The only scrap of culture that this group of aesthetes rescued from its East European Jewish past was the one that everyone else had discarded: the anonymous Yiddish folksong, the love song, in particular.[52] Di Yunge valued these songs for their "secularity," for being lyrical and personal rather than didactic and bombastic. As Ruth Wisse has shown in her study of this group, it was their search for a truly individuated voice that paradoxically moved Di Yunge to explore the rigorous conventions of the Yiddish folksong. Di Yunge, according to Wisse, returned to an indigenous cultural base once they discovered how anemic and derivative their own personalism had become. Above all it was Mani Leyb (1883–1953) who sought to imitate the rhythms, rhymes, and musical forms of the Yiddish folksong and ballad as a way of laying the aesthetic foundations for a modern, formal poetry.[53]

There was one member of the group, Moyshe-Leyb Halpern (1886–1932), who turned his unrequited love of the past into parodic anger. Halpern played the bad boy and street drummer to Mani Leyb's humble shtetl craftsman. Once, in a rare moment of lyrical reprieve, Halpern seized upon the golden peacock as a symbol of love and longing for death—a poem later set to an exceptionally poignant melody by the American-Yiddish composer Ben Yomen.

> Di zun vet aruntergeyn untern barg,
> vet kumen di goldene pave tsu flien
> un mitnemen vet zi undz ale ahin,
> ahin vu di benkshaft vet tsien.
>
> (The sun will set beneath the hill; / The golden peacock will then appear, / And whisk us all away with her / To that place for which we yearn.)

Fig. 6.9. Moyshe Leyb Halpern, "Di zun vet aruntergeyn," from *Mir trogn a gezang! Favorite Yiddish Songs of Our Generation*, ed. Eleanor Gordon Mlotek. 2nd rev. ed. (New York: Workmen's Circle Education Department, 1977), p. 181.

"Us all" included the young Yiddish poets, whose ocean crossing left them sporadically yearning for home.[54]

Halpern was not content until he had turned that longing against itself. Who could better serve as an antisymbol or countersymbol than *The Golden Peacock* (1924), the legendary bird now stripped of its golden feathers in order to subvert any vestige of nostalgia for the Old World, to parody the pretensions to beauty still harbored by Yiddish poets writing in America, and to present Yiddish "folklore" in its coarsest, angriest, garb.[55] *The Golden Peacock* lays bare all the lies that the immigrant masses lived by: their claim to a hallowed shtetl past; to loving, pious grandparents; to group solidarity; to a covenantal relationship with God. It is a huge family saga, peopled with grotesque uncles, aunts, American cousins, and adopted family ("Moyshe Nadir's Leyzer-Elye, the One from the Old Home"). It is a genealogy of morals, which traces man's stupidity and coarseness back to the Creation. It is a mock literary history, starring Zarkhi, the aged poet-philosopher-and-beach-bum. The only island of repose is the poet's nuclear family: Royzele his wife, and their son. The monosyllabic, antipoetic rhymes are reminiscent of a badkhn's doggerel; for indeed, "Moyshe Leyb" is the learned, witty, New World master of ceremonies, here making his last public appearance.

Halpern's double use of the peacock—as mascot of group longing and as idol of false consciousness—is a cultural watershed for yet another reason. With the republication of his first book of poems in 1927, he became the single most popular and influential Yiddish poet in Poland.[56] From this we learn that the Golden Peacock made a return flight back across the ocean, this time adorned with brand new plumage. The energy of America, the boldness of its rhythms and rhymes, its unabashed display of sentiment and rage, its ideological *im*purity—all these made the new poetry and song culture irresistible.

Through sheet music, return migration, and "Vagabond Stars" (the new class of professional Yiddish actors), the American Yiddish song repertory penetrated deep into the East European Jewish heartland. "Der rebe Elimeylekh," a comical adaptation of "Ol' King Cole Was a Merry Ol' Soul" composed in New York City by Halpern's best buddy Moyshe Nadir, made it to the top of the neohasidic hit parade on both sides of the Atlantic. Lifshe Schaecter-Widman spent all of six years in America before returning to her native Bukovina—just long enough for her to add Reingold's irreverent "A Year after My Wedding" and Shmulewitz's supersentimental "Orphan Song" to her permanent repertory. In the Warsaw ghetto, Miriam Eisenstadt "moved even the stone hearts of the Ghetto and police officials" with her rendition of *Eyli, eyli* ("My God, My God"), which had premiered on Second Avenue in 1896. Herman Yablokoff's Depression-era song "Papirosn" (Cigarettes) was adapted far and wide in the Nazi ghettos.[57]

Even if Halpern's parodies were never set to music, his poetry exposed the worst and the best about American Yiddish culture as a whole: the mishmash of sentiment and satire, of patriotism and traditional piety, of sex and schmaltz; the impossible amalgam that went by the name of *shund*. Shund, meaning "trash," or "rubbish," became the central legacy of American Yiddish song.

Lebedeff and the Aesthetics of Shund

The aesthetics of shund, if one can use such a paradoxical phrase, had nothing to do with affecting a folk style, with covering up one's modern, European sensibility behind the traditional forms of Jewish self-expression. The whole point of shund was to let the seams show through, to let form and content clash and short circuit one another. Shund exploited the traditional pieties of the audience as well their desperate desire to break loose from the shtetl. Shund poked mercilous fun at the hasidic rebbe while allowing his daughter in the very same act to express the most heartfelt religious sentiments. Shund raised the double entendre and sexual innuendo to artistic heights that hadn't been reached since Elizabethan times. Off-color "Deutschifying" lyrics could thus be sung to sacred liturgical settings. The glory of shund was that you could eat your cake and have it, too.

Given these irreconcilable positions, shund could enjoy no support from among the American Yiddish intelligentsia, for among other things, the official ideologues were extremely puritanical about sex. Sex was a diversion from the class struggle and from the rebuilding of Zion.

Shund resisted any attempt at ideological pigeonholing. Shund, by definition, combined nostalgia for the shtetl with pragmatic acceptance of America; songs about the Sabbath, *kugl*, and Palestine with Catskill and California honeymoons. In shund, there was something for everyone.

After 1918, however, the battle lines hardened, and no more would the intellectuals' noblesse oblige extend to Yiddish Tin Pan Alley. Shmulewitz might still be kosher, because he was passé, but the moment Second Avenue entered into its period of greatest creative energy, it posed a real threat to competing claims for cultural hegemony.

Onto this battleground for the hearts and minds of the Jewish immigrant masses burst Aaron Lebedeff.[58] Fresh from his command performances on the Russian musical stage, he arrived here in September 1920, at the age of forty-seven. Legend had it that in Harbin, Manchuria, he had performed on alternate nights before Kerensky, Lenin, and Trotsky, adapting his repertory to the politics of each. But the key to Lebedeff's genius, I believe, was not his ability to tailor each performance to the needs of a specific audience. Rather it was the way he brought the tension between two disparate cultures to the fore. Knowing both Russian and shtetl culture at their source, he could celebrate the fusion and confusion that characterized Jewish life in American exile.

Lebedeff, whose most famous roles were Lyovke the Smart Lover, played in Russian, and the Romanian Litvak, played in Yiddish; Lebedeff—who could affect a *sabesdiker losn*, the provincial dialect of northern Litvaks, while never appearing in public without his straw hat and faultlessly tailored clothes—knew that the vitality of Yiddish culture lay in its clash of opposites. Linguistic and ideological purity were the kiss of death.

Here is Lebedeff at his most outrageous, celebrating the unbridled Jewish appetite for wine, women, and song (both the lyrics and music are his own):[59]

> Di Rumener trinken vayn
> un esn mamelige.
> ver es kisht zayn eygn vayb
> akh, yener iz meshige.
> Zets, tay didl di dam . . .
>
> *Yikum purkon min shmayo,*
> shteyt un kisht di kekhne, Khaye,
> ongeton in alte shkrabes
> makht a kigl lekoved shabes
>   Zets, tay didl di tam . . .

> (The Romanians drink wine / and eat *mamelige*. / And he who kisses his own wife / must be out of his bean. // MAY FROM HEAVEN COME SALVATION— / stop and kiss the cook named Khaye / dressed in rags and tatters / she makes a pudding for the Sabbath.)

If it weren't so hilarious, and delivered with such exuberance, this song could get one arrested for sacrilege. Khaye, the cook, who offers herself to all male callers, rhymes with an Aramaic prayer from the Sabbath morning service. (*Yikum purkon min shmayo* must have had comical associations back in the Old Country as well.) Here, the salvation it announces comes not from heaven but from that source of very earthly pleasures. Only

Lebedeff could have turned Romania into a parodic version of paradise lost.[60]

The kind of Jewish parody offered up by Lebedeff & Co. affirmed group norms and cultural codes by stretching them to new and impossible limits. Usually, the sacred and profane messages were delivered side by side, in line with the conventions of Vaudeville. Such was the case with the musical comedy *Der litvisher Yankee*, Aaron Lebedeff playing the lead.

In one justly famous song (lyrics by Lebedeff, music by Sholom Secunda), the Litvak Yankee takes pot shots at the rapid physical and moral assimilation of the Jewish immigrants to America:

> I spared no effort to get to Ameriker
> Thinking I'd become a rabbi and grow a beard.
> I had a beautiful pair of *peyes*, like every observant Jew,
> Now, instead of the beard, I've lost the *peyes*, too!
>
>> So you may ask me, why and how?
>> Dear friends, I'll give you the answer right now:
>
>> What can you do? It's America!
>> Where all the fancy dressers come from the hoi polloi.
>> What can you do? It's America!
>> Even the Jew has the face of a Goy!

The English-Yiddish refrain says it all: on the surface, *vot ken you makh, es iz Amerike*, bespeaks an ironic acceptance of the price that America exacts; beneath the surface, one cannot but laugh at how vulgar and ridiculous these Jews look without their beards and peyes.

Despite the risqué character of the song, which is primarily what recommended it to Kapelye, from whose wonderful recording I learned to sing it, the message of the play as a whole is very conservative.[61] It is a warning to the audience not to throw the baby out with the bathwater. And the song that brings the curtain down has the inviolability of *yidishkayt* as its parting message. Though betrayed from within by self-hating Jews and attacked from without by "the enemy," the "sacred flame" of yidishkayt, their matinee idol assures them, continues to burn on all corners of the earth.[62] Obviously, one does not expect a musical comedy to provide a theological gloss on what this yidishkayt means precisely. But the fierce note of national pride is unmistakable, and one longs for the day when our born-again klezmorim will feel comfortable enough in their own artistic identity to include this side of Aaron Lebedeff's repertory as well. Meanwhile, from other songs that Lebedeff made famous, one may conclude, at the very least, that *A yidish meydl darf a yidishn boy*, that Jews should marry in and not out.[63]

Parody, Memory, and Popular Culture

Yes, the Golden Peacock lost more than a feather when she made the ocean crossing to America. But not until the demise of Second Avenue did she lose her voice. When that happened, American Jews lost the art of spoofing that which they hold most sacred. Second Avenue preserved and perfected the art of Jewish parody. If ever there was a time and place where Jews needed to indulge in a sacrilegious joke, it was during their painful rebirth in America. What the badkhn was allowed at weddings and the folk was allowed at Purim became the sanctioned release mechanism for the largest mass of migratory Jews in history.

Jews lost an effective venue for their politics as well. Now that all the utopian ideologies have collapsed, either through failure or success, one can appreciate the pragmatism of Yiddish popular culture that tried to toe the line somewhere between the real and the ideal. One can marvel at how the anger and guilt over leaving the shtetl were worked through and finally resolved by creating a myth of paradise lost. The terrible disappointments of America were similarly conjured away by repeating the same rags-to-riches plot in one musical comedy after another. Second Avenue took both the restorative and the revolutionary impulses of the Promised Land and played them off each other.

Most importantly, Jews have lost the key to their immediate past. Second Avenue was the folk repository of Jewish collective memory, just as the handwritten songbooks brought over by Jewish immigrants preserved a partial record of prior upheavals. In World War I, the stars of the Yiddish stage could send their own *grus fun di trentshes*, greetings from the trenches, and end with a messianic hope for the success of the Jewish Legion. After the war, Yiddish Vaudeville performers could immortalize the transatlantic flight of the Jewish millionaire-entrepreneur Charles A. Levine, who almost beat Lindbergh to the finish line.[64]

> Levine, Levine, you're the hero of your race
> Levine, Levine, you're the greatest Hebrew ace.
> We got a thrill when Chamberlain flew
> But you were right there, too,
> We're proud of you!
> Levine, Levine, just an ordinary name

But you brought it everlasting fame.
We welcome you home from over the foam
Levine with your flying machine.

Second Avenue charted the ebb and flow of Jewish pride and patriotism. Second Avenue preserved the Jewish memory of world events.

Now, the memory of American Jews preserves only two events, neither of which happened here: the Holocaust and the birth of the State of Israel (or three, if one adds the Exodus of Soviet Jewry). And as for their own immigrant roots, there is only "Sunrise, Sunset," glitzy, sentimental, mass-marketed ethnic pop.

So if today Yiddish folksong revivalists are singing a different tune, it is because they have discovered—a generation too late—that the loss of Jewish parody, of pragmatic Jewish politics, and the loss of the immediate Jewish past were the price they paid for the death of Second Avenue. As usual, it is Aaron Lebedeff who said it best, in a patois of English, Yiddish, and Russian: *Vot ken you makh? Es iz Amerike! Amerike un bol'she nitshevo.*

7 A Revolution Set in Stone: The Art of Burial

> In modern times, Pantheons are also built, not for mythical figures, but for great men who brought new worlds, spiritual realms, into being. In our days a Pantheon is a temple of glory dedicated to the spiritual leaders of one's people.
>
> —M. Ivenski, 1939

Among Jews, there is no such thing as a potter's field. Regardless of their place of origin, Jews have always regarded burial as a *khesed shel emeth*, the supreme act of loving kindness for which there is no earthly reward. Wherever they settled, they organized a Hevra Kadisha, or Holy Society, to secure and oversee a Jewish cemetery. For reasons of ritual purity, the dead were segregated from the living and the Jewish cemetery occupied a hallowed space outside of secular time. However far Jews wandered, the Hevra Kadisha always retained its absolute control over the rites of burial and preserved the eternal resting place of the dead.[1]

Of all the changes modernity wrought—in the way Jews remember, record, sing, talk, work, dress, and educate their young—the last and most stubborn holdout of tradition is the way they bury their dead. The surest sign, then, of an irrevocable break with the past was when Jewish burials began to ape those of the Gentiles. This first occurred in the very cradle of Jewish modernity, Berlin.

They called themselves *Die Gesellschaft der Freunde* (the Society of Friends) and, having acquired their own burial ground in 1792, set about introducing innovations. The dead were buried in coffins instead of shrouds; to prevent the possibility of premature burial, the event was postponed for three days; epitaphs were written in German, not exclusively in Hebrew; the dates of the deceased were given according to the Gregorian, not only the Jewish, calendar; modest-sized tombstones were replaced by ones that far exceeded the height of a human being; and allegorical motifs lifted from Greek and Roman iconography came into fashion: obelisks, urns, bas-reliefs of sword-wielding, bare-breasted women.[2]

But only in the New World could Jews wipe the granite slab completely clean. Here they could redefine the meaning of being a Jew altogether by joining a fraternal order organized by place of origin or by political persuasion, or both. Landsmanshaftn began as benefit societies meant to provide for their members from cradle to grave, with burial aid listed as a main attraction. "Our cheverah kadishah," wrote the president of the Ponevezher landsmanshaft, "not only assumes the responsibility for burying the body according to the laws of Israel but also immortalizes the name of each member by repeating the prayer in memory of the departed soul on the day of yiskor. They do everything in their power to prevent the name of a member from being erased from the memory of the living."[3]

Through voluntary membership in a neotraditional society organized by place of origin, the Old Home reasserted itself in the New. But secular workers' orders—the Workmen's Circle (1900), the Jewish National Arbeter Farband (1910), and the International Workers' Order (IWO, 1930)—offered a completely new form of Jewish affiliation. For the first time in history, burial was removed from the most conservative wing of society and placed in the hands of agnostic radicals.

With full awareness that a new chapter of Jewish life had begun, the Workmen's Circle established a New York Cemetery Department in 1907 and boasted in its first *Yearly Report* that henceforth the religious establishment would no longer be able to bar freethinkers and other iconoclasts from proper burial. The latter had found a noble resting place at last, one that was fully consistent with the revolutionary ideals by which they had lived. Soon the Department began to issue literary supplements in Yiddish and English that offered nonreligious words of comfort and printed eulogies for secular heroes. Whether writing in Yiddish or English, whether neotraditional or radical, the new fraternal orders dispensed with one key word: the Old World *besoylem* was permanently replaced with the New World *semeteri*.

The time had come to break ground for a cultural revolution. First to go was the traditional Hebrew, replaced in whole or in part by Yiddish and English. Gone too was the prayer for the immortality of the soul, abbreviated *taf-nun-tsadik-bet-hey*; even the initials *pey-nun*, for *po nitman*, ("here lies"), were all but banished from the grave. Gone, more often than not, was the Jewish date of death, without which the surviving family would not know when to recite the kaddish. And almost nothing remained of the old iconography. Instead of two hands raised in priestly blessing, to denote a Kohen, or a hand holding a water jug, to denote a Levite, a new set of symbols appeared: eagles, feathers, torches, lyres, sheaves of wheat. A hierarchy made up of "*lerer*/teacher," "*khaver*/comrade," "*pionir*/pioneer," and "*kemfer*/fighter," replaced "Rabbi," "the wealthy," "the noble."[4] The party

Fig. 7.1. Entrance to the Workmen's Circle Plot,
Old Mount Carmel Cemetery, Queens, New York.
Photograph by Allan Ludwig.

Fig. 7.2. Feather on the headstone of Bernard Gorin (Yitskhok Goido),
"Novelist. Critic. Historian of the Yiddish Theatre." Flanked on the right by
Mordecai Spector's vandalized headstone, which lacks its bronze bas-relief.
Photograph by Tim Davis. © 1998 by Tim Davis.

Fig. 7.3. Sheaf of wheat atop the headstone of Jacob Goldstone (1871–1940). The Yiddish epitaph reads: "The Jewish Bakers' Union Is My Eternal Monument." Photograph by Allan Ludwig.

Fig. 7.4. Insignia of the Yugnt-Bund in Poland.
Detail from the headstone of Nachman Natan Szafran
in the New Mount Carmel Cemetery.
Photograph by Allan Ludwig.

Fig. 7.5. Headstone of Elias Reisberg. The Yiddish epitaph reads: "The Path of His Struggle Illuminated with the Glow of Refined Spirit."
Photograph by Allan Ludwig.

faithful were buried with the insignia of the Workmen's Circle, the Jewish Labor Bund, the Yugnt-Bund, or the International Ladies Garment Workers Union (ILGWU).

With one tomb, that of Aaron Shmuel Liberman, several taboos were broken at once. The thirty-five-year-old "Pioneer of Jewish Socialism" had arrived in America in 1880, only to shoot himself in the head a few months later in Syracuse, New York. There he lay until 1934, when his body was reinterred with great pomp and circumstance in the Workmen's Circle Mount Carmel Cemetery in Queens. According to tradition, a suicide must be buried *untern ployt,* beneath the fence, as an outcast whose soul is consigned to perdition. But the Workmen's Circle buried Liberman in the Honor Row, the second grave to the right of the archway. What's more, a beautiful, stately bust was commissioned—in violation of the Second Commandment.

Liberman's burial was part of a trend toward funerals as pageants—celebrations of the collective struggle for redemption. The First Amendment right of freedom of assembly combined with the unprecedented concentration of so many Jews in small urban areas like the Lower East Side had given rise to a new form of communal observance, a ritual of collective affirmation: the mass public funeral. The first to mobilize were Orthodox Jews, thousands accompanying the plain pine coffin of their beloved chief rabbi, Jacob Joseph, in 1902. Unique to the New World was the mass public funeral of Kasriel Sarahson, the dynamic editor of the Orthodox *Tageblat* who died in 1905. Not until 1909 did the secular street get its moment in the sun, when the great Yiddish dramatist Jacob Gordin, author of *Mirele Efros* and *God, Man, and the Devil,* passed away. Hoping for a funeral that would eclipse that of Ulysses S. Grant, the secular Yiddish press mobilized the masses, and the veteran labor leader Joseph Barondess presided over a gala memorial meeting that included the Halevi Choral Society singing the "Pilgrims' Chorus" from Wagner's *Tannhäuser.* Gordin's stately coffin stood open on the stage, in flagrant violation of Jewish law.[5]

Radical Jews in America sorely lacked martyrs of their own. The East European Jewish Labor Bund, still in its infancy, already boasted the cobbler's apprentice Hirsh Lekert of Vilna as one of its martyred sons. Since the tsarist police had buried him in an unmarked grave, the Bund turned the anniversary of Lekert's hanging into an occasion for commemorative protest gatherings. Nothing comparable occurred in New York City until the infamous Triangle Shirtwaist Company Fire of March 25, 1911, most of the 146 victims of which were Jewish women. Protest rallies growing in size and vehemence took place for three days in succession, culminating in a mass funeral march and public burial of the last seven unidentified bodies

Fig. 7.6. The grave of Aaron Shmuel Liberman,
"The Pioneer of Jewish Socialism."
Photograph by Tim Davis. © 1998 by Tim Davis.

on April 5. In the Mount Zion cemetery, the Workmen's Circle erected a large monument in memory of all those garment workers, Jews and Italians, who, in the words of the *Forverts*, "were murdered by the profit fiend named capitalism."[6]

Only one man succeeded in uniting all sectors of the Jewish community, from Orthodox to anarchist, and he did so only in death. That man was Solomon Rabinovitsh, universally revered as Sholem Aleichem. His funeral, on Monday, May 15, 1916, drew close to a quarter of a million mourners. The event itself was a unique blend of rigorous adherence to Orthodox rite and Yiddishism. The ritual purification of Sholem Aleichem's corpse was performed by "three old Jews with long beards" from the Pereyaslev landsmanshaft society, but from that moment until the start of the funeral procession, one hundred secular Yiddish writers working in shifts guarded the body. Children from both the Orthodox Talmud Torah and the National Radical schools accompanied the coffin while reciting chapters of Psalms.

Overlooked at the event was the fact that Sholem Aleichem had neither wanted to die in American exile nor to be turned into a secular icon. He had left instructions that he be reinterred in Kiev after the war. Going against tradition, however, he had insisted on being buried "not among aristocrats, but among ordinary Jewish working folk." His epitaph, which he himself had composed after an earlier run-in with death, drove home this self-effacing message: "Here lies a simple-hearted Jew," it read, "In whose Yiddish womenfolk delighted; / And all the common people, too, / Laughed at the stories he indicted."

In 1921, when it became clear that Kiev was destined to remain under Soviet domination, the Cemetery Department of the Workmen's Circle made the family an offer it could not refuse. An Honor Row was to be established at the entrance to its new Mount Carmel plot, and the first occupant was to be Sholem Aleichem. For the first year, his large black marble tombstone stood there all by itself. But as the Row started filling up with the graves of Jewish labor leaders and other, less famous, writers, the "simple-hearted" Jew from Russia became, retroactively, the founding father of secular Yiddish culture in the New World. From that pageant, an American Yiddish Pantheon was born.[7]

Of Sholem Aleichem's closest neighbors, only Meyer London, the first Socialist to be elected to Congress (d. 1926), and Boruch Vladeck, a founder of the American Labor Party and the Jewish Labor Committee (d. 1938), were to receive a hero's burial of even grander proportions. During the interwar years, the Jewish labor movement continued to rally the masses

Fig. 7.7. The grave of Sholem Aleichem.
Photograph by Allan Ludwig.

around its dead leaders with a secular rite commensurate with its radical ideology: the exposed body lay in state in an open coffin in the Forward Building the entire day prior to the funeral, under the protection of "red" honor guards, and the graveside ritual concluded with the singing of revolutionary hymns.[8]

How did Sholem Aleichem, a synagogue-attending, card-carrying Zionist who called himself "How-Do-You-Do" come to rub headstones with the likes of such radical men? By the right of his very pen-name. The most revered figure in the Workmen's Circle Honor Row was neither "Solomon Naumovitsh Rabinovitsh" from Kiev nor "Sholem, son of Nokhem-Vevik" from Pereyaslev, but a self-invented "Sholem Aleichem" from Yiddishland. Were it not for his wife, Olga Rabinovitsh, who was buried at his feet, and the Hebrew translation of his epitaph on the obverse side, to which his son-in-law I. D. Berkowitz added his full Jewish name, there would be no evidence whatsoever of his "true" identity. Thus did Sholem Aleichem pioneer a major trend in modern Jewish culture, whose history was in large part the history of its hidden identities.

The persona, mask, or assumed identity obliterated one's real origins, whether geographic, linguistic, or genealogical, whether for reasons of secrecy, as in a *nom de guerre*, or for reasons of artistry, as in a *nom de plume*. Three brothers lie buried in the old and new Honor Row of the Workmen's Circle; only one of them, Daniel Charney (1888–1959), carries his family name alone. The other two—the literary critic S. Niger (1883–1955) and Boruch Charney Vladeck (1886–1938)—provide their family connection in parentheses. Except for a husband-and-wife, family members are scattered here, there, and everywhere in both the old and new Workmen's Circle plots. Whatever group allegiance the individual claimed transcended the parochial boundaries of family, religious faith, or place of origin.

Most astonishing is the grave of the pioneer of Yiddish socialist poetry, Morris Winchevsky, a.k.a. Leopold Benedict (1856–1932), or so claims his stone. Once upon a time, there was a Russian Jew named Lipe Ben-Tsiyon Novakhovitsh. Of him the only trace that remains is the distant, vaguely Central European "Leopold Benedict," who in turn made one more stopover in England, to become "Morris Winchevsky," before immigrating to the United States of America, there to be buried in what one recent visitor dubbed a Yiddish "witness protection cemetery."

The Honor Row in the old Mount Carmel cemetery is a silent community that bears false witness to an apparently seamless chronology. Although everyone buried there was born outside the United States and came over at different times, their birthplaces are never given. And although they often

Fig. 7.8. The grave of Morris Winchevsky.
Photograph by Tim Davis. © 1998 by Tim Davis.

fought on opposite sides of the barricades, they now make up three consecutive generations of Yiddish writers who seemingly worked in harmony with a unified Jewish labor movement. These are the generations of Adam.[9]

First come the pioneers of Yiddish secular culture: Sholem Aleichem, Mordecai Spector (1858–1925; immigrated 1921), and Morris Winchevsky. The bronze bas-relief of Spector was unfortunately vandalized some ten years ago, during a spate of similar acts all over Queens, which were economic, not antisemitic, in motive. What remains is the epitaph: "His whole life Yiddish, Jews, yidishkayt." Like his close friend Sholem Aleichem, Spector's burial in America was an accident of history.

The generation of the classicists begat the Yiddish poets and prose writers who were nothing if not American: Avrom Lyessin, a.k.a. Avrom Valt (1872–1938; immigrated 1896); Phillip Krantz, a.k.a. Yankev Rambro (1858–1922; immigrated 1890); and Morris Rosenfeld (1862–1923; immigrated 1882, 1886). They in turn begat the generation of aesthetes called Di Yunge, who, as befits young upstarts, are not buried in the Honor Row: Moyshe-Leyb Halpern, Zishe Landau, the folklorist J. L. Cahan, and the theatrical director, David Herman. They were the harbingers of the aesthetic revolution, as each of their tombstones eloquently testifies. Halpern's is in the shape of a scroll. Zishe (and Reyzl) Landau's bear only their names, in the distinctive typeface used in his volumes of poetry. Cahan's is in the shape of a book, with his dates on the spine and the following inscription on the cover: "The wellsprings of the folksong / he did open / the charm of the folktale / he did reveal." The standard square lettering is here replaced by stylized Ashkenazi script. The bas-relief on David Herman's tomb recreates a theatrical poster for his most famous production, *The Dybbuk,* featuring the Rabbi of Miropolye and the lovers Khonon and Leah.

Aaron Shmuel Liberman's regal bust, meanwhile, still stands alone, as befits the progenitor of the Jewish socialist idea. The first-generation leaders of the socialist and anarchist movements in England and the United States are located mostly to the left of the archway: Winchevsky, Krantz, Benjamin Feigenbaum, Abraham Cahan, Saul Yanovsky, and the founders of the Bund, Vladimir Kosvosky, a.k.a. Nokhem Levinson, Yekusiel Portnoy, a.k.a. "Noyakh," and Vladimir Medem.

Their origins are not the only thing that is effaced. So too the deep divisions that split their ranks. The schism during the 1890s between the anarchists and social democrats was mere child's play as compared with the communist putsch within the trade union movement during the late 1920s. One grave tells the whole story, even as it covers it: that of Morris Winchevsky who, in the last years of his life, betrayed his socialist roots and

Fig. 7.9. The grave of Judah Leib Cahan.
Photograph by Tim Davis. © 1998 by Tim Davis.

Fig. 7.10. The grave of David Herman.
Photograph by Allan Ludwig.

went over to the communists. A year before he died, the Jewish section of the Communist Party celebrated Winchevsky's seventy-fifth birthday in Madison Square Garden. After the funeral, however, when Winchevsky's family refused to have him buried in a Party-approved cemetery, the New York City police were called in to protect the cortege from stone-pelting Party faithful.

Less dramatic was the fate of Morris Rosenfeld, who spent several years lecturing at Ivy League universities only to outlive his welcome in the New World and die an embittered, lonely man. The Germanicized verse on his obelisk-style tombstone, topped by an enshrouded eagle and urn, bears eloquent testimony to an aesthetic whose time had come and gone. "The poet's pure soul has risen supernal," his long epitaph reads in conclusion, "To glow there, amongst lights eternal."[10]

What began, in 1921, as an ad hoc decision to honor the greatest of Jewish émigré writers, and quickly evolved into an Honor Row for the socialist aristocracy, became, in the wake of the Great Depression and the rise of Hitler, a memory-site of national significance. By then, the front ranks of the Jewish labor movement were rapidly thinning. It was easier to buttress them from behind, by resurrecting the memory of Aaron Shmuel Liberman, for instance, than it was to recruit new leaders. By the mid-1930s, moreover, America was becoming the refuge for an increasing number of already-established Polish- and Russian-Jewish intellectuals and labor leaders. The Honor Row was indeed honored to boast the likes of I. J. Singer, who immigrated from Poland in 1933, or the historian Shoyel Ginzburg, who reached these shores in 1930. Two leaders of the Bund were rescued from Poland when the war broke out, both to die almost upon arrival: Yekusiel Portnoy and Vladimir Kosovsky. Several glorious chapters in the history of Jewish self-determination were coming to a very rapid close. It was time to cast the revolutionary past in stone, and elevate it to a new status.

"What the Pantheon is to France," declared M. Ivenski, a member of the National Board of Directors of the Workmen's Circle, "what Westminster Abbey is for England, the Victory Boulevard in Berlin's Tiergarten for Germany, and Arlington Cemetery—for the United States of America, the Honor Row on Mount Carmel must now become for the Jews." Dispersed among the nations, the Jews are united behind a set of ideals, the crown of which is the twin ideal of justice and brotherhood. This is the banner under which the Jewish labor movement has always fought. But because the American-Jewish community is so relatively young, and because it has been so derelict in honoring its spiritual leaders, it is incumbent upon organized Jewish labor to enter the breach. It alone can and must "repay the national debt of the Jewish people." Henceforth and in perpetuity, the Workmen's Circle cemeteries will memorialize the Jewish people's greatest spiritual heroes.[11]

The next-to-last to be buried in the Honor Row in the Old Mount Carmel cemetery, imperious in death as he was in life, was the long-time editor of the *Forverts*, Abraham Cahan (1860–1951; immigrated 1882). Not coincidentally, his was the last funeral pageant to be staged by the Jewish labor movement. When Yoysef Baskin died (1880–1952; immigrated 1907), his being the final gravestone to be unveiled, the Jewish immigrant masses could look upon the Honor Row as a collective monument to their secular ideals. His epitaph summed up their credo in three languages: "Fighter for Truth, Justice and Brotherhood," it read in English, Yiddish, and very flowery Hebrew.

Few of those buried in the Honor Row had espoused the Jewish national cause; most were socialist internationalists. But once again, thanks to Sholem Aleichem's presence, it was possible to retroactively impose the new national consciousness of the Jewish radical sector. His universal Jewish stature rubbed off on his neighbors. An unending stream of dignitaries and pilgrims would deposit pebbles and rocks on his grave as a sign of respect: personal memory on top of national memory.

In the early 1950s, a new Honor Row began to take shape in the new Mount Carmel Cemetery just up the hill; fifty-one monuments from start to finish as compared to the thirty-seven down below. But the new Honor Row was much more than an extension of the old. The Row was now evenly divided between professional writers and political activists. Writers who had been young upstarts in the decades before had achieved preeminence; Yiddish culture was now as precious—and endangered—as the fight for truth, justice, and brotherhood. Here and there, an (English) epitaph still memorialized an "Internationalist" (Meyer Davidoff) or "Humanitarian" (Louis Goldberg). In the case of I. N. Steinberg, the English recalled him as a "Man of Letters Man of Action Man of Faith," while the Yiddish allowed for a more parochial legacy: a "Fighter in Word and Deed for Humanity and [his] People."

The people—what had happened to the people? Most had perished in Europe. And this terrible fact cries out from epitaph to epitaph, whether the deceased had witnessed the slaughter from afar, had miraculously survived it, or had borne witness to it—by taking their own lives.

"Over the mound of the Jewish catastrophe," reads the inscription on Yankev Pat's stone, "over the mighty ocean of Jewish anguish and calamity / a great light will yet shine!" (from *Ash and Fire*, 1946, his travelogue about postwar Poland). "O Lord," begins the more muted inscription on Khayim Liberman's grave, "preserve the sun for the sake of the world / and my people for the sake of the nations" (from his only nonpolemical work, *De profundis*, 1942). Zusman Segalovicz (1884–1949), identified as a "Yiddish poet and threnodist of murdered Polish Jewry," similarly displays a passage from his Holocaust-related work, which appears in cursive script just below the traditional abbreviations, dates, and data, duly reinstated. *Khaver* Bernard, a.k.a. Bernard Goldstein, is memorialized as a "Leader of the [Jewish] Self-defense, a Fighter in the Warsaw Ghetto," and as one who "Dedicated his Life to the Bund."

It is the heroism and tragedy of the Bund, the leading Jewish movement in interwar Poland, that is given pride of place in the new Honor Row. Thanks to his compatriots in America, the "Pioneer and Builder of the Bund," Franz Kurski, a.k.a. Shmuel Kahn (1877–1950), found a safe haven, as did the popular "Yiddish Writer Thinker and Bundist" I. J. Trunk (1887–1961). The golden chain of dedication to the cause had never been severed, for here lay Emanuel Nowogrodzki, "Builder of the Bund in Poland and America / General Secretary 1920–1961." But Nowogrodzki's headstone also honored his wife Sonia, "Teacher in the TSISHO Schools Bundist Leader Active in the Warsaw Ghetto / Murdered in Treblinka."[12]

Separated spatially and architecturally on the extreme left is the tomb of "Artur (Shmuel Mordecai) Zygelboim 1895–1943 / Member of Central Committee of the Jewish Labor Bund in Poland / Bund Representative in Polish Parliament in Exile." Containing his ashes that were brought over from London after the war, his tomb is the first memorial to the Holocaust on American soil. Martyrdom is its operative term. The biographical side of the tomb concludes with the words: "May 11, 1943, in London Chose Martyr's Death." The liturgical side speaks of Zygelboim's "free heroic suicide," which is read as an expiation for the involuntary martyrdom of "The 6 Million Jews / Victims of Nazi Genocide." The flame atop his stone is their Eternal Light.

Martyrdom and suicide bracket the legacy of the Jewish labor movement. On the other side of the ocean lay the unmarked grave of Hirsh Lekert of Vilna, the Bund's first martyr to the cause. Magnificently entombed in America lay Arn-Shmuel Liberman, who had given birth to the Jewish socialist dream in Russia-Poland, before taking his own life. In the new Honor Row lay Artur Zygelboim, who took his own life rather than preside over the burial of that dream.

All the American-Yiddish writers buried in the new Honor Row lived long enough to see their own dreams come to naught as well. Yet a lyrical,

Fig. 7.11. The memorial grave of Artur Zygelboim, with
an excerpt from his suicide note in Yiddish and English.
Photograph by Allan Ludwig.

almost liturgical, tone informs their epitaphs. The most irreverent is Daniel Charney's (1888–1959):

> Keyner veyst nit dem eygenem sof
> vi er veyst nit dem onheyb fun zikh.
> Eyner shtarbt beneshike in shlof
> der tsveyter in kragn un shikh.

(No one knows how he'll reach his end / nor how he was begat. / One dies in his sleep with a divine kiss / the other—in starched collar and spats.)

The most upbeat is Abraham Reisen's:

> Zing, neshome, zing!
> Kurts der veg tsi lang.
> S'endikt say vi say
> vi a vayt gezang.
>
> Zing, neshome, zing!
> Lebn heyst gezang
> un dernokh vet zayn
> sheyn der viderklang.

(Sing, my soul, sing! / Whether life's road is short or long. / Either way it ends / Like a distant song. // Sing, my soul, sing! / The meaning of life is song. / And thereafter a beautiful echo / will resound.)

Nearly all the key figures of Di Yunge, most of whom died in the 1950s and 1960s, are reunited here, with samples of their own verse: H. Leivick, a.k.a. Leivick Halper, and Mani Leib, a.k.a. Brahinsky, among them. In death, as in life, they are accompanied by the noted critic and literary historian S. Niger. Just behind the Honor Row lie the poet David Ignatoff and prose writer Joseph Opatoshu. The *Inzikhistn*, or arch-modernists, who sought to supplant them, are represented by A. Glantz Leyeles in the Honor Row (right next to Zygelboim) and N. B. Minkoff in the second tier.

A rhetorical self-confidence emanates from their epitaphs, the confidence of a generation that had achieved two radically different goals: the sanctification of the lowly jargon called Yiddish, and the shaping of this folk vernacular into a supple and modern vehicle of self-expression. While the writer Pat and the activist Liberman used Yiddish to express their na-

Fig. 7.12. The grave of Abraham Reisen.
Photograph by Allan Ludwig.

tional-collective yearnings, the epitaphs of H. Leivick and Mani Leib are statements of faith in themselves as the anointed by God:

> Ikh lig a fardekter un her vi mayn shtern
> git iber mayn nomen tsum har fun di shtern.

> (I lie covered over and hear my own star / conveying my name to the Lord of the Stars.)

and

> Fun shtoyb hot got mikh ufgeheybn
> un mikh derhoybn iber aykh
> az ikh zol ayer koved loybn
> az ikh zol greysn ayer nomen
> az ven ikh vel nit zayn mit aykh
> zol zayn mit aykh mayn nomen. Omeyn.

> (God raised me from the dust / set me above other men / to have me sing your worth / to have me praise your honor / that when I returned to earth / my name remain among you. Amen.)[13]

Yiddish culture had laid claim to both the heavens and the earth. The earthly claim, represented by its revolutionaries, labor leaders, and martyrs, was now a thing of the past. Only a Pantheon remained to the fallen gods. The poets, most of whom had eked out a living at the margins of organized labor, laid claim to the heavens. Judging from their epitaphs, that claim was still pending.

Two women lie among them, separate from their spouses, and just behind the Honor Row. One is the sculptor, prose writer, and poet Rosa Walinsky (1888–1953), whose epitaph celebrates the lasting magic of a poem, of life experiences, and of the sun's play on a person's eyelids.[14] The poet's last gaze is directed upward. Not so the epitaph of Anna Margolin, a.k.a. Rosa Lebensboym Ayzland (1887–1952), written twenty-one years before she died. So brutal is its downward spiral and so explicit its imagery that the Cemetery Department of the Workmen's Circle expunged the first two lines:

> [Zi, mit di kalte marmorne brist
> un mit di shmole likhtike hent,]
> zi hot ir sheynkayt farshvendt
> af mist, af gornisht.

Fig. 7.13. The grave of Anna Margolin.
Photograph by Allan Ludwig.

Zi hot es efsher gevolt, efsher geglust
tsu umglik, tsu zibn mesers fun payn
un fargosn dem lebns heylikn vayn
af mist, af gornisht.

Itst ligt zi mit a tsebrokhn gezikht.
Der geshendter gayst farlozt di shtayg.
farbaygeyer, hob rakhmones un shvayg—
zog gornisht.

[She with the cold marble breasts / and the narrow bright hands,/]
She wasted her life / on trash, on nothing. // Maybe she looked for
misfortune / and lusted for the seven knives of pain / and poured out
her life / on trash, on nothing. // Now she lies with a shattered face / her
dishonored soul has quit the cage. / Passerby, pity her and be still. Say
nothing.)[15]

It was the fate of modern artists to be misunderstood and to fail in their
own self-estimation. How much more so the modern *Yiddish* artists, sons
and daughters of a people who had squandered their treasures left and right.
Anna Margolin's epitaph is different only in degree but not in kind from
the first epitaph unveiled in the old Honor Row back in 1921, that of Sholem
Aleichem. The world-class artist who, in the opening stanza, passed himself off as a simple folk writer for women, went on to portray himself as
Pagliacci, smiling on the outside, crying inside: "Most often when his audience / applauded and was laughter-ridden, / he ailed, which God's omnis-
cience / alone remarked. He kept it hidden."

Yet all of them—men and women, poets and politicians, cosmopolitans
and nationalists, aesthetes and arch-modernists, rebels and martyrs—had
found a collective, sanctified, resting place, a memory-site made of granite
and marble, so designed that decades later, when all their own aspirations had been ground to dust, young Jews in search of models of self-
determination and self-transcendence might know where to look.

Ivenski was wildly off the mark when, in 1939, he compared the Work-
men's Circle cemetery in Queens to the French Pantheon, Westminster
Abbey, Arlington National Cemetery, not to speak of the Victory Boule-
vard in Berlin. The radical sector of the American-Jewish street bore no
resemblance to nation-states that had coalesced over centuries. Rather, the
Yiddish cultural revolution invites comparison with the other Brave New
Worlds of the twentieth century: the Soviet Union and the Palestinian
Yishuv. There too cemeteries took shape to honor revolutions.

The vast Novodevichy cemetery in Moscow is where Khrushchev and

Mikoyan, Soviet generals and fighter pilots all lie buried in sumptuous tombs. There is but one Hebrew gravestone, that of the nineteenth-century landscape painter Isaak Levitan. Otherwise, the price of admission to the Soviet pantheon was to expunge all signs of one's Jewishness; the price paid by the popular composer Dmitri Pokrass so that he could lie just down the row from the Russian opera star, Chalyapin, and by the great film director Sergei Eisenstein, that he might lie a stone's throw away from Gogol.

The mass exodus of Russian Jews, among them many doctors, engineers, painters, filmmakers, and composers, suggests that they got tired of waiting for the Revolution to deliver on its promise. Most ended up settling within commuting distance of Tel Aviv, the "First Hebrew City." So rapidly has it grown that no one even notices the small, walled-off cemetery smack in the heart of town, and not the nicest part, either. Here the Zionist leadership had carved out a properly segregated space for the major Hebrew writers, the mayors and councilmen, the martyrs of the Arab pogroms, and the most influential Zionist ideologues. A native-born generation sick and tired of ideology and martyrdom is not beating down the cemetery's gates to revisit the past. Yet even as I sit here writing in New York City, theatergoers in Tel Aviv are enjoying a new play, ʿAl hahayim veʿal hamavet (A matter of life and death) by Eldad Ziv, set in the Old Tel Aviv cemetery. By all accounts, Ziv's play rescues the forgotten Zionist writers and politicians as people of flesh and blood.[16]

That is why I lead a biannual pilgrimage of students to the Workmen's Circle plots in Mount Carmel: on the chance that the gravestones will lend new life to the spirit that animated the men and women they memorialize, and inspire young Jews today, in search of a usable past.

A cemetery isn't much to show for such colossal effort, for such utopian dreams, for so radical a reinvention of Jewish life. Still, there is reason to hope. According to tradition, when the People of Israel left Egypt, they salvaged only the remains of their ancestor, Joseph; but look at what *they* went on to create in their Promised Land.

8   A City, a School, and a Utopian Experiment

We will forever search for the echo of chords sounded long ago that were
never forgotten. Sounds, melodies, smells, and memories. What we thereby
seek is both our childhood, lost irrevocably, and the total yidishkayt that was
possible under certain conditions once prevalent in the small shtetl but
impossible to reproduce here in the metropolitan American exile. That
longing and unhappiness is an important psychic factor in our lives.

—Shloime Wiseman, 1948

Ideology Begins at School

Somewhere between the ages of three and four, Jewish boys received their first instruction in the alphabet. In a typical East European
heder, the teacher sat down next to the child, opened to the first page in
the prayer book printed in large letters, and began to chant as follows:

> Zogt a yingele mit kheyshek: pasekh shin vi makht?
> Sha.
> Vayter, gikher: Da.
> Da-yud?
> Day.
> Makht dos in eynem?
> Shaday.
> Derunter mit dem?
> E.
> Segel mem?
> Me.
> Mem sof?
> Mes.
> Makht dos in eynem?
> Emes.
> In eynem makht dos?
> Shaday emes, shaday.

(This is what a little boy should recite with zeal: What does *pasekh-shin* spell? *Sha.* Next, now be quick: *Da. Da-yud? Day.* Together what does it spell? *Shaday.* What's underneath [the letter]? *E. Segel-mem* [spells what]? *Me. Mem-sof? Mes.* Together what does it spell? *Emes.* And all together? *Shaday emes, shaday.*)

Induction into reading was synonymous with induction into the first principle of faith: *Shaday emes* means "God is truth."[1]

Spurred on by a different ideology, one that stressed social activism, secularism, and universalism, German-born Felix Adler (1851–1933) founded the New York Society for Ethical Culture; and almost at once (in 1878) he established a kindergarten (the first in the eastern United States) designed to inculcate ethics and productivity in the very young.[2]

Equally committed to the three principles of social activism, secularism, and universalism, Russian-born Abraham Kazan (1889–1971) built the first and largest middle-income cooperative housing project in the United States. George Bernard Shaw may have dreamt about such a place, but it came to pass through the joint efforts of the Jewish labor movement and the New York State legislature. The year was 1927. For Kazan, the cooperative ideal was the center of the vision, very different from Adler's teaching of citizenship and individual responsibility. Thus, among the manifold cooperative services that the Amalgamated Housing Corporation in Bronx, New York, offered its tenants were secular Yiddish afternoon schools that covered the political spectrum from Zionism to communism. Here, several generations of American-born youth, living in a New World equivalent of the shtetl, studied the works of I. L. Peretz and Sholem Aleichem in the Yiddish original. This lasted until the 1970s, when — as the *Encyclopedia of New York City* puts it so diplomatically — the Amalgamated projects became "more ethnically diverse, . . . like the rest of the city."[3]

Which of these three (Jewish-inspired) institutions of learning is still around, lo these many years later? With kindergartens now part of the state apparatus, which must observe the separation of church and state, children are being presocialized in independently run day care centers throughout the country. If my son's experience in a nonsectarian day care center is any guide, they are still being taught Felix Adler's curriculum, with an overlay of political correctness. The revival of separatist Jewish communities, meanwhile, based on an antiliberal, religiously conservative ideology, has allowed the old-style heders to flourish anew. Here, the ritual of learning *Shaday emes*, with or without the melody, means that for the Hasidim, the perpetuation of Judaism is an end in itself. But the network of Yiddish secular schools has almost vanished from the urban landscape, victims of their own success. Since collectivism was merely a stepping stone to achieving the higher end of a universal, secular, and liberal polity, the graduates of these schools eventually moved out—and married out. Liberalism, their new religion, saw the existence of separate schools taught in foreign languages as something anomalous, if not downright barbaric. There was room in the American landscape for the confessional school only because Tom Sawyer had gone to one, on Sundays.

The modern Jewish school was the first child of Jewish modernity, and its final victim. A Jewish school uncompromising both in its modernity and its Jewishness may no longer be a viable option anywhere outside of Israel—and some would say, even in Israel. Before it disappears forever, therefore, I propose to revisit the one place on the North American continent where such a school not only survived but thrived well beyond the period of mass immigration, one experiment in utopian living whose ideological and institutional foundations withstood the great upheavals of the twentieth century. That place is Montreal, Canada, and Yiddish was the crucible of its modern Jewish curriculum.

The Shaping of Yiddish Culture in Montreal

Exploiting what was and still remains a unique configuration of religious and ethnic groupings, the second wave of Yiddish-speaking immigrants to the island of Montreal established a collective presence and a collective vision that should not be dismissed as being merely anomalous; for Montreal Yiddish culture provides a usable model of a creative Jewish Diaspora and a successful example of Jewish self-determination in the face of unprecedented freedom.

It has five distinguishing features:

(1) Montreal Yiddish culture was a utopian venture. Nothing like it existed anywhere else on earth and therefore it had to be invented from scratch.

(2) It was neither a pragmatic compromise with the ethnic makeup of Quebec nor a freak occurrence. It was a cognitive and above all ideological construct, the work of a tiny group of secular Zionist intellectuals.

(3) The break-up of the old order and the destruction of traditional faith were a given to this group of recent immigrants. There was no going back. Therefore one had to ensure that the New Jew to be born would be a redeemer and not a golem.

(4) While elsewhere in the Jewish world national liberation was pursued

through a divide-and-conquer strategy, through permanent revolution, the Montreal Yiddish intelligentsia fought for a restorative and integrative program that would create a sense of wholeness both within Jewish life and within the fragmented world at large.

(5) Through extraordinary self-sacrifice and in the face of bitter infighting, this cadre of young ideologues established a network of institutions to embody their bold utopian vision: a Yiddish press, a Jewish public library, a Vaad Ho'ir (the Jewish Community Council), afternoon and day schools, a teacher's seminary, amateur Yiddish theater groups, summer camps, and book stores.

The key to this utopian venture was the word *folk*. The word asserted itself in the names of new institutions and publications alike: *Di yidishe folks-bibliotek, di yidishe folkshuln, Di yidishe folks-entsiklopedye*. When the "Jewish People's Library" finally opened its doors, in rented quarters, on May Day 1914, it amalgamated two earlier collections belonging to the Dorshei Zion and Poalei Zion (both Labor Zionist groups). Reuven Brainin, a Hebrew-Yiddish-German publicist of some renown, was invited to preside over the new institution, whose motto was "By the People, Through the People, For the People."[4]

The choice of Folkshule was no less programmatic. The Yiddish secular schools were called into being at the Fifth Poalei Zion Convention held in Montreal on October 20, 1910. They were to be known as *Natsyonale Radikale shuln.*[5] The Peretz School, founded in 1913 as a Saturday and Sunday school, continued to boast of this pedigree in its official anthem. But ideological differences arose among the Poalei Zion activists over the place of Hebrew in the curriculum and the emphasis on traditional subject matter. With the Peretz School holding out for a more exclusively Yiddish and radical orientation, Yehuda Kaufman broke away to establish the *Folkshule*. His heir and chief disciple, Shloime Wiseman, would spend forty years of his life trying to preserve the folk character of the Folkshule in the face of attacks from the right and from the left.

The ideology of serving the broadest interests of the "folk" extended even to classical text editions produced in Montreal. Thus, in his Hebrew translation of the Zohar, Yudl Rosenberg only included the exegetical portions connected to the Bible. Replying in the *Keneder odler* to criticism leveled against him by the young Shimshen Dunsky (March 31, 1931), Rosenberg argued that one mustn't reveal the esoteric Kabbalah to the simple folk.[6] A dozen years later, Simcha Pietruszka created his *Jewish Folk Encyclopedia* in order to refamiliarize the Yiddish-speaking masses with the traditional roots of their culture, while in his Hebrew-Yiddish *Mishnayes*

(The Mishnah), Pietruszka adopted a highly conservative approach to the textual apparatus.[7] Dunsky, now older and wiser, adopted a similar approach to textual emendation in his own *Midrash Rabba*. All these scholars went by the same principle: to speak for the folk meant that one had to respect its boundaries.

The anomaly of Yiddish in Montreal is that a group of "lay Jewish revolutionaries," as David Rome so felicitously calls them, took upon itself the arduous task of guarding Jewish cultural boundaries.[8] To be sure, the ideological foundations of cultural nationalism had been laid elsewhere: by Aḥad Haᶜam (1858–1927) and Chaim Zhitlowsky (1865–1943), the major theoreticians of the Hebrew and Yiddish revival. By the same token, the postwar treaties negotiated on minority rights and cultural autonomy, not to speak of the Balfour Declaration, had everything to do with Jewish political aspirations in French Canada. But while the roots of the Yiddish cultural revolution in Montreal were decidedly East European, its particular flowering—and the fruits that it ultimately bore—were nowhere else to be found.

To be more specific, it was on this northernmost outpost of the New World that members of the Labor Zionist movement (the Poalei Zion) actualized their party platform. As opposed to those radical Zionists who prepared themselves solely for the rigors of agricultural life in Palestine, the Labor Zionists stressed *Gegenwartsarbeit*, working in the Diaspora to raise Jewish productivity and consciousness.[9] While the other radical groups had a monolingual policy—the Bund committed only to Yiddish, the Hashomer Hatsair only to Hebrew and the assimilationists only to the coterritorial language—the Labor Zionists fought to maintain an internal Jewish bilingualism. The use of both Hebrew and Yiddish had become a matter of ideology precisely because Jewish culture was no longer unified and internally coherent. Whereas once, before the Emancipation, Jews could move effortlessly back and forth between Yiddish and *Loshn-koydesh* (the Holy Tongue, Hebrew) simply on the basis of utility, now an ideological bulwark was needed to keep Humpty Dumpty from falling down. If East European Jewish writers wished to address the entire Jewish body politic, they had to write the *same work* in both Hebrew and Yiddish—or pay to get it translated. The act of self-translation that was so characteristic of secular Jewish culture in Eastern Europe prior to World War I was an act of will, a last-ditch effort to reimpose a sense of cohesion on an ever more fragmented reality. Internal Jewish bilingualism was an ideological tactic for combatting the centrifugal forces at work politically, socially, and geographically.[10]

Adopting this bilingual scheme to the exigencies of the New World, the lay Jewish revolutionaries of Poalei Zion discovered a special place for Yid-dish. Yiddish would evoke memories of Paradise Lost; would be a vehicle for revolutionary action; would be a bulwark against assimilation. Yiddish, the language of the immigrant community, of the "generation of the wilderness," would cut across all classes and all ideological sectors. Yiddish would be the key to history and to *lebns-shteyger* (folkways). Yiddish would be the bridge to Loshn-koydesh and to modern Hebrew.

This utopian experiment could only be carried out on virgin soil, be-cause everywhere else the battle lines had already been drawn. As early as 1907, Yitzhak Ben Zvi was forced to close *Der onfang*, the official organ of Poalei Zion in Palestine, and Hebrew was adopted as the language of the party.[11] Then a year later came Czernowitz, at which the resolution to pro-claim Yiddish as *the* national Jewish language was only narrowly defeated.[12] Meanwhile, the Yiddish press in the United States, regardless of its ideo-logical stripe, was successfully promoting the process of Americanization.[13] Against this backdrop of language wars and rapid acculturation, a Yiddish-Hebrew ideological program with an overlay of folksiness was more than merely a radical alternative. It was a full-fledged eschatology.

At this point, armchair sociologists will counter that the qualitative dif-ferences of Montreal Jewry were not a function of ideology, much less of eschatology. External factors alone can explain the differences: the eth-nic makeup of Quebec, with Jews caught between two inhospitable groups (French-speaking Roman Catholics and English-speaking Protestants); the parochial school system; the later immigration; the climate. There is even the Litvak Connection. With so many of the founding fathers—Brainin, Wiseman, Dunsky, Rabinovitsh, and David Rome—hailing from Lithu-ania, is it any wonder that education and culture loomed so large?

Environment or pedigree do very little, however, to explain how a tiny group of recent immigrants with no political clout and with no traditional sources of authority to fall back on, how these lay Jewish revolutionaries took their case for a separate Jewish school panel all the way to the Privy Council of England; how, when their legislative efforts failed, they created the very first day schools in Montreal, which were also the first *Yiddish* day schools anywhere in North America. Indeed, it was on the Jewish School Question that raged in Montreal from 1923–1931 that the Labor Zionists took their stand and became—despite their lack of Canadian roots—a ma-jor integrative force in the community.

To prepare for battle, the secular revolutionaries led by the Poalei Zion established the Vaad Hoʿir, also known as the Jewish Community Council. Included in this council, according to David Rome, were sixty-six labor unions, Zionist groups, mutual and sick benefit societies, fraternal groups, synagogues, Yiddish schools, rabbis, journalists, and scholars.[14] In addition to rationalizing the distribution of kosher meat, this unlikely coalition of bearded rabbis, atheist socialists, Zionists, and anti-Zionists, were to lobby the Canadian government for a separate Jewish school system under the provisions of the British North America Act. Needless to say, there was no unanimity among the members of the labor caucus about the necessity of separate Jewish schools, especially if it involved collaborating with the Orthodox. The party line was finally hammered out at a series of labor conferences, one of which, at Communist insistence, met on Yom Kippur, at yizkor time. The Orthodox, for their part, had made their opposition to the secular Yiddishists eminently clear as far back as July 5, 1916. In a protest resolution published in the *Keneder odler* they had accused the National Radical Schools and the Folkshule of replacing the sacred Torah with Yiddish songs.[15] Let the education of the young, they pleaded, remain in the same hands as before.

A more powerful opposition emanated from the Uptown Jews. A certain Rabbi Corcos articulated the horror with which the Jews of Westmount viewed the prospects of a separate Jewish school panel:

> The originators of this mad scheme, whoever they may be, are not only enemies of God . . . but they are also the worst enemies of their country, since nothing but calamity and misfortune can come to a country that is divided against itself. . . . They would mean the creation of a state within a state. They would mean the revival of a ghetto and the return of the dark ages of ignorance and superstition; they would mean the perpetuation of their horrid jargon known as Yiddish, and thus the province of Quebec will become a veritable tower of Babel with so many confused dialects.[16]

And so, for one very powerful group of Montreal Jews, Yiddish represented a return to the Dark Ages, to poverty, superstition, and segregation, whereas for the Orthodox, it meant precisely the opposite: the dangers of subversion from within. Given the Yom Kippur caucuses, their fears were certainly not unfounded.

What, then, did Yiddish and yidishkayt mean to that tiny group of ideologues led by Yehudah Kaufman, Simon Belkin, Moshe Dickstein, and Shloime Wiseman? It was Wiseman who, on that Yom Kippur day in 1923, had to rush off from shul to confront the Jewish communists and other radical leftists. It was he, on the strength of his graduate degree from McGill, who was called upon to defend the Yiddish-speaking Downtown Jews in the pages of the Montreal *Star*. It was he, in a remarkable series of analytic and programmatic essays written in the 1940s, who became the chief theoretician of the Yiddish secular schools in North America. In his classic essay "The Jewish Holidays and Jewish Education," first published in the massive *Shul-pinkes* and later reprinted in the *Shloime Wiseman bukh*, he argued for the place of yidishkayt in the Yiddish cultural revival.[17] The reason this culture had to be reinvented, he explained in a rare outburst of passion, was that everything of value had already been destroyed.

> We of the old generation will never feel at home in the new American yidishkayt. We will always feel that it "just isn't it." We will keep right on running from one synagogue to another; no shul will truly satisfy. We will forever search for the echo of chords sounded long ago that were never forgotten. Sounds, melodies, smells, and memories. What we thereby seek is both our childhood, lost irrevocably, and the total yidishkayt that was possible under certain conditions once prevalent in the small shtetl but impossible to reproduce here in the metropolitan American exile. That longing and unhappiness is an important psychic factor in our lives. It can become a constructive force if it stimulates us in our protest against the pale and anemic yidishkayt in America to create those maximal conditions for improvement and strengthening that are still possible even under our unfavorable conditions. (pp. 224; 115)

The brave new world of Yiddish and yidishkayt, he revealed in this extraordinary passage, was built on the ruins of traditional Jewish life. The real destruction, the irrevocable loss, had occurred the moment these young men and women left the organic communities of Eastern Europe. There was no going back to that world of wholeness. Forever would their generation wander from shul to old-style *shtibl* trying to recapture the lost sounds and smells. Out of their unrequited longing, however, they would establish a new Jewish calendar, making the old festivals yield new meaning. In a cynical age of minimalism they would dedicate every ounce of their energy to creating a *maximalist* culture of yidishkayt.

That invented yidishkayt, Wiseman went on to argue, however insufficient it might seem to themselves, would be real and existentially compelling to their students. The native-born generation would have no other measure of authentic yidishkayt. Besides, it would be the task of Jewish educators to keep alive the longing for a more total and more beautiful yidishkayt. When the students grew up, they would then be motivated to work toward that restorative vision.

Insofar as Yiddish was a key to *lebns-shteyger*; insofar as Yiddish literature extolled the beauty of Jewish holidays; insofar as Yiddish was symbiotically tied to Loshn-koydesh; insofar as Yiddish was the living link to a living people—Yiddish would be the crucible of past, present, and future. Insofar as the new cultural institutions embodied this integrative vision, Yiddish would become the embodiment of yidishkayt.

A new brand of Diaspora nationalism was thus created by Wiseman and his fellow Labor Zionists, designed to combat the fragmentation within and the seductions from without. Wiseman spelled out the nationalist agenda in no uncertain terms. Our purpose, he wrote at the beginning of the same essay, is to condition our students so that they couldn't live *other than as Jews*. To achieve this end one must create a total environment, both within the school and without—by teaching them to live in two Jewish languages; by celebrating all the holidays in a meaningful way; by instilling within them a sense of responsibility for Jewish history and Jewish destiny. What a sophisticated educational philosophy! What a utopian, and at the same time, pragmatic vision!

In practice, however, things didn't turn out quite so well. The first thing to go, as Wiseman was to recall in his unfinished memoirs, was spoken Yiddish.[18] It was simply impossible to enforce Yiddish speaking among the students themselves. The best that could be hoped for was that students and teachers would communicate solely in that language.

Besides, the 1920s and 1930s were a time of competing utopian visions. Many were the forces vying for the souls of Jewish youth, especially those who were already committed. For the longest time, Wiseman recalled in that same memoir, the Folkshule *klubn* were kept separate from Habonim, the youth movement of the Labor Zionist Federation, because Habonim honored only Hebrew. More painful still—and Wiseman was not one to forget or forgive—were the rebellious group of Shule graduates who, in flyers they circulated in 1933, repudiated the yidishkayt curriculum as so much petty bourgeois apologetics.[19] They called instead for workers' solidarity and for a more positive attitude to their Soviet brethren.

But ideologies came and went. What Wiseman and his cohort understood is that only institutions, or what the Israelis would later call "creating facts," would insure the transmission of their integrationist lifestyle. Small wonder then that it was they and not the leaders of the Talmud Torah who pioneered the Jewish day school in Montreal—in 1928. Wiseman argued in an essay devoted specifically to the topic that only the day school, with its integrated curriculum, could counteract the dualism of *goles* (the Diaspora).[20] Only the day school could make yidishkayt central to the students' experience rather than an occasional late afternoon appendage. Only the day school could forge a Jewish elite that would someday assume leadership positions in the community.

The first graduating class of the Folkshule graduated in 1940, only one year after the Shule finally received full accreditation from the Protestant School Board. The Shule occupied its new building on Waverly Street in 1941. At about that time, a teacher from the Folkshule named Chaim Pripstein set up a summer camp where the Yiddish-Hebrew curriculum shifted toward sports and waterfront activities but was maintained nonetheless. In 1946, a Jewish Teachers' Seminary was established that ran in two parallel tracks: one in Yiddish-Hebrew and the other in Hebrew only. Eventually the two were combined. Later still, in 1956, Dora Wasserman organized a Yiddish Drama Group under Folkshule auspices. A large part of its repertory would be translated and adapted from Hebrew by teachers from the Shule.[21] This institutional growth spell, this coming of age of the Montreal integrationist utopia, coincided with the collapse of Yiddish cultural life almost everywhere else on the globe.

Montreal Yiddish Culture a Generation Later

Now, the durability of a utopian experiment is never really tested until at least one generation after its founding. In our case, the new generation came of age just as the world of East European Jewry was totally destroyed and dispersed. Of course, there would be an influx of refugees and survivors—my own parents among them—who would replenish Montreal Yiddish culture from the native, East European soil; but if the institutional and ideological foundations had not been sound to begin with, no amount of transplantation would have saved the day. Many great Jewish movements collapsed under the weight of history: Territorialism, the Jewish Labor Bund and the Jewish Section of the Communist Party. That the Yiddish-Hebrew-and-yidishkayt equation of the founding fathers weathered the storm is, I think, its ultimate vindication.

The Montreal Yiddish-Hebrew intelligentsia was prepared for the Holocaust because, as Shloime Wiseman revealed in that remarkable passage, the destruction of their world had already happened. Destruction and loss were the very stuff that Jewish dreams were made of. Because there was no going back to a world of orthodox faith and communal autonomy, they invented a surrogate yidishkayt embodied in an all-encompassing network of cultural institutions. They came as close as one could to establishing the "state within a state" that Rabbi Corcos was so afraid of. The actual, physical destruction of Jewish Eastern Europe only intensified the longing for a more whole and beautiful yidishkayt that had long ago become part of the hidden curriculum.

If the vast bloodletting in Europe could be turned into a source of creative longing for the past, there was even greater scope in the Zionist vision of the future. In a wonderfully evocative essay called "A Goles Education," my sister Ruth Wisse recalls how she and her fellow students in the Folkshule vicariously experienced every act in the drama of Israel's independence. "I was startled," she writes, "when an Israeli friend said to me, about her education in Rehavia, 'You would never have known that we were living through the most memorable period in Jewish history.' As for us, we were never in doubt."[22]

Yet the very success of the Zionist revolution might have overwhelmed the modest achievements of the mini-utopia on North American soil. As committed Zionists, the Yiddish-Hebrew intellectuals of Montreal had to acknowledge, as Wiseman did in an essay written in December 1943, that only in Erets-Yisroel could Jews fulfill themselves (oyslebn zikh) as Jews nationally and spiritually.[23] And indeed, other Zionist ideologues viewed with scorn any attempt to instill a sense of belonging to America. But America, Wiseman countered, offered something else: the unique opportunity to integrate one's yidishkayt within a multi-ethnic and culturally diverse American lifestyle.[24] That, according to Wiseman, was the challenge facing Jewish educators in the latter half of the twentieth century. He now openly lamented that the exclusive emphasis on Yiddish and Hebrew had made for an elitist attitude toward English-speaking Jews and a denigration of North America. American Jewry was finally coming of age, and who could tell what spiritual forces that newfound independence might unleash?

Yiddish, then, was invaluable as an integrative force, as a means of holding the diverse parts of the culture together. The claims of the immediate severed past could best be made through Yiddish in conjunction with Loshn-koydesh. The drama of a people reclaiming its ancient homeland could be conveyed in Yiddish, in conjunction with Hebrew.[25] And as for America, the story of that miraculous new haven of East European Jewry had already been played out primarily in Yiddish; it could now be retold in conjunction with English.

Conclusion

Yiddish glue did not put Humpty Dumpty together again. The integrationist ideology fell apart when faced with renewed fragmentation from within and the totally unexpected challenge of French Canadian ethnic supremacy from without. The East European Jewish past, the North American present, and the Zionist future have gone their separate ways. Still, there is much to be learned from that brief sojourn in utopia.

First, that all Jews live after the *ḥurban beit hamidrash*, the destruction of traditional faith, but out of that loss, a new and viable culture can be reinvented. Just as alienated intellectuals looking to reinvent themselves as traditional Jews gave Yiddish literature its most compelling vision of the East European Jewish past,[26] radical educators built a cradle-to-grave alternative to the old way of life with the Yiddish day school inheriting the place of the synagogue.

Second, that a community cannot be built without an ideology, without a collective vision that somehow integrates past, present, and future. Those who believe the Marxist canard that ideologies are tools of the ruling class are fated to be ruled by their own lack of vision.

Third, that some ideologies are better than others. The radical secularists who tried to tear Yiddish completely away from yidishkayt, who believed that a humanist-socialist faith could be totally self-sustaining, could never adapt to the profoundly religious character of both Judaism and America. In contrast, the young Jewish rebels of the late 1960s, who tried to establish monastic orders of neohasidic mystics, disbanded once their apocalyptic fervor waned and the war in Vietnam was over.

The lay Jewish revolutionaries in Montreal succeeded beyond one generation because they were collectivists with a restorative, neoclassical bent who operated in the public domain. They organized, they fought, they lobbied, they built institutions from the bottom up, they went from house to house collecting the fifty cents a month tuition for the afternoon school. Their ideology was predicated on peoplehood, not prophecy; on language not divorced from the liturgy; on getting their hands dirty in the nitty-gritty of communal and, when need be, of national politics.

Yiddish in their scheme was never an end in itself; it was a means toward achieving cultural integration: of reuniting East and West, the folk and the intelligentsia, the *frume* and the *fraye*. Yiddish was to be the vehicle of national liberation.

9 Zionism, Israel, and the Search for a Covenantal Space

Sound the great shofar for our freedom; lift up the banner to bring our exiles together, and assemble us from the four corners of the earth.
—Daily Prayer Book

but all these buildings no longer had any future because they were old and ill adapted to modern tastes and lifestyles, and especially because the sky-rocketing prices of land and apartments had turned their existence into a terrible waste and enabled their owners to come into fortunes by selling them, and Goldman, who was attached to these streets and houses because they, together with the sand dunes and virgin fields, were the landscape in which he had been born and grown up, knew that this process of destruction was inevitable, and perhaps even necessary . . .
—Yaakov Shabtai, 1977

First-time visitors to Israel routinely learn two Hebrew words. "Shalom" is one. "Tiyyul" is another. One could write a short history of modern Israel drawn entirely from that one word, "Shalom," which the secular Zionists, intent upon creating a "normal" polity, had hoped to strip of its sacred connotations (the "Angels of Peace" who attend every Friday night meal), and apply it solely to the mundane realm of saying "hello" and "goodbye"; but then, as one war followed another, shalom, the elusive prize that promised to bring an end to Israel's isolation in the world and to allow Jewish parents to sleep through the night, became the all-embracing slogan of the Israeli Left; until finally, with the assassination of Yitzhak Rabin in November 1995, "shalom" became a martyrological code word, elevated back into the domain of the sacred by the president of the United States and informed this time not by Judaism but by Christianity, with the Jew cast in the role of Christ figure. Yes, a semiotic study of the word "shalom" would make for a gripping narrative.

An alternative reading of the Zionist enterprise would begin and end with the neologism "tiyyul," which does not resonate with anything liturgical, political, or eschatological. Yet tourists, the moment they embark upon their first hike, or guided tour, of some small piece of modern-day

Israel, are in effect retracing a very long itinerary that culminated in the triumph of Zionism.

It began, as do all the major trends of modern Jewish life, in the late eighteenth century; in this case, not with the Ba῾al Shem Tov, and not with the Gaon of Vilna, but with the Physiocrats. As sons of the French Enlightenment, they took their cue from nature. This spoke to their disciples in faraway Galicia and Russia-Poland, who launched a critique of Jewish society as being cut off from nature, and therefore, parasitic and unproductive. Only by returning to the soil, said the Maskilim and their various heirs, could Jews liberate themselves from the bondage of the medieval "ghetto." It was not enough to conquer one's fear of the outdoors, to venture forth outside the two thousand ells prescribed by the Halachah, which Jews are forbidden to exceed when walking on the Sabbath. It was necessary to restructure the economic base of the Jewish artisan and merchant classes along agricultural lines, and if this was not possible in Eastern Europe, where Jews were generally forbidden to own any land, then in Palestine, the Argentinian Pampas, or, failing that, in Louisiana, South Dakota, and Oregon.

The rise of nationalism, at the end of the nineteenth century, added a historical dimension to the Jewish reclamation of the land. Wherever Jews lived, they needed landmarks, not merely to their rabbis and zaddikim lying in sanctified burial grounds, but to their collective presence. In Poland, between the two world wars, a Jewish movement for tourism and knowledge of the landscape, called *landkentenish*, became popular among members of the urban middle class. One strand, represented by my uncle, Hirsh Matz, upheld the original Enlightenment mandate. In 1935, he produced a detailed Yiddish guide to *Health Resorts and Tourism in Poland*, complete with advice by sixteen medical doctors as to which Polish spas and regions were best suited to cure which ailments. Zalmen Szyk, meanwhile, chairman of the Vilna branch of the Landkentenish Society, set out to rescue "Yerusholaim deLite" (the Jerusalem of Lithuania) as a universal Yiddish memory-site. His lavishly illustrated and thoroughly professional guidebook to *1000 Years of Vilna* was designed to serve his people into the next millennium.[1]

While the spas and health resorts would nurse the sick body of Polish Jewry back to life, and the local guidebooks would instill a sense of national pride in a landscape of fiercely competing nationalisms, the Zionist youth groups prepared for the rigors of agricultural labor in Palestine by setting up model farms throughout Poland. At a recent exhibition of "Visual Images of Zionism, 1897–1947" mounted at Beth Hatefutsoth in Tel Aviv, I saw an interwar map of such Hakhsharah points in Poland.[2] They are, to put it mildly, off the beaten track. No place name resonates either with the eight-hundred-year-old past of Polish Jewry or with the pride of the modern Polish Republic. So who could have guessed that among all the maps and countermaps, only these vicarious and precarious Jewish farms stood any chance of survival, after being transplanted to some permanent space, on the other side of the world?

There, on the other side, the return-to-nature movement and the historical geography movement gave birth to the Ḥevra Lehaganat Hateva, the Society for the Protection of Nature. In a country riven by political and ethnic differences, the Hevra brings all Israelis together, offering them courses in geography and nature studies, organized tours and lessons in nature preservation. It is the closest thing to a grassroots movement that Israel is ever likely to have. Today, the most colorful *kova tembels*, the most elaborate tours, the sexiest guides, the longest hiking trails, and the best maps of Israel are available through the various centers of the Ḥevra, and the word "tiyyul" trips off the tongues of Israelis and tourists alike as easily as the word for hello and goodbye.[3]

Because the Land of Israel is everybody's dreamscape, reality rarely stands in the way of ideological purity. Surely one of the most surreal sights a tourist will ever see is a three-story brownstone visible from the Tel Aviv to Jerusalem highway. It is a replica of 770 Eastern Parkway in Crown Heights, which stands in Kfar Habad. Why has this Brooklyn brownstone been transplanted into a typically rural Israeli setting? The Hasidim believe that the zaddik is the *axis mundi*, the pivot around which the cosmos revolves. In the old days, it was enough for the disciples to make a pilgrimage to the Rebbe's court, or to visit his grave on the anniversary of his death, in order to realign their souls with that cosmic center. Walking, according to one scholar of Hasidism, was itself redefined as a religious act.[4] We also know that the Habad, or Lubavitsh, Hasidim, are radical messianists. Although during his entire sojourn in America, Menachem Mendel Schneerson left his home only long enough to visit *his* father's grave, his followers in Israel believed that if you built it, he would come. Their "bayyit shlishi," or Third Temple, as they call it, even replicates the Rebbe's bedroom, furniture and all.[5] So while a radical fundamentalist sect called Ateret Kohanim was preparing to rebuild the Second Temple, there to resume the sacrificial cult, the Lubavitsher pinned their hopes on the Rebbe ushering in the messianic era by taking up residence in his home-away-from-home. Now that the Rebbe is dead, they believe this more fervently than before.

Is this good news or bad? On the one hand, to gather all the centers of holiness unto Zion is consistent both with normative Judaism and classical Zionist thought. Arnold Eisen has demonstrated how Zionist thinkers, children of the Enlightenment, demystified and de-routinized the concept of the Land, so that the words of the daily prayer, "Sound the great shofar for our freedom; lift up the banner to bring our exiles together, and assemble us from the four corners of the earth," were turned into a radical, political, agenda.[6] From a secular Zionist perspective, building the Rebbe a replica of his home in a theologically neutral part of the state might seem quixotic, but it would not be viewed as aberrant—provided the rebbe actually moved there. As an absentee landlord, however, the rebbe stands for the reconsecration of the Diaspora.

Does the proliferation of pilgrimage sites undermine the basic tenet of classical Zionist thought? Can Zionism be reconciled with the more even distribution throughout the world of Jewish sacred space? Does the competing traffic between hikers and pilgrims within the Land of Israel itself spell the doom of the Zionist enterprise as a whole? Allowing that Zionism has already scored a spectacular success in the geopolitical arena, many have argued that its ideology, if not bankrupt, is obsolete. But, like Marxism, the Zionist idea precedes and transcends its political agenda. For while Marxism set out to eliminate the "alienation of labor," Zionism's chief objective was to alleviate and resolve the alienation of space. *Kapital* is to Marxism as *Galut* (Exile) is to Zionism. Can it be that the first, having failed to liberate the workers of the world, and the second, having failed to monopolize on Jewish sacred space, are equally bankrupt?

The analogy to Marxism suggests a possible answer. As a methodology, Marxism is still going strong, despite its manifest failure as a political-economic system. Zionism, in contrast, despite its notable success, has yet to be adopted as a serious analytic tool. I therefore propose that we substitute "exile" for "capitalist society" and paraphrase the Marxist critic Georg Lukács to say as follows: "the contradictions of exile provide thus the key for the understanding of the modern literary imagination."[7] Only Zionism, I submit, lays bare these contradictions and offers a coherent reading of the Jewish, and exilic, condition. Zionism, I am claiming, raised the territorial and national consciousness of all Jews everywhere, whether or not they openly espoused a Zionist ideology. Zionism stimulated a reclamation of space both in the political present and the reimagined past; both in Crown Heights and Kfar Habad.

As in every success story, by solving one anomaly, Zionism gave rise to many others. Zionism, as Eli Barnavi reminds us in his *Historical Atlas of the Jewish People,* "offered the possibility of rejoining 'heart' and 'body,' " which is to say, of actualizing the metaphoric and messianic journey to Palestine, while on the other hand, Zionism recreated the anomaly of Jewish space. "In the contemporary Jewish world," he writes, "the model of the isolated *shtetl* applies above all to the State of Israel."[8] In her analysis of Israeli literature of the 1990s, Zvia Ginor reveals a disturbing recidivism in the representation of the modern Jewish state. She frames her analysis in terms of the historical archetypes of exodus and exile so as to drive home the point that increasingly, perhaps inevitably, one becomes an exile even in the Promised Land.[9]

Does this mean that we throw the baby out with the bathwater? Do we therefore conclude, with Sidra Ezrahi, that until the middle of the twentieth century, Jewish space was seen primarily as something "protean and permeable, bounded at its outer limits only by the extremes of exilic time — as above all, nonterritorial"?[10] And do we then adopt the term "territorial" as a dirty word that carries with it a decidedly leftist, postcolonialist, and — why not admit it — anti-Zionist, connotation?

For exile, in the cyclical nature of things, has once again been elevated to near-theological status, this time not by the Hasidim but by secular academics. Eighteen scholars, most of them displaced Jews, held a symposium in 1996 on "Creativity and Exile." They opened with a genealogy of exile from Isaiah to Salman Rushdie.[11] (Never mind that Ezekiel, the greatest prophet of exile, spent his entire sojourn in Babylonia imagining the restoration of the Temple in Jerusalem, down to the minutest detail. And never mind that at least one member of the pantheon, Alexander Solzhenitsyn, is permanently ensconced back in Mother Russia.)

The celebration of exile is as predictable as it is time-bound. At the last fin-de-siècle, a disproportionately large number of Jewish intellectuals were locked in ideological debate about culture at the nexus of time and space. Most of them staked out a universalist position in defiance of the Zionist claim to a specific territory, an ancient tongue, and an unbroken history. Zionism, then as now, represented the path of national liberation not taken. Thus the 1996 symposium (published where else but in Tel Aviv) is designed to repudiate Zionism's central axiom — that true creativity and exile are mutually exclusive. Today's academic elite does not care if the Rebbe takes up residence in Kfar Habad. It would be much happier if he stayed put in Crown Heights, to prove the quasi-theological proposition that exile is, always has been, and always will be the seat of the creative spirit. Zionism, therefore, has lost none of its bite, and has an important role to play as a critical — and counterexilic — methodology.

The *Ba'al-Guf*: Defending the Land

The rise of European nationalism profoundly affected the collective representation of the Jews. In Odessa, we recall, the leading members of the Jewish intelligentsia—Abramovitsh, Aḥad Ha'am, Ben-Ami, and Simon Dubnov—debated the proposition that the Jews of Eastern Europe had a secular history worthy of being preserved.[12] What, they asked themselves, would the life of the Jewish people look like when viewed from within? What would its gender be? After all, the rising nation-states of Europe seemed to demand a female icon: a stately and matronly Britannia; Marianne, with one breast exposed.[13] So, too, the people of Israel, who, in ancient times, had been allegorically rendered either as the widow Zion or (by the prophets Isaiah, Jeremiah, and Ezekiel) as an unfaithful wife: she acts like a harlot and enters into alliances with men who will betray her in a time of need.[14] Turning this biblical trope on its head in 1873, Abramovitsh introduced *Di klyatshe*, a talking mare, the allegorical embodiment of stoic Jewish suffering down through the ages. Russian-Jewish readers had absolutely no trouble deciphering the novel's allegorical code, and *Di klyatshe* immediately entered into the Yiddish language as Israel in Exile, universally abused and abandoned.[15]

The practice of collective representation, of imagining the Jews as a distinct people inhabiting a discrete plot of land, obviously predates the making of a Zionist ideology and the creation of the sovereign State of Israel.[16] The Mare and the literary image of the shtetl were but two of the modern constructs of the Jewish collective that later helped to shape and to sharpen the Zionist response.

The main "contradiction of exile" (paraphrasing Lukács) is that one could be on the land and not of it. The fictional town of Tuneyadevke was clearly situated somewhere in the Ukraine, as attested to by the -*evke* suffix; yet Benjamin of Tuneyadevke could not speak one word of the native language, Ukrainian.[17] At issue also was whether the Jews had any territory they could call their own. The consensus among nineteenth-century Jewish writers was that the sole piece of real Jewish property was the shtetl burial ground. "It never occurs to the Eastern Jews," writes Karl Emil Franzos in 1873, "to plant trees or sow annuals there; but the fresh green grass is allowed to cover the graves, and blossoming elders grow by every headstone. Their burial-ground was the only bit of land these people were allowed to possess until a few years ago!"[18] Writing ca. 1895, I. L. Peretz has a nameless shtetl Jew deliver the following verdict: "Our poor folk live on hope, our merchants live on air, and our grave diggers make a living from the soil. . . ."[19]

No wonder that these "eastern Jews" seized the first opportunity when they reached the New World to speculate in real estate. One of the earliest Yiddish novels about American-Jewish life is Leon Kobrin's *Ore di bord* (ca. 1918) about the real estate boom in Brownsville. One of the earliest Canadian-Jewish novels is Mordecai Richler's *The Apprenticeship of Duddy Kravitz* (1959), whose eponymous bad-boy hero is instructed by his grandfather Simcha that "a man without land is nobody."

Duddy Kravitz, as it happens, stands in a long line of Jewish low-lives, originally called *baᶜalei-guf,* who entered into fiction in response to the ideological demand that Jews stop abdicating the physical realm for the spiritual.[20] Sholem Asch promoted the figure of the *baᶜal-guf* so as to provide the shtetl with a masculine profile, and he reclaimed a place called "Kola Street" in order to stake a territorial claim. "The Jew native to this region," Asch asserts in deliberate provocation, "partakes more of the flavor of wheat and of apples than of the synagogue and the ritual bath."[21] Asch's young readers, now divided along party lines, decoded his message as follows. Bundists read it as a blueprint for the future brotherhood of "productive" Jews and Gentiles on Polish soil. Zionists read it as a call to transplant these Jewish peasants to Palestine. But to the self-defense units then being organized by Socialists and Zionists alike in the face of a new wave of pogroms, Asch had this to say: "The Three-Trade Synagogue was in Kola Street. This street was not in the Diaspora, as it were; there no Jew was ever beaten" (ibid.). If not in the Diaspora, "as it were," then where could it be? In a place where frontier justice prevailed; where Jews were ready to fight to protect their own turf, and where even the most unlettered among them remained fiercely loyal to the tribe.[22] Territory entailed, above all, the exercise of power.

The baᶜal-guf enjoyed something of a vogue between 1910 and the 1930s, both in fiction and on stage. There were writers, like Zalman Schneour, who specialized in this type, whether male (*Noyakh Pandre,* 1939) or female ("The Girl," 1906); and others, like Isaac Babel, who could rescue nothing from the sunny Odessa of his youth save for Benya Krik and his Gang. At a time of universal Jewish powerlessness, readers must have thrilled at the sight of healthy, earthy, Jews flexing their collective muscle. Just as today, at a time of unprecedented Jewish power, there are those who recoil at the sight. The critic Paul Breines has gone so far as to trace the "Political Fantasies and the Moral Dilemma of American Jewry" back to stories such as these, and to critics, like myself, who write about them.

Commenting on the Howe and Greenberg *Treasury of Yiddish Stories*, where "Kola Street" and other explicit baʿal-guf narratives first appeared in English translation, Breines writes: "Roskies, like Sholem Asch, Fishel Bimko, and Isaac Babel, is on the lookout for tough Jews. Irving Howe and Eliezer Greenberg were not."[23]

Precisely. Zionism, I repeat, raised the territorial and national consciousness of all Jews everywhere, whether or not they openly espoused a Zionist ideology. Zionism stimulated a reclamation of space both in the Uganda and Palestine of the political present and the Kola Streets of the reimagined past.

Two fictional types arose in opposition to the proto-Zionist hero of action. One was the schlemiel, the other was the *talush* (lit. "dangling man"). The schlemiel, for those who have not had the benefit of reading Ruth Wisse's classic study on the subject, becomes a hero when real action is impossible and reaction remains the only way a man can define himself.[24] Although this literary type has not been heard from for many years and Wisse pronounced his "requiem" as far back as 1971, it is startling to see him resurrected in the name of exilic consciousness.

Sidra Ezrahi believes that the English-language publication of I. B. Singer's schlemiel-story "Gimpel the Fool" in 1954 was a defining moment in the history of American-Jewish letters, just as she believes that Singer's nonterritorial shtetl became an authentic Jewish geography. The evidence presented in chapter 4 of this book suggests otherwise. As for "Gimpel the Fool," it is the tale of a saint, and saints by definition transcend the boundaries of time and space. Singer actually has much to say about the national plight of the Jews, but his shtetl stories are not where he says it.[25]

Who, then, *does* speak for the contradictions of exile? The baʿal-guf, by all accounts, was a transitional type designed to model heroic behavior in a setting close to nature. He lives on in various macho guises that are not the exclusive property of the Jews. The schlemiel was likewise a transitional type who, as Wisse has shown, made the successful ocean crossing to America. But nowadays it is almost impossible to convince one's students that Gimpel the Fool is in any way heroic. I have tried on numerous occasions here in New York City, and have failed just as miserably in Tel Aviv. The only contemporary setting where Gimpel's victory-in-defeat makes any sense is Moscow.[26]

The fictional type who embodies the contradictions of exile is the third member of the triad, the talush, or superfluous man, who was imported into Jewish fiction by writers steeped in nineteenth-century Russian literature.[27] A protean figure, the talush comes into his own as a specifically *Jew-*

ish type the moment he settles in the Land of Israel. Where but in Zion can a Jewish intellectual feel the split more profoundly between the utopian ideal and the fragmented reality? The Zionist *talush* is a modern Hebrew writer by any other name.

The Talush: Exile in the Promised Land

The *talush* is usually a young man, thus underscoring the identification between author and character. Not so in Yosef Hayyim Brenner's "Hamotsa" (The way out, 1919), subtitled "A Reportage from the Most Recent Past."[28] Written in the immediate aftermath of World War I, Brenner describes the low point in the history of the Yishuv. As the din of battle between the Turks and the British can be heard in the distance, a pioneer settlement prepares for its own onslaught, the arrival of yet more starving Jewish refugees, out of which there emerges the figure of a Bible-quoting old pioneer teacher, a talush-in-khakis. Through the teacher, Brenner—the fiercest Jewish critic of Zionism who ever set foot on Palestinian soil—delivers a moral indictment of his own people. The teacher then succumbs to death as the only "way out."

Unlike Brenner, who conjures up a single, apocalyptic landscape, Hayyim Hazaz offers his Hebrew readers a choice between two competing landscapes in his superbly programmatic tale, "Rahamim" (1933).[29] Menashkhe Bezprozvani inhabits an arid, emotionally barren landscape even in the land of his dreams. While the "Menashe" part of his name invokes the biblical promise, "God hath made me forget all my toils and my father's house," the second part, meaning "man-without-a-name" in Russian, drags along the Diaspora legacy. Luckily, this angry and alienated intellectual has a chance encounter with Rahamim, a baʿal-guf from Kurdistan, a double-man, "his face bright as a copper pot and his chest uncommonly virile and broad" (p. 258). While Menashke (in addition to all his other complaints) suffers from the excessive heat on this mid-July day, Rahamim reflects the sun off of his coppery visage. At home in the natural landscape, Rahamim tries to console Menashke with his down-to-earth philosophy, rendered in faulty Hebrew.

One would expect the native-born generation of Hebrew writers to finally dispense with the *talush* once and for all and, pace Paul Breines, embody their neocolonialist fantasies in the macho figure of the baʿal-guf. The conquest of the land did awaken fantasies in some, of returning to a Canaanite "New Middle East," led by a virile, neopagan cadre of Hebrew Youth, but this Canaanite "heresy," according to Yaakov Shavit, had a significant impact only on Israeli poetry; none on Israeli politics.[30] Meanwhile, the real conquest of the land exacted a terrible toll. Alongside and in response to the outpouring of *sifrut ha'izavon*, memorial books for a whole generation of Hebrew Youth who were killed while securing Israel's military victory over the combined Arab armies, who should rear his ugly head if not the talush? No longer relegated to the margins, the talush now reemerged in the very heat of battle. Beginning with S. Yizhar's gallery of depressive characters in his controversial war stories, "Ḥirbet Ḥizʻeh," "The Prisoner," and "Midnight Convoy"; continuing with A. B. Yehoshua's word-weary forest ranger in "Facing the Forests"; with Aharon Appelfeld's stable of male and female *telushim*-as-Holocaust survivors; and culminating in Yaakov Shabtai's neurotic threesome in *Past Continuous*, the talush has come to define the moral center and moral angst of present-day Israel.[31]

Much has been written about this phenomenon, dubbed "the morning after" syndrome by the literary critic Nurit Gertz.[32] Thanks to the efforts of Dan Miron, Gershon Shaked, and Robert Alter, these very works have assumed canonical status, both in Hebrew and in English translation. The antiheroic talush, plagued by self-doubt, also builds upon the left-wing legacy, which sees moral doubt as a source of strength. When Israeli soldiers returned from the Six-Day War to voice their moral repugnance at the price of victory, the edited transcripts of their reflections became an international best-seller which, for a brief moment in time, cast Israel in a positive light.[33] Other critics, like Ruth Wisse, view this as *Schöngeisterei*, the root cause of Israel's moral crisis.[34]

I shall take a different approach and try to put all the pieces together. If, for Ezrahi, the schlemiel is the standard-bearer of an exilic consciousness, "protean and permeable, bounded at its outer limits only by the extremes of exilic time," and "above all, nonterritorial"; and if, for Breines, the baʻal-guf embodies the atavistic desire to seize control of someone else's territory, then the talush represents the Zionist alternative: living the dilemma and the dream of a covenantal space at one and the same time.

The talush is left "dangling" between awareness of loss and unrequited longing. Although a dreamer and closet romantic, the talush is cerebral, and painfully self-aware. His medium—indirect interior monologue, first-person narrative, stream-of-consciousness—is the message. Unlike the schlemiel, who is something of a pilgrim, the talush remains rooted in a secular landscape. Yehoshua's forest ranger insists on studying the Crusades "from the human, that is to say, the ecclesiastical aspect" (p. 366). When Goldman is not otherwise occupied sitting shiva or walking the streets of

Tel Aviv, he works on a translation of Kepler's *Somnium*. First and foremost, the talush is estranged from his father.

Shabtai's *Zikhron devarim* (*Past Continuous*, 1977) begins with the family sitting shiva for Goldman's father after Goldman fils has already killed himself. The whole protocol is a fantasy of a life continuing after the subject is gone.[35] It is a protocol, moreover, disembodied from national memory. The intellectual and spiritual quests of its three main protagonists take place outside the realm of Jewish or Israeli sources. Each of the friends is engaged in mimicking: Israel copies music, Caesar is a photographer, and Goldman is a translator. The various memory-sites strewn about the landscape are emblems of tragic loss: the poinsettia regia and ficus at the foot of which they discovered the body of Kaminskaya; the enlarged photo of sister Naomi, killed in a motorcycle crash; the Czech tea set over which Goldman received a beating from his father; and the grotesque lamp in Goldman's room, an unreturned wedding present.

But the one memory-site to which Goldman returns obsessively carries rich and variegated meanings: the wooden shacks on the outskirts of Tel Aviv. This is where the first generation of his family put down stakes, among them grandfather Baruch Chaim, grandmother Hava, Uncle Lazar, Aunt Zipporah, and Shmuel and Bracha, whose garden remains lovingly implanted in Goldman's mind. While the others eventually abandoned the rickety, overcrowded shacks for life in the city, or, in Uncle Lazar's case, for servitude in Spain and the Gulag, Aunt Zipporah—selfless, awe-inspiring Aunt Zipporah—settled on a moshav, where young Goldman spent many a blissful summer vacation doing arduous farm work. Of course, there is no going back to this paradise lost, and when Goldman pays a visit to Chaim-Leib, who stubbornly refuses to move out of the renovated shack that had once belonged to Uncle Lazar and Rachel, he, Goldman, is filled at first with a feeling of disappointment, then, of existential despair, and finally, of apocalyptic rage. For Goldman, who has never traveled outside of Israel, the experience of *ḥurban*, of a destruction at once national and cosmic, is the relentless urban renewal of Old Tel Aviv and the final destruction of these dilapidated shacks. What he salvages from the ruins is the credo of Uncle Lazar, or Lazarus, risen from the dead: the existentialist, antiredemptive credo of doubt, soberness, being-in-the-world.

Goldman is the quintessential talush, caught between loss and longing. For Shabtai, the end of the Zionist dream in the aftermath of the Six-Day War has nothing to do with Israeli militarism, religious fanaticism, or the Palestinian conflict. It has to do with the economic miracle that destroyed the land. That palpable, excruciating, personal sense of loss permeates every urban landmark, and every narrative perspective. Here, told ostensibly from Israel's point of view, is a passage describing one of three central events in the novel, the murder of Kaminskaya's pet dog, whose name, Nuit Sombre, represents everything that is anathema to Goldman's father:

> After he had killed Nuit Sombre, Goldman's father hurried to wash the hammer, his hands and whole body shaking, and then he put the dog's body into a sack and carried it off and threw it far away in one of the big uncultivated fields covered with thorns and brambles and weeds, stretching as far as the orange groves and sabra hedges of the Arab villages, which disappeared a few years later with the uncultivated fields and the cultivated plots and the melon patches and vineyards and the little eucalyptus glade and the jackals which devoured Nuit Sombre's carcass—disappeared because of the new buildings going up on them one after the other, and the city streets along one of which the bus made its way toward the last stop. . . . (p. 14)

Just as the talush represents that liminal state between loss and longing, isolation and belonging, exile and homecoming, Shabtai's Tel Aviv represents their objective correlative. Never mind that Shabtai's neurotic litany of changeability is decidedly "post-Zionist" and that all of Zionism's sacred cows are being slaughtered along with Nuit Sombre: the Palmach myth of the invincible sons who eliminate their fathers from view; the heroic narratives of the War of Independence with their homoerotic male bonding experiences.[36] Shabtai succeeds—brilliantly, poignantly—in bringing to life his beloved city of Old Tel Aviv amidst the detritus of urban renewal and shattered dreams.

Israel as Covenantal Space

Exile is a literary contruct. And so is Zion. Since its earliest articulation in the Torah, the foundational document of Judaism, the idea of exile implies that there is a place, or community, that was left behind.[37] This is another way of saying that the Torah is a postexilic document about the drama of homecoming. The Torah, furthermore, as Zali Gurevitch argues, is rife with internal contradictions vis-à-vis the "double site of Israel." The very Covenant that governs the relationship between the People of Israel and the God of Israel was delivered outside of Israel. So too other key revelations that are essentially placeless.[38]

But does it follow that there exists a cognitive dissonance between text and territory? Does it follow, to quote Ezrahi quoting George Steiner, that if "our homeland [is] the text . . . our text [is] our [only] homeland"?[39] The new exilic school believes that this is so. The Israeli school of Zionist thought rejects this dichotomy by swallowing it whole. The resurrected figure of the talush gives that cognitive dissonance a name and Shabtai's Tel Aviv gives it an address.

Zionism continues to enrich the Jewish literary imagination by introducing *competing* ideologies of space. There was never any question of imposing one, neocolonialist, exclusionary vision of Jewish territoriality. Since when would the Jews ever have bought into something like that? Like messianism, to which it is often compared, Zionism has both a revolutionary and a restorative impulse.[40] As a radical response to the Jewish state of exile, as a frontal attack on "the alienation of space," Zionism represents a transvaluation of traditional Jewish values. The "Negation of the Diaspora" runs like a bold thread through Zionist thought, from Aḥad Haʿam to the Canaanites.[41]

On the restorative side of the ledger, Zionism sounded the shofar of Jewish freedom and reawakened the possibility of actual, physical reclamation. Without Zionism, without a place that some Jews call home, modern Jewish writing would be devoid of any national construct. Even Diasporism, lately espoused by Philip Roth, only makes sense in a world in which the actualization of Jewish space has become a reality.[42] Zionism vivified the concept of home. It gave East European Jews back the shtetl. To American Jews it restored a sense of the family as the last line of collective defense. And for Israeli Jews it quickened the longing for the old Yishuv, for the Mandate period, for the good old days of the Zionist Gemeinschaft.

Part of the Zionist agenda, then as now, is to realize the metaphor of the tallith, in which all "four corners" are assembled. A covenantal space that marks the end of exile is one that gathers in unto Zion all Jewish presents and pasthoods, all Jewish dialects, jargons, social speech types, professional, and other discourses. It is a polyphonic and heteroglossic space. A. M. Klein, the poet laureate of Canada, already gave voice to this polyphony in the "Deuteronomy" chapter of *The Second Scroll* (1951), which celebrates the revival of modern Hebrew in Israel.[43] Even Klein, the committed Zionist, could not have forseen the renaissance of the Hebrew novel that was ushered in by the publication of Shabtai's *Zikhron devarim* and has still not run its course. Zionism in the wake of Operation Exodus, and after the fall of the Iron Curtain, no longer means (if it ever meant) the desire for cultural hegemony.

Zionism is protean, inclusive, and heteroglossic. Within the discourse of Zionism the language of exile coexists with the language of covenantal space. Pilgrims and hikers meet at its crossroads. It is home to baʿalei-guf and schlemiels and telushim. Zionism is predicated on the idea that human life is enriched by participation in a covenantal community that will some-day be at home in the natural landscape of a particular place.

Afterword

May He who blessed our ancestors, Abraham, Isaac, and Jacob, bless this
entire congregation, together with all holy congregations: them, their sons
and daughters, their families, and all that is theirs, along with those who
unite to establish synagogues for prayer, and those who enter them to pray,
and those who give funds for heat and light, and wine for Kiddush and
Havdalah, bread to the wayfarer and charity to the poor, and all who
devotedly involve themselves with the needs of this community and the
Land of Israel.

— The Morning Service on Sabbaths and Festivals

We have journeyed through some densely populated Jewish landscapes,
following in the footsteps of poets, playwrights, songwriters, novelists,
chroniclers, critics, educators, graphic artists, and filmmakers, or as members of an organized tour. The sponsors of these group tours have also been
many—about as many as there are belief systems that modern Jews live by.

To complicate matters, our search has taken us on parallel and crisscrossing high roads and byroads, for time travel is an ongoing process that
occurs simultaneously at the grassroots as well as in the literary salon,
among the so-called "ruling elites" and the hoi polloi. Our travels have
shown that there is little to commend the Marxist model, which situates
the "invention of tradition" solely among the ruling elites, in *their* attempt
to impose a colonialist or nationalist hegemony.[1] Jews, to put it bluntly,
refuse to take marching orders from anyone; not from Hitler, not even (par-
don the proximity) from Ben-Gurion. While it is certainly true that the
modern police state has been able to manipulate and obliterate the past
in ways heretofore undreamed of, methods of replication and preservation
have also grown apace, and no police state, not Stalin's and not Brezhnev's,
achieved absolute control over the means of memorial production.[2] As for
the Jews, both memory and counter-memory always come into play when
they recall and record, regardless of age, social status, ideological persuasion, or domicile.

By and large, our route has skirted the deserts, mountains, valleys, and
steppes and has taken us instead through cities and towns, some real, some
imaginary. This is because, ever since the Babylonian Exile, the Jews have
been city dwellers and have learned, since the Destruction of the Second

Temple, to compensate the loss by building communities, which in turn sustain an impressive network of religious, social, and educational institutions. Part of what makes Sholem Aleichem's Tevye so poignant a figure is that he represents the last village Jew rooted in the soil of Russia. He doesn't need a quorum of ten men to pray with because he talks directly to God. But Tevye's surviving daughters will move to the big city, sooner or later.

To judge from the Jewish experience, the DNA of group memory is transmitted not through individuals, not even through families, but through institutions, and never with greater mobility than in modern times. We began our tour with the institutionalization of Jewish memory *in extremis*—with the heroic efforts to document the Jewish destruction in Kishinev, in Kiev, and later, in the Nazi ghettos and extermination camps. Emanuel Ringelblum, for all that he espoused the return-to-nature program of the landkentenish movement, was in practice a pioneer of urban history and sociology. The shtetl, the stand-in for the Jewish community in East European exile, provided a convenient grid of interlocking, urban, institutions. One axis connected the Jews to their God; another bound Jews to other Jews; while somewhere in the middle, Jews rubbed shoulders with their peasant clientele. When the grid began to come apart, a complex and layered image of the shtetl was fashioned to stand-in for the thing itself. In this way, the shtetl became at one and the same time a neo-Platonic Model City and an Augustinian City of God.

The oldest and most exclusive of Jewish institutions was the rabbinate. As such, it came under scrutiny and attack from young, secular writers intent upon reform and subversion. When the writers couldn't beat them, they joined them, by inscribing their own rebellion into the literary representation of rabbis and rebbes. Yet in the peculiar push-and-pull of Jewish modernity, the sacred and secular realms keep getting mixed and matched. Today, Milton Steinberg's *As a Driven Leaf* is recommended reading for students entering Hebrew Union College, the rabbinical school for Reform rabbis; at the Jewish Theological Seminary, I require all my rabbinical students to read Isaac Bashevis Singer's *Satan in Goray* and Cynthia Ozick's "The Pagan Rabbi"; and at Yeshiva University, most students have read Chaim Potok's *The Chosen* while still in high school. Institutions such as the modern rabbinate weather the sea changes that modernity has wrought by subverting the modernist subversion.

Even songs, seemingly so ephemeral, fared best within an institutional body, whether sacred or secular, that rolled with the punches. From the Brody Singers to Goldfaden to Second Avenue, Yiddish song culture found a new home designed for mobility and adaptability. It is surely no accident that of all the New World settings, New York City, with its vaudeville shtick divided along ethnic lines, provided fertile ground for the Jewish immigrants to "do their own thing."[3] Nothing comparable existed in Paris or Buenos Aires. In all of Metropolitan New York, however, no other ethnic group could boast of its very own music union, its own Klezmer Union, as early as 1889—the Russian Progressive Musical Union No. 1 of America.[4]

Ideologies—whether "progressive" or "regressive"—are central to the search for a usable past. If Zionism has figured in our travels at virtually every bend in the road, it is because no other modern ideology had so much invested in reinventing the Jewish past. From its ranks there emerged such brilliant engagé historians as Fritz Baer, Ben-Zion Dinur, and Gershom Scholem.[5] (To this Jerusalem-based pantheon of Zionist historians I would add Lucy S. Dawidowicz and Gerson D. Cohen, both born and bred in New York City.) Nowadays, the vigor of Zionism can best be measured by its loyal opposition—by Jewish and Israeli critics like Jonathan Boyarin, Nurit Gertz, Anita Shapira, and Yael Zerubavel, who are intent on challenging the "myths," "master narratives" and "national traditions" of the Jewish State.[6]

Another constant throughout our travels has been the availability of a shul. A "shul," mind you, not a synagogue; a shul where you *davven*, where you engage God—and other Jews—in fierce dialogue. Step into a shul and you enter the cyclical realm of historical archetypes, where the Akedah, the Exodus, the Revelation at Sinai, the Destruction, and the hoped-for Restoration occurred both in ancient times and are apprehended anew in every generation. Notions of progress—or apocalypse—are reconfigured within the structure of the fixed liturgy. So many of our secular tour guides end up saying kaddish over the ruins of a lost faith (Peretz, Sholem Aleichem, and Babel; Auerbach and Wiseman; Singer and Shabtai) that it almost seems as if the whole of Jewish modernity were nothing more than an interval between late afternoon and evening prayers.

And so, for all that our tour has led inexorably from the Old World to the New—through rows of stately tombstones honoring the American-Jewish Left; through a modern school dedicated to secular ideals of folkhood; through a contentious fictional landscape peopled with gangsters, losers, and misfits—this journey through secular time has turned into a pilgrimage. At century's end, a customary time of quest, one feels a strong urge to go off alone in search of something immutable, transcendent, sacred. Not so much to search as to find that which others have found before: that confluence of time and place that was once to be found only in the Holy of Holies; that center of all centers where, as Eleanor Munro writes in *On Glory Roads: A Pilgrim's Book about Pilgrimage*, heaven and earth are joined, "the unnatural with the natural, the unseen and longed-for with the inevitable."

Willy-nilly, the manifold ruptures of the twentieth century have turned all Jewish memory-sites into pilgrimage sites. The dedicated traveler through Jewish space needs more than a guidebook grounded (as this one seeks to be) in the mental curriculum of the landkentenish movement. History, language, custom, and culture occupy but one, horizontal, axis. The other is vertical. The Jewish pilgrim's progress through modernity also follows a covenantal compass.

Notes

Chapter 1

1. See *The Literature of Destruction: Jewish Responses to Catastrophe*, ed. David G. Roskies (Philadelphia: Jewish Publication Society of America, 1989), secs. 1–22.

2. Idem, *Against the Apocalypse: Responses to Catastrophe in Modern Jewish Culture* (Cambridge: Harvard University Press, 1984), chap. 2.

3. *In Praise of the Baal Shem Tov [Shivḥei ha-Besht]: The Earliest Collection of Legends about the Founder of Hasidism*, trans. and ed. Dan Ben-Amos and Jerome R. Mintz (Bloomington: Indiana University Press, 1970); to be read in conjunction with Moshe Rosman, "In Praise of the Baʿal Shem Tov: A User's Guide to the Editions of *Shivḥei haBesht*," *Jews in Early Modern Poland*, ed. Gershon David Hundert (= *Polin*, vol. 10) (London: Littman Library of Jewish Civilization, 1997), pp. 183–99.

4. Nahman of Bratslav, *The Tales*, trans. and ed. Arnold J. Band (New York: Paulist Press, 1978); David G. Roskies, *A Bridge of Longing: The Lost Art of Yiddish Storytelling* (Cambridge: Harvard University Press, 1995), chap. 2.

5. See *Di komedyes fun der berliner haskole*, ed. Max Erik (Kiev-Kharkov: Melukhe-farlag far di natsyonale minderhaytn, 1933); Aaron Wolfson, *Kalut daʿat utseviʿut*, ed. Dan Miron (Tel Aviv: Siman kriʾah, 1977).

6. Ismar Schorsch, *From Text to Context: The Turn to History in Modern Judaism* (Hanover, N.H.: Brandeis University Press and University Press of New England, 1994).

7. Ibid., "The Myth of Sephardic Supremacy," p. 81.

8. Heinrich Heine, *The Rabbi of Bacherach, a Fragment*, trans. E. B. Ashton (New York: Schocken Books, 1947).

9. Schorsch, *From Text to Context*, "Breakthrough into the Past: The *Verein für Cultur und Wissenschaft der Juden*," p. 213.

10. *Zeitschrift für die Wissenschaft des Judentums* 1 (1822): 277–384.

11. Karl Emil Franzos, *The Jews of Barnow*, trans. from the German by M. W. Macdowall (1883; reprint, New York: Arno Press, 1975); Joseph H. Udelson, *Dreamer of the Ghetto: The Life and Works of Israel Zangwill* (Tuscaloosa: University of Alabama Press, 1990), pp. 41–48.

12. Shmuel Feiner, *Haskalah vehistoria: toldoteha shel hakarat-ʿavar yehudit modernit* (Haskalah and history: The emergence of a modern Jewish awareness of history) (Jerusalem: Zalman Shazar Center for Jewish History, 1995).

13. Abraham Mapu, *Ahavat Tsion* (The love of Zion, 1853), and *Ashemat Shomron* (The guilt of Samaria, 1865). Only a small fragment of his novel on Sabbatianism, *Ḥozei ḥezyonot* (The visionaries, 1858), was ever pub-

lished. See Ruth Shenfeld, *Min hamelekh hamashiaḥ veᶜad lemeleh basar vadam: ᶜiyyunim baroman hahistori haᶜivri bameᵓah haᶜesrim* (Tel Aviv: Papirus, 1986), chap. 1.

14.   Michael Stanislawski, *Tsar Nicholas I and the Jews: The Transformation of Jewish Society in Russia 1825–1855* (Philadelphia: Jewish Publication Society of America, 1983); Adina Ofek, "Cantonists: Jewish Children as Soldiers in Tsar Nicholas's Army," *Modern Judaism* 13 (1993): 277–308.

15.   *Yidishe folkslider fun Rusland*, S. N. Ginsburg and P. S. Marek, eds.; photographic offset of 1901 ed. with a new introduction by Dov Noy (Ramat-Gan: Bar-Ilan University Press, 1991), no. 49; trans. David G. Roskies and Hillel Schwartz, in *Literature of Destruction*, pp. 120–21.

16.   Ginsburg and Marek, *Yidishe folkslider*, no. 50; Roskies, *Literature of Destruction*, p. 119.

17.   Mendele Moykher-Sforim (Sholem-Yankev Abramovitsh), "Petiḥtah" to *Bayamim hahehm* (1897), in *Kol kitvei Mendele Mokher Sefarim* (Tel Aviv: Dvir, 1966), p. 259; trans. Raymond P. Scheindlin as "Of Bygone Days," in *A Shtetl and Other Yiddish Novellas*, ed. Ruth R. Wisse, 2nd rev. ed. (Detroit: Wayne State University Press, 1986), p. 272. I should like to thank Professor Marcus Moseley for identifying the real-life counterparts in Reb Shloyme's fictional salon.

18.   See Mendele Moykher-Sforim, "The Mare," in *Yenne Velt: The Great Works of Jewish Fantasy and Occult*, ed. Joachim Neugroschel (New York: Wallaby, 1978), pp. 545–663.

19.   See Israel Bartal, "The Ingathering of Traditions: Zionism's Anthology Projects," and Mark Kiel, "*Sefer haᵓaggadah*: Creating a Classic for the People and by the People," in *The Jewish Anthological Imagination*, ed. David Stern, *Prooftexts* 17 (1997): 77–93, 177–97.

20.   Yosef Hayim Yerushalmi, *Zakhor: Jewish History and Jewish Memory* (Seattle: University of Washington Press, and Philadelphia: Jewish Publication Society of America, 1982).

21.   Roskies, *A Bridge of Longing*, chap. 5.

22.   All quotations are from Sholem Aleichem, *Tevye the Dairyman and The Railroad Stories*, trans. Hillel Halkin (New York: Schocken Books, 1987).

23.   Pierre Nora joins a distinguished line of French-Jewish structural anthropologists who have changed the way we think about history and memory. See his "Between Memory and History: *Les lieux de mémoire*," trans. Marc Roudebush, in *Memory and Counter-Memory*, ed. Natalie Zemon-Davis, special issue of *Representations* 26 (Spring 1989): 7–25.

24.   The scholars working behind the scenes are Khone Shmeruk, "*Tevye der milkhiker*: letoldoteha shel yetsirah," *Hasifrut* 26 (1978): 26–38; Seth Wolitz, "The Americanization of Tevye or Boarding the Jewish *Mayflower*," *American Quarterly* 40 (1988): 514–36; Ken Frieden, "A Century in the Life of Sholem Aleichem's *Tevye*" (Syracuse University, The B. G. Rudolph Lectures in Judaic Studies, 1993–1994); and Ruth R. Wisse, in a chapter on *Tevye* from her forthcoming book *Modern Jewish Literature*. See also

Sholem Aleichem and the Critical Tradition, Prooftexts 6:1, special issue (January 1986).

25.   See Khone Shmeruk, "The Frankist Novels of Isaac Bashevis Singer," in *Literary Strategies: Jewish Texts and Contexts*, ed. Ezra Mendelsohn, vol. 12 of *Studies in Contemporary Jewry* (1996): 120; Anita Norich, "Isaac Bashevis Singer in America: The Translation Problem," *Judaism* 44 (1995): 208–18; Roskies, A *Bridge of Longing*, pp. 304–306.

26.   Khone Shmeruk, "Yiddish Literature in the U.S.S.R.," in *The Jews in Soviet Russia since 1917*, ed. Lionel Kochan (London: Oxford University Press, 1970), pp. 232–68; Roskies, A *Bridge of Longing*, chap. 6.

27.   Barbara Diamond Goldin, *Bat Mitzvah: A Jewish Girl's Coming of Age* (New York: Viking, 1995).

Chapter 2

1.   H. J. Zimmels shows how the European rabbis applied this legal term to the unfolding Nazi terror. See "How far can the Nazi Holocaust be termed 'shaath ha-shemad' (religious persecution)?" in *The Echo of the Holocaust in Rabbinic Literature* (London: Marla, 1976), chap. 7. *Bishʿat hahashmada* is my own coinage.

2.   The prooftext for the law of *sheymes* is Deut. 12:3–4, quoted in the epigraph. Based on the juxtaposition of the two verses, the tannaitic rabbis interpreted the biblical injunction to "cut down the images of their gods, obliterating their name from that site" as follows: While *their* name is to be destroyed, God's name must never be erased, not from stone, not from parchment, not from paper (Rashi, ad loc., quoting Sifre, B. Makkot).

3.   All subsequent quotations are drawn from *Literature of Destruction*.

4.   "Proclamation of the Hebrew Writers' Union," trans. Zvia Ginor, *Literature of Destruction*, p. 158.

5.   For more on this epoch-making poem, see Alan Mintz, *Ḥurban: Responses to Catastrophe in Hebrew Literature* (New York: Columbia University Press, 1984), chap. 4, and Roskies, *Against the Apocalypse*, chap. 4.

6.   Bialik's commanding presence in the Nazi ghettos and concentration camps deserves a separate study. For some preliminary evidence, see *Against the Apocalypse*, chaps. 8–9, and two remarkable documents from the Lodz ghetto, Simkhe-Bunem Shayevitsh's "Spring 1942" and Jozef Zelkowicz's "Nightmarish Days," in *Lódź Ghetto: Inside a Community under Siege*, ed. Alan Adelson and Robert Lapides (New York: Viking, 1989), pp. 250–62, 320. Shayevitsh's poem is both a continuation and parody of Bialik's "In the City of Slaughter." Likewise, the intertext of Zelkowicz's "Son of man, go out into the streets" is Bialik's poem.

7.   Abraham Lewin, A *Cup of Tears: A Diary of the Warsaw Ghetto*, ed. Antony Polonsky (Oxford: Basil Blackwell, 1988), entry for July 26, 1942. Jewish literary and biblical references in Lewin's diary, including this one, are not identified in Polonsky's otherwise scrupulous edition.

8. "Appeal to Collect Materials about the World War," trans. David G. Roskies, *Literature of Destruction*, p. 210. Judging from the Appeal's staccato style and Germanicized diction, one may assume that Peretz was its main author.

9. For excerpts in English, see *Literature of Destruction*, sec. 53, and *The Dybbuk and Other Writings by S. Ansky*, ed. David G. Roskies (New York: Schocken Books, 1992), pp. 171–208.

10. The Akedah or Binding of Isaac on Mt. Moriah became the archetype of individual sacrifice. Ḥurban signifies the Destructions of the Temple in Jerusalem in 587 B.C.E. and 70 C.E. and became the archetype of national catastrophe. Kiddush Hashem, the Sanctification of God's Name, is the Hebrew term for martyrdom, eventually defined as an act carried out in public during times of religious persecution. For a fuller discussion, see *Against the Apocalypse*, chap. 2.

11. See *Against the Apocalypse*, chap. 10.

12. Cited by Zosa Szajkowski in his epilogue to Elias Tcherikower, *Di ukrainer pogromen in yor 1919* (New York: YIVO, 1965), p. 333. Szajkowski is my source on the Ukrainian pogroms.

13. See Max Weinreich, *Der veg tsu undzer yugnt: yesoydes, metodn, problemen fun yidisher yugnt-forshung* (Vilna: YIVO, 1935); Moses Kligsberg, *Child and Adolescent Behavior under Stress: An Analytic Topical Guide to a Collection of Autobiographies of Jewish Young Men and Women in Poland (1932–1939) in the Possession of the YIVO Institute for Jewish Research* (New York: YIVO, 1965). On the revolutionary import of the autobiography contest in the history of the genre, see Marcus Moseley, "Jewish Autobiography in Eastern Europe: The Prehistory of a Literary Genre," Ph.D. diss., Oxford University, 1990, chap. 7.

14. See the slightly abridged translation of Emanuel Ringelblum, "*Oyneg Shabbes*," dated January 1943, trans. Elinor Robinson, in *Literature of Destruction*, sec. 71. All subsequent quotes are from this translation.

15. For sample questionnaires, monograph outlines, and other research projects of the Oyneg Shabes archive, see *To Live with Honor and Die with Honor! . . . : Selected Documents from the Warsaw Ghetto Underground Archives*, ed. Joseph Kermish (Jerusalem: Yad Vashem, 1986 [should be 1988]).

16. Rachel Auerbach, "Yizkor, 1943," trans. Leonard Wolf, *Literature of Destruction*, sec. 78.

17. Two memory lapses: Hannah's prayer is recorded in 1 Sam. 1, not in Judges. Eli did not drive Hannah from the Temple.

Chapter 3

1. For a preliminary, groundbreaking study, see Alan Rosen, "The Language of Survival: English as Metaphor in Spiegelman's *Maus*," *Prooftexts* 15 (1995): 249–62.

2. See Emanuel Ringelblum's unsigned editorial in the inaugural issue of *Landkentenish* (Warsaw) 1 (1933), the official organ of the Jewish Society for Knowledge of the Land in Poland. A bilingual publication, its Polish title was *Krajoznawstwo*. For more on the landkentenish movement, see chapters 4 and 9 of this book.

3. The main sourcebook on the Ringelblum Archive is the unwieldy and unevenly translated *To Live with Honor and Die with Honor!: Selected Documents from the Warsaw Ghetto Underground Archives "O.S." ["Oneg Shabbath"]*, ed. Joseph Kermish (Jerusalem: Yad Vashem, 1986 *[sic]*). For a historical evaluation, see Ruta Sakowska, "Two Forms of Resistance in the Warsaw Ghetto—Two Functions of the Ringelblum Archives," *Yad Vashem Studies* 21 (1991): 189–219. In contrast to his English-language anthology, Kermish published an almost complete Hebrew edition of the underground press, meticulously edited and translated: *ʿItonut-hamaḥteret hayehudit beVarsha*, 6 vols. (Jerusalem: Yad Vashem, 1979–1997). The first of a projected twelve-volume scholarly edition of the Ringelblum Archive in Polish appeared in 1997 under the editorship of Ruta Sakowska. See *Archiwum Ringelbluma: Konspiracyjne Archiwum Getta Warszawy*, vol. 1: Letters from the Holocaust (Warsaw: Jewish Historical Institute, 1997). The six thousand documents represent the first and second parts of the Archive. The third part was never found. See p. vii of Sakowska's preface.

   In the early 1950s, the historian Ber Mark oversaw the publication of Yiddish prose fiction and reportage from the Oyneg Shabes Archive. These are the subject of the present chapter.

4. See Gila Flam, *Singing for Survival: Songs of the Lodz Ghetto, 1940–45* (Urbana: University of Illinois Press, 1992); Mordecai Gebirtig, *Krakow Ghetto Notebook*, CD produced by Bret Werb for the United States Holocaust Memorial Museum (Austria: Koch International Classics, 1994); and *Rise up and fight! Songs of Jewish Partisans*, CD produced by Bret Werb (Washington, D.C.: United States Holocaust Memorial Museum, 1996).

5. See Hamutal Bar-Yosef, *Hareshima kez'aner shel maʿavar mireʾalizm lisimbolizm basifrut haʿivrit* (Tel Aviv: Katz Institute for Hebrew Literature, 1989).

6. See Roskies, *A Bridge of Longing*, chaps. 4–5.

7. The only volume of his collected ghetto writings published thus far is Yozef Zelkowicz, *Bayamim hanoraʿim hahem: reshimot migeto Lodz'*, trans. Aryeh Ben Menahem and Yosef Rav (Jerusalem: Yad Vashem, 1994). For a diverse selection translated into English by Joachim Neugroschel, see *Lódź Ghetto: Inside a Community under Siege*. Zelkowicz's name is the most prevalent among the signed works listed in *The Documents of the Lodz Ghetto: An Inventory of the Nachman Zonabend Collection*, ed. Marek Webb (New York: YIVO, 1988), and *Nachman Zonabend Collection on the Lodz Ghetto (Record Group O-34)*, ed. Michal Unger (Jerusalem: Yad Vashem, 1992).

8. Emanuel Ringelblum, "Oyneg Shabbes," trans. Elinor Robinson, in *Literature of Destruction*, p. 389.

9. The fullest available edition is *Reshimot*, ed. Zvi Shner and trans. Avraham Yeivin (Tel Aviv: Ghetto Fighters' House and Hakibbutz Hameuchad, 1970).

The Yiddish version, *Reportazhn fun varshever geto* (Warsaw: Yidish-bukh, 1954), is incomplete and censored. Opoczynski is very poorly represented in Kermish's *To Live with Honor and Die with Honor!* See pp. 102–11, 157–63, and 650–53. Opoczynski's prewar writings are partially collected in his *Gezamlte shriftn*, ed. Sh. Tenenboym, with a biography by Rina Oper-Opoczynski (New York, 1951).

10. Peretz Opoczynski, "House No. 21," trans. from the Yiddish by Robert Wolf, in *Literature of Destruction*, sec. 73.

11. Peretz Opoczynski, "Der yidisher brivtreger," *Reportazhn*, p. 75; trans. from the Yiddish by E. Chase as "The Jewish Letter Carrier," in *Anthology of Holocaust Literature*, ed. Jacob Glatstein and Israel Knox (Philadelphia: Jewish Publication Society of America, 1969), pp. 75–88. I have revised Chase's translation to make it more colloquial. For the unaltered version, see "Nose-hamikhtavim hayehudi," in *Reshimot*, pp. 153–76.

12. Translated by Lucy S. Dawidowicz in idem, *A Holocaust Reader* (New York: Behrman House, 1976), pp. 197–207. For a more complete translation see *Reshimot*, pp. 139–52.

13. Cf. Sholem Asch, "Kola Street" (1905–1907), trans. Norbert Guterman, in *A Treasury of Yiddish Stories*, ed. Irving Howe and Eliezer Greenberg, 2nd rev. ed. (New York: Penguin, 1989), pp. 260–75. For more on the *baᶜal-guf*, see chapter 9 of this book and Michael C. Steinlauf, "Fear of Purim: Y. L. Peretz and the Canonization of Yiddish Theater," *Jewish Social Studies*, n.s. 1:3 (1995): 52–53 and the relevant notes.

14. "Eulogy Read at a Commemorative Evening in Honour of Yitshak Meir Weissenberg, 13 September 1941," appendix to Abraham Lewin, *A Cup of Tears: A Diary of the Warsaw Ghetto*, ed. Antony Polonsky (Oxford: Basil Blackwell, 1988). The Yiddish original was published anonymously in *Tsvishn lebn un toyt*, ed. L. Olicki (Warsaw: Yidish bukh, 1955), pp. 17–19.

15. On Yiddish prose between the two world wars, see the following essays by Khone Shmeruk: "Jews and Poles in Yiddish Literature in Poland between the Two World Wars," *Polin* 1 (1986): 176–95; "Yisroel Rabon and His Novel *Di Gas*," *Polin* 6 (1991): 231–52; "Responses to Antisemitism in Poland, 1912–1936: A Case Study of the Novels of Michal Bursztyn," *Living with Antisemitism: Modern Jewish Responses*, ed. Jehuda Reinharz (Hanover, N.H.: University Press of New England, 1987), pp. 275–95. The same shift from social realism to a metahistorical perspective occurred in the writings of I. J. Singer, I. B. Singer, Joseph Opatoshu, and Sholem Asch when these Polish-born authors emigrated from Poland. This subject, as scholars are wont to say, awaits a much fuller treatment.

16. Marian Turski, "Published Diaries from the Lodz Ghetto in Polish and German," in *Holocaust Chronicles: Individualizing the Holocaust through Diaries and Other Contemporaneous Personal Accounts*, ed. Lucjan Dobroszycki and Robert M. Shapiro (Hoboken, N.J.: Ktav, 1998). Michael André Bernstein developed a similar line of argument in his *Foregone Conclusions: Against Apocalyptic History* (Berkeley: University of California Press, 1994).

17.   Leyb Goldin, "Chronicle of a Single Day," trans. from the Yiddish by Elinor Robinson, in *Literature of Destruction*, sec. 74.

18.   Survivor testimonies written soon after the liberation sometimes recapture the sense of durational time. I am thinking in particular of Primo Levi's "The Story of Ten Days," the last chapter of *Survival in Auschwitz*, written in 1946, and Leyb Rochman's *The Pit and the Trap: A Chronicle of Survival*, published in book form in 1949 but based on a diary that he kept in hiding.

19.   Yehoshue Perle, "Khurbm Varshe," in *Tsvishn lebn un toyt*, pp. 100–41. Although the manuscript is dated "3 August–2 October 1942," a careful reading allows us to distinguish between the brief time of its composition and the time span it encompasses. Perle took pen in hand on the fortieth day of the slaughter.

20.   Ber Mark, "Yudenratishe 'Ahvas yisroel' (an entfer oyfn bilbl fun H. Leyvik)," *Bleter far geshikhte* 5:3 (1952): 63–115.

21.   See "*Oyneg Shabbes,*" in *Literature of Destruction*, p. 391. Wisse's critique is presented most systematically in *If I am Not For Myself . . . : The Liberal Betrayal of the Jews* (New York: Free Press, 1992).

22.   Cf. the censored version of Yitzhak Katzenelson, *Vittel Diary*, trans. Moshe Cohn (Israel: Ghetto Fighters' House, ca. 1964) with his *Ktavim aharonim begeto Varsha uvemahane Vittel*, ed. Shlomo Even-Shoshan (Israel: Ghetto Fighters' House and Hakibbutz Hameuchad, 1988). My source on the destruction of Huberband's *Kiddush Hashem* is David E. Fishman, who edited and translated the book into English.

23.   Yehoshue Perle, "4580," trans. Elinor Robinson, in *Literature of Destruction*, sec. 76; *Tsvishn lebn un toyt*, pp. 142–49.

24.   The answers to the questionnaires distributed among members of the Jewish intelligentsia in the Warsaw ghetto were published in *Bleter far geshikhte* 1:2 (April–June 1948): 111–22; 3–4 (August–December 1952): 188–202. The questionnaire itself is reprinted in the latter issue on pp. 186–87. See Dawidowicz, *A Holocaust Reader*, pp. 218–25, for the replies of Zeitlin and Milejkowski. See also Kermish, *To Live with Honor and Die with Honor!* sec. xv. For Shayevitsh, Kalmanovitsh, and Shapira, see *Literature of Destruction*, secs. 89–91; Nehemia Polen, *The Holy Fire: The Teachings of Rabbi Kalonymus Kalman Shapira, the Rebbe of the Warsaw Ghetto* (Northvale, N.J.: Jason Aronson, 1994).

25.   See Ber Mark, *The Scrolls of Auschwitz*, trans. from the Hebrew by Sharon Neemani and adapted from the Yiddish original (Israel: Am Oved, 1985). This may be read in conjunction with Zalmen Gradowski's "The Czech Transport," *Literature of Destruction*, sec. 93. See also Nathan Cohen, "Diaries of the *Sonderkommando*," in *Anatomy of the Auschwitz Death Camp*, ed. Israel Gutman and Michael Berenbaum (Bloomington: Indiana University Press in association with the United States Holocaust Memorial Museum, 1994), pp. 522–34.

26.   Originally published in *Di goldene keyt* 46 (1963): 29–35; trans. Leonard Wolf, in *Literature of Destruction*, sec. 78.

27. The *Mitteylungen* and six issues of *Wiadomości* are translated in ʿ*Itonut-hamaḥteret hayehudit beVarsha*, vol. 6: March 1942–July 1944, ed. Israel Shaham (Jerusalem: Yad Vashem, 1997). On the significance of the change from Yiddish to Polish, see Shaham's introduction, p. xi.

Chapter 4

1. See Dan Miron, *Der imazh fun shtetl: dray literarishe shtudyes* (Tel Aviv: I. L. Peretz, 1981), pp. 21–138; idem, "The Literary Image of the Shtetl," *Jewish Social Studies*, n.s. 1:3 (1995): 1–43; idem, introduction to *Tales of Mendele the Book Peddler*, ed. Dan Miron and Ken Freiden (New York: Schocken Books, 1996). For Dik, see Roskies, *A Bridge of Longing*, pp. 80–91.

2. On this, see Miron, "Literary Image of the Shtetl," pp. 34–35.

3. S. Y. Abramovitsh, "The Brief Travels of Benjamin the Third" (1878), trans. Hillel Halkin, in *Tales of Mendele the Book Peddler*, p. 305. Halkin, I am sorry to report, is also guilty of translating *besmedresh* as "synagogue" and renders *gzeyres* (evil decrees) as "pogroms," which is both inaccurate and anachronistic.

4. Abraham Cahan, "The Imported Bridegroom" (1898), in *Yekl and the Imported Bridegroom and Other Stories of Yiddish New York* (New York: Dover Books, 1979), p. 103.

5. Dan Miron, *A Traveler Disguised: The Rise of Modern Yiddish Fiction in the Nineteenth Century*, 2nd ed. (Syracuse: Syracuse University Press, 1996).

6. On [train]-travel-as-exile, see S. Y. Abramovitsh, "Shem and Japheth on the Train" (1890), Sholem Aleichem, "The Wedding that Came Without Its Band" (1909), and Lamed Shapiro, "The Cross" (1909), anthologized in my *Literature of Destruction*, secs. 40, 49–50.

7. The classic text in this regard is still Mark Zborowski and Elizabeth Herzog, *Life Is with People: The Culture of the Shtetl*, 3rd ed., with an introduction by Barbara Kirshenblatt-Gimblett (New York: Schocken Books, 1995).

8. For a convenient sourcebook, see *The Shtetl Book: An Introduction to East European Jewish Life and Lore*, ed. Diane K. Roskies and David G. Roskies, 2nd rev. ed. (New York: Ktav, 1979).

9. M. J. Rosman, *The Lord's Jews: Magnate-Jewish Relations in the Polish Commonwealth during the 18th Century* (Cambridge: Harvard University Press, 1990); Gershon David Hundert, *The Jews in a Polish Private Town: The Case of Opatów in the Eighteenth Century* (Baltimore: Johns Hopkins University Press, 1992).

10. See Israel Bartal, "The *Porets* and the *Arendar*: The Depiction of Poles in Jewish Literature," *Polish Review* 32 (1987): 357–69.

11. Roskies, *Against the Apocalypse*, pp. 163–72.

12. Sholem Aleichem, *Stempeniu: A Jewish Romance*, in *The Shtetl: A Creative Anthology of Jewish Life in Eastern Europe*, trans. Joachim Neugroschel

(New York: Richard Marek, 1979), chap. 9; Mendele Moykher-Sforim [Sholem-Yankev Abramovitsh], "Of Bygone Days," trans. Raymond P. Scheindlin, in *A Shtetl and Other Yiddish Novellas*, ed. Ruth R. Wisse, 2nd rev. ed. (Detroit: Wayne State University Press, 1986), pp. 254–358; "On the Threshold of the House of Prayer," trans. Harry H. Fein, in *Selected Poems of Hayyim Nahman Bialik Translated from the Hebrew*, ed. Israel Efros, 2nd rev. ed. (New York: Bloch, 1965), pp. 23–27.

13. See Khone Shmeruk, introduction to Sholem Aleichem, *Ktavim ᶜivriᵓim* (Jerusalem: Bialik Institute, 1976), pp. 25–28; Miron, "The Literary Image," p. 13.

14. Israel Bartal, "Dmut halo-yehudim vehevratam biytsirat Shalom Aleikhem," *Hasifrut* 26 (1978): 46. Jan Mazepa (né Kolodynski, 1644–1709) became the *hetman*, or warlord, of the eastern Ukraine in 1687 and instigated an uprising against Russia.

15. Isaac Meir Dik, "Habehalah (1867), rpt. in *Huliyot: dappim lemehkar sifrut yidish vetarbutah* 1 (1993): 61.

16. S. Y. Abramovitsh, *Dos vintshfingerl*, in *Ale verk fun Mendele Moykher-Sforim* (Warsaw: Farlag Mendele, 1928), vol. 11.

17. Sholem Aleichem, "Di shtot fun di kleyne mentshelekh" (1901), in *Kleyne mentshelekh mit kleyne hasoges*, vol. 6 of *Ale verk* (New York: Folksfond, 1917–1925), p. 14. For a translation, see *The Old Country*, trans. Julius and Frances Butwin (New York: Crown, 1946), pp. 9–17.

18. See Miron, "The Literary Image of the Shtetl," pp. 34–35.

19. Y. Dobrushin, "Tsvey grunt-oysgabn fun Sholem-Aleykhems 'Kleyne mentshelekh mit kleyne hasoges,'" *Visnshaftlekhe yorbikher* 1 (1929): 147–62. Karl Emil Franzos, "Nameless Graves," in *Jews of Barnow*, pp. 297–334.

20. I. L. Peretz, "Impressions of a Journey through the Tomaszow Region," trans. Milton Himmelfarb, in *The I. L. Peretz Reader*, ed. Ruth R. Wisse (New York: Schocken Books, 1990), pp. 20–74; "The Pond" appears on pp. 74–84, "The Dead Town," trans. Hillel Halkin, on pp. 162–71; the quote is on p. 163.

21. Bartal, "The *Porets* and the *Arendar*," pp. 368–69; Miron, *Der imazh fun shtetl*, pp. 102–16.

22. See Mikhail Krutikov, "Representations of Crisis in the Yiddish Novel, 1905–1914," Ph.D. diss., New York, Jewish Theological Seminary, 1998, chap. 2.

23. Translated by Meyer Levin as "The Little Town" in Sholem Asch, *Tales of My People* (Freeport, N.Y.: Books for Libraries Press, 1970), pp. 3–143.

24. For the literary-historical background, see S. L. Shneiderman, *The River Remembers* (New York: Horizon Press, 1978).

25. Sholem Asch, "Kola Street," trans. Guterman, *A Treasury of Yiddish Stories*, p. 261.

26. Translated by Ruth R. Wisse, in *A Shtetl and Other Yiddish Novellas*, pp. 29–78.

27. Reprinted in vol. 3 of Kipnis's *Geklibene verk* (Tel Aviv: I. L. Peretz, 1973).

28. Quoted from an excerpt of the novel in trans. by Leonard Wolf, in *Literature of Destruction*, pp. 334–35.

29. See Esther Rosenthal-Shneiderman, "Itsik Kipnis, azoy vi ikh ken im," *Di goldene keyt* 61 (1967): 123–36.

30. See Hayyim Hazaz, "Revolutionary Chapters" (1924), trans. Jeffrey M. Green, in Roskies, *Literature of Destruction*, sec. 62.

31. No history of this important movement has yet been written. The YIVO Library in New York possesses an almost complete run of the two major publications, *Land un lebn*, ed. Dr. I. Lejpuner (1927–1928) and *Landkentenish/Krajoznawstwo*, ed. Emanuel Ringelblum (1933–1938).

32. I. Lejpuner, "A siem-haseyfer in a poylish shtetl," *Land un lebn* 3–4 (March–April 1928): 1–2.

33. See M. Bursztyn, "A nayer faktor in yidishn lebn," *Landkentenish*, no. 1 (1933): 9–13. For other significant statements by Bursztyn, see "Vilner reministsentsn," in *Landkentenish*, no. 2 (1934): 63–67; "Der mehus fun regyonalizm," ibid., pp. 25–33; "Araynfir tsu der metodik fun landkentenish," no. 1(19) (1935): 1–2; and "Landkenerishe arbet oyf di kolonyes un vanderlagern," no. 2(20) (1935): 3–5.

34. Reprinted in Rokhl H. Korn, *9 dertseylungen* (Montreal, 1957).

35. The gap between theory and practice in Bursztyn's *Bay di taykhn fun Mazovye* is discussed by Khone Shmeruk in "Jews and Poles in Yiddish Literature in Poland between the Two World Wars," *Polin* 1 (1986): 185–87.

36. See, most provocatively, Dan Miron, *Histaklut beravnekher: ʿal 'Hakhnasat kalah' meʾet Shay Agnon useviveha* (Tel Aviv: Hakibbutz Hameuchad, 1996). The 1937 translation of *The Bridal Canopy* by A. M. Lask was reissued in a photo-offset edition by Schocken Books in 1967. On its non-reception in English, see Miron, *Histaklut beravnekher*, pp. 28–30.

37. S. Y. Agnon, *A Simple Story*, trans. Hillel Halkin (New York: Schocken Books, 1985); idem, *A Guest for the Night*, trans. Misha Louvish (New York: Schocken Books, 1968).

38. Isaac Bashevis Singer, "Concerning Yiddish Literature in Poland (1943)," trans. Robert Wolf, *Prooftexts* 15 (1995): 121–22.

39. J. Baum, "Short Resume" [of] *Felshtin zamlbukh: tsum ondenk fun di felshtiner kdoyshim*, ed. Jonah Baum (New York: First Felshteener Benevolent Association, 1937), English section, pp. 20–21.

40. See Ewa Morawska, "Changing Images of the Old Country in the Development of Ethnic Identity among East European Immigrants, 1880s-1930s: A Comparison of Jewish and Slavic Representations," *Going Home*, ed. Jack Kugelmass, vol. 21 of the *YIVO Annual* (1993), pp. 298–311. On the shtetl as a cheap movie set, see J. Hoberman, *Bridge of Light: Yiddish Film between Two Worlds* (New York: Museum of Modern Art and Schocken Books, 1991), chap. 18.

41.	Morawska, "Changing Images," p. 312; H. Leivick, *The Golem,* in *The Dybbuk and Other Great Yiddish Plays,* trans. Joseph P. Landis (New York: Bantam Books, 1966), Scene III. Leivick wrote *The Golem* in New York City between 1917 and 1920.

42.	See *From a Ruined Garden: The Memorial Books of Polish Jewry,* ed. Jack Kugelmass and Jonathan Boyarin, 2nd expanded ed. (Bloomington: Indiana University Press, 1998); Miriam Shmuelevitsh-Hoffman, "Denkmol un zikorn: an oysforshung funem tsunoyfshtel fun zvoliner yizker-bukh," *YIVO-bleter,* n.s., 1 (1991): 257–72; and the first Yizkor book translated in its entirety into English, *Luboml: The Memorial Book of a Vanished Shtetl,* ed. Berl Kagan, no translator credited (Hoboken: Ktav, 1997).

43.	Theo Richmond, *Konin: A Quest* (New York: Pantheon Books, 1995).

44.	Marzynski's film, which was aired on PBS in April 1996, inspired Eva Hoffman's *Shtetl: The Life and Death of a Small Town and the World of Polish Jews* (Boston: Houghton Mifflin, 1997). While considerably richer and more nuanced than the film, Hoffman's shtetl portrait rarely transcends its linguistic limitations. A book that purports to be about "the world of Polish Jews," it is written without knowledge of Yiddish, Hebrew, or Jewish civilization.

45.	Melvin Jules Bukiet, *Stories of an Imaginary Childhood* (Evanston: Northwestern University Press, 1992); Rebecca Goldstein, *Mazel* (1995; New York: Penguin Books, 1996); Steve Stern, *A Plague of Dreamers* (New York: Charles Scribner's Sons, 1994). See also Stern's prior collection of stories, *Lazar Malkin Enters Heaven* (1986; New York: Penguin Books, 1988).

46.	Allen Hoffman, *Small Worlds* (New York: Abbeville Press, 1996).

Chapter 5

1.	Sholem Asch, "Kola Street," trans. Guterman, in *A Treasury of Yiddish Stories,* p. 264.

2.	See Emanuel Etkes, "The Relationship between Talmudic Scholarship and the Institution of the Rabbinate in Nineteenth-Century Lithuanian Jewry," in *Scholars and Scholarship: The Interaction between Judaism and Other Cultures,* ed. Leo Landman (New York: Ktav, 1990), pp. 107–32. On the maggid as front man for the Maskil, see my *A Bridge of Longing,* chap. 3. On the Crown rabbis as agents of modernity, see Eli Lederhendler, *The Road to Modern Jewish Politics: Political Tradition and Political Reconstruction in the Jewish Community of Tsarist Russia* (New York: Oxford University Press, 1989), chap. 4.

3.	See Isaac Joel Linetzky, *The Polish Lad,* trans. Moshe Spiegel, with an introduction by Milton Hindus (Philadelphia: Jewish Publication Society of America, 1975); Henry Roth, *Call It Sleep,* with an introduction by Alfred Kazin and an afterword by Hana Wirth-Nesher (New York: Farrar, Straus and Giroux, 1991). Despite the grotesquely ineffectual figure that Reb Yidl Pankower cuts as he makes his way through the secular streets of New York's

Lower East Side in August 1913, he remains the most fully realized portrait of an East European heder teacher in all of American Jewish literature.

4. There is a rich literature on this subject. The *locus classicus* is Joseph Perl's Hebrew-Yiddish novel *Revealer of Secrets* (1819), now translated and annotated by Dov Taylor (Boulder, Colo.: Westview Press, 1997). For the background, see Raphael Mahler, *Hasidism and the Jewish Enlightenment: Their Confrontation in Galicia and Poland in the First Half of the Nineteenth Century*, trans. Eugene Orenstein, Aaron Klein, and Jenny Machlowitz Klein (Philadelphia: Jewish Publication Society of America, 1985).

5. See Roskies, *A Bridge of Longing*, pp. 73–80.

6. See Michael Stanislawski, *For Whom Do I Toil? Judah Leib Gordon and the Crisis of Russian Jewry* (New York: Oxford University Press, 1988), chaps. 7–8.

7. Isaak Erter, *Hatsofe levet yisraʾel* (1836–1845), ed. Yehuda Friedlander (Jerusalem: Bialik Institute, 1996).

8. Mendele Moykher-Sforim, *Haʾishon hakatan/Dos kleyne mentshele*, ed. Shalom Luria (Haifa: Haifa University Press, n.d.). The English translation by Gerald Stillman, *The Parasite* (New York: T. Yoseloff, 1956), is of the expanded edition of 1879. Here the rabbi has a bit more scope. On "Mendele" representing the counternorm, see Dan Miron, *A Traveler Disguised: The Rise of Modern Yiddish Fiction in the Nineteenth Century*, 2nd ed. (Syracuse: Syracuse University Press, 1996), chaps. 7–8.

9. Raymond P. Scheindlin's translation, *Of Bygone Days*, appears in *A Shtetl and Other Yiddish Novellas*, ed. Ruth R. Wisse, 2nd rev. ed. (Detroit: Wayne State University Press, 1986), pp. 254–358. For the two unfinished sequels, published in 1912 and 1917, which describe young Shloyme's travails in the Slutsk yeshiva, see parts 1–2 of "Fun mayn seyfer-hazikhroynes" in the so-called second volume of *Shloyme reb Khayims*, vol. 19 of *Ale verk fun Mendele Moykher-Sforim* (Warsaw: Farlag Mendele, 1928). On Abramovitsh's changed attitude to Hasidism, see Max Weinreich, *Bilder fun der yidisher literatur-geshikhte fun di onheybn biz Mendele Moykher-Sforim* (Vilna: Tomor, 1928), p. 338.

10. Sholem Aleichem, "Di vibores" (1883), in *Ale verk*, vol. 1 (Moscow: Ogiz, 1948), pp. 50–53; never included in any of the editions of the *Collected Works* over which Sholem Aleichem presided. From 1880–1883, Solomon Rabinovitsh worked as a government-appointed rabbi in the town of Luben, a painful experience to which he returned only in the last years of his life.

11. For a discussion of these works, see Roskies, *Against the Apocalypse*, pp. 167–83.

12. H. N. Bialik, "The Short Friday," translated I. M. Lask, in *Modern Hebrew Literature*, ed. Robert Alter (New York: Behrman House, 1975), pp. 109–24. For Bialik's direct source, see [Eliyohu] L[evi]n, "Der kurtser fraytog," *Der yid*, no. 27–28 (1899).

13. Alan Mintz, *"Banished from Their Father's Table": Loss of Faith and Hebrew Autobiography* (Bloomington: Indiana University Press, 1989).

14. See Itzhak Bacon, *Hatsaʿir haboded basiporet haʿivrit (1899–1908)* (Tel Aviv: Aggudat hastudentim, Tel Aviv University, 1978); Nurit Govrin, *Alienation and Regeneration* (Tel Aviv: MOD Books, 1989).

15. I. L. Peretz, "Between Two Mountains," trans. Goldie Morgentaler, in *Peretz Reader*, ed. Wisse, pp. 184–95; Roskies, *A Bridge of Longing*, pp. 118–21. However anemic the portrait of the Bialer Rebbe, the story still "works" as a monologue.

16. See Roskies, *A Bridge of Longing*, pp. 121–25.

17. Y. L. Peretz, "Di goldene keyt" (1907; 1912–1913), reprinted in *Dramatishe verk: ale verk* (New York: CYCO, 1947), vol. 6, pp. 102–79. There is no translation into English of this enormously influential play. For a textual history, see Khone Shmeruk, "Hamaḥaze haʾḥasidi' shel Y. L. Perets," in *Tsadikim veʾanshei maʿaseh: meḥkarim beḥasidut polin*, ed. Israel Bartal, Rachel Elinor, and Khone Shmeruk (Jerusalem: Bialik Institute, 1994), pp. 293–315.

18. Khone Shmeruk, *Peretses yiesh-vizye: interpretatsye fun Y. L. Peretses Bay nakht afn altn mark* (New York: YIVO, 1971), pp. 39–40; Abraham Novershtern, "Moyshe Kulbaks 'Meshiekh ben Efrayim': a yidish-modernistish verk in zayn literarishn gerem," *Di goldene keyt* 126 (1989): 188.

19. For a fuller—and startlingly original—interpretation of the play, see Ruth R. Wisse, "A Monument to Messianism," *Commentary* (March 1991): 37–42. On Reb Shloyme as pure invention, see Shmeruk, "Hamaḥaze haʾḥasidi' shel Y. L. Perets," p. 314, and p. 313 for Peretz's debt to Polish Romanticism. Shmeruk rejects the widely accepted view that Reb Shloyme is based on the Kotsker Rebbe, of whom more anon. Cf. Abraham J. Bick, *Khsides-motivn in der yidisher literatur un in lebn* (New York: IKUF, 1944), pp. 44–48.

20. For the relevant sources, see "Monish," and "The Rabbi of Tishevitz," in *Peretz Reader*, ed. Wisse, pp. 3–15, 32–34. In *My Memoirs* (pp. 267–359), Peretz fondly recalls the rabbi of his native Zamość, Rabbi Moyshe Wahl (1797–1873). But in Peretz's fiction, Rabbi Wahl is the stuff of legend, not of life.

21. Chaim Grade, *Di agune: roman* (New York: Yidish natsyonaler arbeterfarband, 1961), pp. 5–6, trans. Michael Stern. This important preface does not appear in Curt Leviant's authorized translation of *The Agunah* (New York: Menorah, 1974).

22. See, for example, Khone Shmeruk, " 'Prinzessin Sabbat' by H. Heine in a Yiddish Translation by H. N. Bialik," in *Jewish History—Essays in Honour of Chimen Abramsky* (London: Peter Halban, 1988), pp. 379–89.

23. *The Book of Legends Sefer Ha-Aggadah*, ed. Hayyim Nahman Bialik and Yehoshua Hana Ravnitzy, trans. William Braude with an introduction by David Stern (New York: Schocken Books, 1992).

24. Hayyim Nahman Bialik, *Law and Legend or Halakhah and Aggada*, trans. Julius L. Siegel (New York: Bloch, 1923), pp. 23–25.

25. A convenient place to begin is with Abraham J. Bick's anthology of *Khsidish lid un balade*, appended to his *Khsides-motivn in der yidisher literatur un in lebn*. On the debate among Hebrew intellectuals, see Allan Nadler, *Ration-*

alism, Romanticism, Rabbis and Rebbes* (New York: YIVO, 1992). On
Buber, see Paul Mendes-Flohr, *Divided Passions: Jewish Intellectuals and
the Experience of Modernity* (Detroit: Wayne State University Press, 1991),
chap. 4, "Fin de Siècle Orientalism, the *Ostjuden*, and the Aesthetics of Jewish Self-Affirmation."

26.   Fishl Schneourson, *Khayim Gravitser (di geshikhte fun dem gefalenem), fun
der khabadisher velt*, vol. 1 (Berlin: Literarisher farlag, 1922), pp. 25–26.

27.   See David G. Roskies, "The Maskil as Folk Hero," *Prooftexts* 10 (1990): 219–
35; and idem, introduction to S. Ansky, *The Dybbuk and Other Writings*
(New York: Schocken Books, 1992).

28.   Y. Opatoshu, *In poylishe velder*, 21st ed. (New York: R. J. Novak, 1947) [in
subsequent text references, "Y"]; *In Polish Woods*, trans. Isaac Goldberg
(Philadelphia: Jewish Publication Society of America, 1938) [in subsequent
text references, "E"].

29.   For partisan reactions to the novel's historicity, see Nachman Meisel, *Yoysef
Opatoshu: zayn lebn un shafn* (Warsaw: Literarishe bleter, 1937), chap. 4,
and Pinkhes Zelig Gliksman, *Der Kotsker rebe* (Piotrkow, 1939; photo-offset
ed., Israel, 1972), pp. 68–72, 149–50.

30.   I. J. Singer, *Yoshe Kalb: roman*, 3rd ed., in Singer's *Geklibene verk* (Warsaw:
Kletskin, 1937); trans. Maurice Samuel as *Yoshe Kalb*, with an introduction
by Irving Howe (New York: Schocken Books, 1988).

31.   See Anita Norich, *The Homeless Imagination in the Fiction of Israel Joshua
Singer* (Bloomington: Indiana University Press, 1991), pp. 24–34, and
Mordecai Strigler, "Yoshe Kalb der ershter," his introduction to *Georemt
mitn vint: historisher roman fun yidishn lebn in Poyln* (Buenos Aires, 1955),
pp. 18–25.

32.   See *In Praise of the Baal Shem Tov [Shivḥei ha-Besht]*, trans. and ed. Dan
Ben-Amos and Jerome R. Mintz (Bloomington: Indiana University Press,
1970); and Moshe Rosman, *Founder of Hasidism: A Quest for the Historical
Baʿal Shem Tov* (Berkeley: University of California Press, 1996). Based on
authentic hasidic sources, Perl's *Revealer of Secrets* goes to town over the sacred relics of the Besht, such as his pipe and his cane.

33.   Robert M. Seltzer, "The Secular Appropriation of Hasidism by an East
European Jewish Intellectual: Dubnow, Renan, and the Besht," *Polin* 1
(1986): 151–62. Simon Dubnov, the dean of East European Jewish historians, began his explorations of the hasidic movement in the pages of the
Russian-Jewish periodical *Voskhod* (1888–1893). There, or in the Polish translations of the Warsaw *Izraelita*, Peretz had surely seen the Baʿal Shem Tov
described as a radical reformer and the tales *In Praise of the Besht* defended
as a latter-day Gospels.

34.   See Hannah Berliner Fischthal, "Sholem Asch and the Shift in his Reputation: *The Nazarene* as Culprit or Victim?" Ph.D. diss., City University of
New York, 1994.

35.   Sholem Asch, *Der tilim-yid*, serialized in *The Jewish Daily Forward*, 1932–
1933; first published Warsaw, 1934; cited here from New York ed., 1946;

photo-offset ed., 1952; *Der Trost des Volkes*, trans. Siegfried Schmitz (Zurich, 1934); and *Salvation*, trans. Willa Muir and Edwin Muir (New York, 1934), 2nd rev. ed. (New York: Putnam, 1951). Mikhail Krutikov has prepared a detailed comparison of the Yiddish, German, and two English editions. His findings do not corroborate Asch's claim, in the preface to the English edition of 1951, that "essential" chapters omitted back in 1934 "because of a conviction that at that time they would not be understood by the general reader" were restored in the new edition. In fact, there are only slight differences between the 1934 and 1951 versions, both of which expunge "earthy," supernatural, and otherwise particularist elements of the Yiddish original. A complete translation of this important novel is in order.

36. I am indebted to Ruth Wisse for her insights on the Christological thrust of the novel.

37. Joshua Karlip, "More Christian than Christ's Followers: Christian Symbolism in the Works of Leivick and Sholem Asch," unpublished paper, November 1997.

38. See Fischthal, "Sholem Asch and the Shift in His Reputation," chaps. 1, 3–5.

39. See Isaiah Trunk, "Ḥomer bilti-yaduʿa shel 'Mishlaḥat An-ski' bashanim 1912–1916," *Gal-Ed* 6 (1982): 236.

40. See Gershon C. Bacon, *The Politics of Tradition: Agudat Yisrael in Poland, 1916–1939* (Jerusalem: Magnes Press, 1996).

41. Yitskhok Bashevis, *Der sotn in Goray*, serialized in *Globus*, January–September 1933; published with a foreword by Aaron Zeitlin (Warsaw, 1935); 2nd ed., *Der sotn in Goray a mayse fun fartsaytns un andere dertseylungen* (New York: Farlag matones, 1943). See now, Ruth R. Wisse, introduction to *Satan in Goray*, trans. Jacob Sloan (New York: Noonday Press, 1996), pp. xxxiv–xxxvi.

42. See Khone Shmeruk, "Der proyekt tsu instsenizirn Yitskhok Bashevises 'Der sotn in Goray,'" *Yerusholaimer almanakh* 25 (1996): 264–69.

43. Jacob Glatstein, "A gute nakht, velt," in *American Yiddish Poetry: A Bilingual Anthology*, ed. Benjamin and Barbara Harshav (Berkeley: University of California Press, 1986), pp. 304–305. For an excellent discussion, see Ruth R. Wisse, "Language as Fate: Reflections on Jewish Literature in America," *Literary Strategies: Jewish Texts and Contexts*, ed. Ezra Mendelsohn, *Studies in Contemporary Jewry* 12 (1996): 140–43.

44. Yitskhok Bashevis, *Mayn tatns bezdn-shtub* (New York: Der kval, 1956), originally serialized in the *New York Daily Forward*. For an abridged translation, see *In My Father's Court*, trans. Channah Kleinerman-Goldstein, Elaine Gottlieb, and Joseph Singer (Philadelphia: Jewish Publication Society of America, 1966). Four additional chapters appear in *An Isaac Bashevis Singer Reader* (New York: Farrar, Straus and Giroux, 1971), pp. 285–313. A sequel was edited and published posthumously by Khone Shmeruk. See *Mayn tatns bezdn-shtub [hemsheykhim-zamlung]* (Jerusalem: Magnes Press, 1996).

45. Chaim Grade, *Di agune*, pp. 5–6.

46.　Idem, *The Agunah*, trans. Curt Leviant (New York: Menorah, 1978), p. 112 (emphasis mine).

47.　This reading is based on an unpublished paper by my student Gabriella Rozansky Spraragen (Spring 1994).

48.　Menahem Boraisha, *Der geyer: kapitlen fun a lebn* (New York: CYCO, 1943); Abraham Joshua Heschel, *Kotsk in gerangl far emesdikeyt*, 2 vols. (Tel Aviv: Hamnoyre, 1973).

49.　See Ruth R. Wisse, "Two Jews Talking," and Benjamin Harshav, "The Semiotics of Yiddish Communication," in *What Is Jewish Literature?* ed. Hana Wirth-Nesher (Philadelphia: Jewish Publication Society of America, 1994), pp. 129–64.

50.　Chaim Grade, "My Quarrel with Hersh Rasseyner" (1953), trans. Milton Himmelfarb, *A Treasury of Yiddish Stories*, pp. 624–51; and cf. David E. Fishman, "The Musar Movement in Interwar Poland," in *The Jews of Poland between Two World Wars*, ed. Yisrael Gutman et al. (Hanover, N.H.: University Press of New England, 1989), pp. 247–71.

51.　Louis Finkelstein, *Akiba: Scholar, Saint and Martyr* (1936; New York: Atheneum, 1970). My thanks to Mark Kiel for the "working class" label.

52.　Milton Steinberg, *As a Driven Leaf* (1939; Northvale, N.J.: Jason Aronson, 1994).

53.　Cynthia Ozick, "The Pagan Rabbi" (1966), in *The Pagan Rabbi and Other Stories* (London: Secker & Warburg, 1972), pp. 3–37. See also Louis Harap, "The Religious Art of Cynthia Ozick," *Judaism* 33:3 (Summer 1984): 353–63.

Chapter 6

1.　On the distinction between internal and external migrations, see Arcadius Kahan's introduction to *YIVO Annual of Jewish Social Science* 18 (1983): xi–xii.

2.　See Joseph and Eleanor Mlotek, *Perl fun der yidisher poezye* (Pearls of Yiddish poetry) (Tel Aviv: I. L. Peretz, 1974). To date, three song books have come out of this column: *Mir trogn a gezang: The New Book of Yiddish Songs*, ed. Eleanor Gordon Mlotek, 2nd rev. ed. (New York: Workmen's Circle, 1977); *Pearls of Yiddish Song: Favorite Folk, Art and Theatre Songs*, comp. Eleanor Gordon Mlotek and Joseph Mlotek (New York: Workmen's Circle, 1988); and *Songs of Generations: New Pearls of Yiddish Song*, comp. Eleanor Gordon Mlotek and Joseph Mlotek (New York: Workmen's Circle, [1997]). References to the cassette recordings appear in the notes below.

3.　Here I am following Moshe Beregovski, "Jewish Folk Music" (1934), in *Old Jewish Folk Music: The Collections and Writings of Moshe Beregovski*, ed. and trans. Mark Slobin (Philadelphia: University of Pennsylvania Press, 1982), pp. 32–36, and what I have learned from my mother, Masha Roskies, who was one of twelve informants extensively recorded in the 1970s for the YIVO project "East European Jewish Folksong Performance in Its Social

Setting: An Analysis of the Social Systematization of Folksong Performance," directed by Barbara Kirshenblatt-Gimblett. See David G. Roskies, "Der mames lider: a kapitl moderne yidishe kultur-geshikhte," *Di pen* 31 (1997): 1–21. See also Petr Bogatyrev, "Folk Song from a Functional Point of View" (1936), trans. in *Semiotics of Art*, ed. Ladislav Matejka and Irwin R. Titunik (Cambridge: MIT Press, 1976), pp. 20–32.

4. See "Songs of Reb Leivi Itzchok Berditchever," in *Folks-gezangen* as interpreted by Chaim Kotylansky (New York: IKUF, 1954), pp. 15–43. They are recorded in *Songs of the Baal Shem*, arranged by Richard J. Neumann and Rafael Adler on the Collectors Guild label.

5. See Judah Leib Cahan, "Dos yidishe folkslid," in *Shtudyes vegn yidisher folksshafung* (Studies in Jewish folklore), ed. Max Weinreich (New York: YIVO, 1952), pp. 27–31.

6. For the text and music of the original "Golden Peacock," see *Mir trogn a gezang*, pp. 106–107. For the Ukrainian parallel, see Moshe Beregovski, "The Interaction of Ukrainian and Jewish Folk Music (1935)," in *Old Jewish Folk Music*, pp. 514–15.

7. See Benjamin Hrushovski, "Habayit hatipusi beshir haᶜam beyidish," in *Sefer Dov Sadan*, ed. S. Werses, N. Rotenstreich and Kh. Shmeruk (Tel Aviv: Hakibbutz Hameuchad, 1977), pp. 111–28; and cf. V. Ja. Propp, "The Russian Folk Lyric," in *Russian Folk Lyrics*, ed. and trans. Roberta Reeder (Bloomington: Indiana University Press, 1993), pp. 1–56.

8. The major source is still E. Lifschutz, "Merrymakers and Jesters among Jews (Materials for a Lexicon)" (1930), translated in *YIVO Annual of Jewish Social Science* 7 (1952): 43–83. See also Avraham Yaari's bibliographical essay "Sifrei badḥanim," *Kiryat Sefer* 35 (1960): 109–26; 36 (1961): 264–72. And see Ezra Lahad, "Habadḥanim," *Bamah Drama Quarterly* 95/96 (1983): 43–68.

9. The relevant verses, as cited by Lahad, "Habadḥanim," pp. 54–57, are from the anonymous *Der krumer marshalik mit a blind oyg* (The crooked jester with a blind eye) (Warsaw, 1875) and Hillel Klibanov, *Di elnte Shulamis* (The lonely Shulamith) (Vilna: Matz, 1893). The first was a folk book cribbed from by many *badkhonim*. On the role of music at weddings, see Moshe Beregovski's introduction to "Jewish Folk Songs (1962)," in *Old Jewish Folk Music*, p. 292.

10. See Roskies, *A Bridge of Longing*, p. 169.

11. On "The Jew from the Holy Land," see Yaari, "Sifrei badḥanim," addenda, pp. 267–68; on impersonating Gentiles, see Lahad, "Habadḥanim," pp. 60–61.

12. Cf. Petr Bogatyrev, "Semiotics in the Folk Theater" (1938), translation in *Semiotics of Art*, ed. Matejka and Titunik, p. 40.

13. The fullest discussion of the badkhn's art is by Mordkhe Schaechter in "Elyokum Tsunzer—der mentsh, zayn velt, zayn shafn," the introduction to

The Works of Elyokum Zunser: A Critical Edition, 2 vols. (New York: YIVO, 1964), 1:29–55.

14. Sh. Ernst, "Tekstn un kveln tsu der geshikhte fun teater, farvaylungen un maskaradn bay yidn," Arkhiv far der geshikhte fun yidishn teater un drame, ed. Jacob Shatzky, vol. 1 (Vilna and New York: YIVO, 1930): 5–37; Purim and the Cultural Poetics of Judaism, ed. Daniel Boyarin, Poetics Today 15:1, special issue [1994]).

15. The origins of the Purim-shpil have been thoroughly researched by Khone Shmeruk and the earliest known texts published by him in Maḥazot mikrai'im beyidish 1697–1750 (Yiddish biblical plays, 1697–1750) (Jerusalem: Israel Academy of Sciences and Humanities, 1979).

16. See Shimon Halamish (Schlaferman), "Mekhirat Yosef," Yeda-ʿam 30 (1965): 132–45. For a description of the costuming and props, see Shmeruk, "Haʿitsuv hassteni shel hadrama hamikra'it beyidish vedarkhei hatsagatah," Maḥazot mikrai'im, chap. 4; Halamish, "Mekorot hakhnasah shel 'Mekhirat Yosef,' " Yeda-ʿam 28/29 (1964): 87–88.

17. Abraham Cahan, "A Ghetto Wedding," in Yekl and the Imported Bridegroom and Other Stories of the New York Ghetto (New York: Dover Books, 1970), pp. 226, 234–35.

18. These are the major sources on his life and work: N[okhem] Shtif, Di eltere yidishe literatur: literarishe khrestomatye (Older Yiddish literature: A literary sourcebook) (Kiev: Kultur-lige, 1929), pp. 195–99; Berl Margulies, Dray doyres (Three generations: The songs of Berl Broder, the feuilletons of Yam Hatsiyoni; narrative and lyric poetry of Ber Margulies) (New York, 1957), pp. 7–32; and Dov Sadan, "Zamarei Brod veyerushatam," Avnei miftan: masot ʿal sofrei yidish, 3 vols. (Tel Aviv: I. L. Peretz, 1962), 1:9–17. Berl Broder's sole publication was the chapbook-format Shirey zimro, 2nd ed. (Lemberg: Salat, 1864), which contains the lyrics to thirty of his songs. Copies of this rare book can be found in the YIVO library in New York and the Widener library at Harvard University.

Of the two competing biographies, I have chosen the "official" version originally pieced together by M. Gelber in Aus zwei Jahrhunderten, and endorsed by his family, over the "revisionist" version of Manye Petshenig in Literarishe bleter. See Shtif for the differences.

19. Reprinted in Shtif, Di eltere yidishe literatur, pp. 200–201.

20. The main biographical source is Zalmen Reisen's Leksikon fun der yidisher literatur, prese un filologye, 2nd rev. ed. (Vilna: Kletzkin, 1927), 2:832a–840.

21. See the combination apologia-autobiography that precedes volume 1 of his Makel noʿam, subtitled (in German translation) Volkslieder in polnischjüdischer Mundart mit hebräischer Uebersetzung (Lemberg: Berl Lorje, 1[8]69), pp. 1–3. I understand aḥotah haḥasidah to be Zbarzher's cryptic name for the Hasidim.

22. The quote is from Reisen's Leksikon, col. 833.

23. For the most complete tally, see Chana Gordon Mlotek, "Velvl Zbarzher Ehrenkrants—tsu zayn 100stn yortsayt," Di tsukunft 90 (1984): 7–12, 47–54.

24. See Mlotek and Mlotek, *Perl fun der yidisher poezye*, pp. 466–69, for the original text and some sample parodies. For the music, see Gordon Mlotek, *Mir trogn a gezang*, p. 125.

25. The full text of *Di nakhtigal* is reprinted in Mlotek and Mlotek's *Perl fun der yidisher poezye*, pp. 470–75. For the later variants and the music, transcribed in 1909, see *Ganovim-lider mit melodyes*, ed. Shmuel Lehman (Warsaw: Pinkhes Graubard, 1928), pp. 7–9, 205–206. On Manger, see Roskies, *A Bridge of Longing*, chap. 7.

26. I. Charlash, "Mikhl Gordon (1823–1890)," *YIVO-bleter* 41 (1957/58): 59–60.

27. For a compassionate study of Gordon junior, a highbrow, Hebrew poet, essayist, and social reformer, see Michael Stanislawski, *For Whom Do I Toil? Judah Leib Gordon and the Crisis of Russian Jewry* (New York: Oxford University Press, 1988). In contrast, Stanislawski's passing references to the older, Yiddish poet, are rather harsh.

28. See his retrospective anthology *Shirey M. Gordon / Yidishe lider fun Mikhl Gordon* (Warsaw: Alapin, 1889), which contains twenty-seven texts. Some of the extensive revisions that Gordon made of his first song collection, *Di bord, un dertsu nokh andere sheyne yidishe lider* (Zhitomir: Shadov, 1868), are discussed by Charlash, "Mikhl Gordon," pp. 65–71. On the folkorization of his songs, see Chana Gordon Mlotek, "A gilgl fun Mikhl Gordons *Di bord*," *YIVO-bleter* 35 (1951): 299–311. The most accessible selections of his song texts are in Shtif, *Di eltere yidishe literatur*, pp. 148–67, and Mlotek and Mlotek, *Perl fun der yidisher literatur*, pp. 27–34, 448–52.

29. Note to *Fun der khupe* ("From the Wedding Canopy"), *Shirey M. Gordon*, p. 88.

30. The identification of the singer as a drunk little Hasid appears only in the first edition of 1868. For the song text and music, see Mlotek and Mlotek, *Pearls of Yiddish Song*, pp. 163–64.

31. In *Kapelye Presents Levine and His Flying Machine*, Shanachie Records (1985) 5SHAN-21006, Side 1, Band 6, and a fuller version sung by Michael Alpert in *Pearls of Yiddish Song*, the Workmen's Circle, ca. 1991 (no catalogue number), Side 1, Band 3.

32. See Zunzer's delightful autobiographical sketch, *Eliakum Zunser: A Jewish Bard*, trans. Simon Hirsdansky, ed. A. H. Fromenson (New York: Zunser Jubilee Committee, 1905), and the fuller Yiddish version in Mordkhe Schaechter's critical edition of the *Works of Elyokum Zunser*, vol. 2, pp. 667–716.

33. For the music and the part of this song that survived into the next century, see "The Plow," *Mir trogn a gezang*, pp. 96–97.

34. *Di yidishe bine*, vol. 2, ed. Yehudo Katsenelnboygn (New York: Hebrew Publishing Co., 1897). I worked from the 1901 reprint at the YIVO Library.

35. The most readable account of Goldfaden's career is by Nahma Sandrow, *Vagabond Stars: A World History of Yiddish Theater* (New York: Harper & Row, 1977), chap. 3. For a more biographical approach, see Reuven Goldberg's introduction to Abraham Goldfaden, *Shirim umahazot* (Poems and

plays) (Jerusalem: Bialik Institute, 1970). The latter reprints Goldfaden's Hebrew poems of 1865.

36. On the sources of Goldfaden's music, see A. Z. Idelsohn, *Jewish Music in Its Historical Development* (New York: Tudor Publishing Co., 1948), pp. 452–53, and Joseph Rumshinksy, "Der liber plagyator: vegn der opshtamung fun Avrom Goldfadns muzik" (1933), rpt. in Avrom Goldfaden, *Oysgeklibene shriftn*, vol. 18 of the Musterverk series, ed. Shmuel Rozhansky (Buenos Aires: Literartur-gezelshaft baym YIVO, 1963), pp. 270–76.

37. See Mark Slobin, *Tenement Songs: The Popular Music of the Jewish Immigrants* (Urbana: University of Illinois Press, 1982), pp. 184–90.

38. For a detailed discussion of the song, its variants and its offshoots, see Menashe Geffen, *Mitaḥat laᶜarisah ᶜomedet gdiyah* (Under the cradle stands a kid [In the footsteps of Jewish song]: Essays and studies) (Tel Aviv: Sifriat Poᶜalim, 1986), pp. 12–68, esp. pp. 20–22.

39. See *Folklor-lider*, vol. 2, ed. Z. Skuditsky and M. Wiener (Moscow: Emes, 1936), pp. 326–56. All the song books I worked with were copied out by male immigrants to America who were versed in Hebrew, Yiddish, and some Russian.

40. Hutchins Hapgood, *The Spirit of the Ghetto,* ed. Moses Rischin (Cambridge: Harvard University Press, 1967), pp. 91–98.

41. Shloyme Shmulewitz, *Lider* (New York: Solomon Small, 1913). The fact that Shmulewitz was his own publisher and distributor is further proof of his entrepreneurial spirit.

42. Slobin, *Tenement Songs*, p. 124.

43. This biographical material on Shmulewitz is from Zalman Zilbertsvayg, *Leksikon fun yidishn teater* 6 (Mexico City, 1969): 5741–52.

44. See Moses Rischin, *The Promised City: New York's Jews, 1870–1914,* 2nd ed. (Cambridge: Harvard University Press, 1977), chap. 8, for the most readable account of Jewish socialist activity on the Lower East Side. The quoted phrase is on p. 152.

45. For a useful, though partisan, guide to the problem, see Leon Kobrin, "From 'Daytchmerish' to Yiddish in America" (1943), trans. Joseph C. Landis, *Yiddish* 2:2–3 (1976): 39–48.

46. Note that by the time Shmulewitz used the SHMARTS:HARTS rhyme, it was already so hackneyed that it could appear embedded within a single line. See l. 7 of his refrain, cited above.

47. See "Mayn tsavoe" (My testament), in *Mir trogn a gezang,* pp. 92–93; trans. Benjamin and Barbara Harshav from a work-in-progress. For a more thorough sampling of Socialist Yiddish poetry, see N. B. Minkoff, *Pionern fun yidisher poezye in Amerike* (Pioneers of Yiddish poetry in America: The social poetry), 3 vols. (New York, 1956).

48. H. Leivick, "Di—on traditsye," *Der inzl* (January 1918), separate pagination, pp. 12–21. See also Mani Leyb, "On traditsyes," *Epokhe* 20 (December

1945): 86–88, for a retrospective statement on American Yiddish poetry in general.

49. Leivick, "Di—on traditsye," p. 15.

50. Zishe Landau, "Introduction to *Antologie, di yidishe dikhtung [in Amerike biz 1919]*," trans. Joseph C. Landis, *Yiddish* 2:2–3 (1976): 64.

51. Ruth R. Wisse, *A Little Love in Big Manhattan* (Cambridge: Harvard University Press, 1988), pp. 4, 60–65; Reuven Iceland, "At Goodman and Levine's," trans. Nathan Halper, in *Voices from the Yiddish*, ed. Irving Howe and Eliezer Greenberg (Ann Arbor: University of Michigan Press, 1972), pp. 300–305.

52. These they discovered from *Yidishe folkslider mit melodyen* (Yiddish folksongs with melodies), collected by Judah Leib Cahan, 2 vols. (New York: International Library Publishing Co., 1912). Part of his up-beat introduction to volume 1 was prepublished in *Literatur* (official organ of the *Yunge*) 2 (December 1910): 122–41.

53. *A Little Love in Big Manhattan*, esp. chaps. 2–3.

54. Moyshe-Leyb Halpern, "Di zun vet aruntergeyn," *In Nyu-york*, 3rd ed. (New York: Farlag Matones, 1954), p. 156; music in *Mir trogn a gezang*, p. 181; and Wisse, *A Little Love in Big Manhattan*, chap. 5.

55. Moyshe-Leyb Halpern, *Di goldene pave*, illus. Yosl Kotler (Cleveland, 1924); 2nd ed. (New York: Farlag Matones, 1954). See also, Kathryn Hellerstein, "The Demon Within: Moyshe-Leyb Halpern's Subversive Ballads," *Prooftexts* 7 (1987): 225–48.

56. Wisse, *A Little Love in Big Manhattan*, p. 200.

57. "Der rebe Elimeylekh": *Mir trogn a gezang*, pp. 168–69; Leibgold and Shmulewitz: *Az di furst avek: Lifshe Schaechter-Widman, a Yiddish Folksinger from the Bukovina*, Global Village Music C111 (1987), Side 1, Band 8; Side 2, Band 6; "Eyli, eyli": *Pearls of Yiddish Song*, pp. 220–22; and "Papirosn": ibid., 267–70.

58. The biographical sketch of Aaron Lebedeff is from Zilbertsvayg's *Leksikon* 2 (Warsaw, 1934): 1133–35, and the dust jacket of *Aaron Lebedeff Sings Rumania, Rumania and Other Yiddish Theatre Favorites* written by B. H. Stambler, Collectors Guild R62–1499 (1962). Aaron Lebedeff's original recordings, and those of Shloyme Shmulewitz, are housed and catalogued in the Max and Frieda Weinstein Sound Archives at the YIVO Institute, New York.

In a project that complements my own, Gila Flam has analyzed the "philosophy of schmaltz" based on the repertory of Lebedeff's contemporary and chief rival, Herman Yablokoff. Paper read at the 23rd Annual Conference of the Association for Jewish Studies in Boston, December 15, 1991.

59. "Roumania, Roumania," in *Aaron Lebedeff*, rereleased on cassette tape by Banner Records, BAS-C-1007, Side A, Band 1. Sholom Secunda's musical arrangement for this show-stopper, copyright 1947, appears in *The New York Times Great Songs of the Yiddish Theater*, ed. Norman H. Warembud (New York: Quadrangle, 1975), pp. 175–81.

60. Elsewhere he sang "In Ades, in Ades / Af der Moldavanke / Kh'hob getantst a polonez / Mit a sharlatanke" [In Odessa, in Odessa, / On the Moldovanka / I danced a polonaise / With a lady who led me false], a song, amazing to say, which made it into Beregovski's "Jewish Folk Song" collection of 1962. See *Old Jewish Folk Music*, p. 406.

61. *Kapelye's Chicken*, Shanachie 21007 (1987), Side 1, Band 4.

62. "Yiddishkeit," in *Aaron Lebedeff Sings Fourteen Yiddish Favorites*, vol. 2 (Brooklyn: Greater Recording Co., 1973), GRC 56, Side B, Band 6.

63. *Aaron Lebedeff*, Side B, Band 2.

64. For the texts of these songs, see Slobin, *Tenement Songs*, pp. 138–39, 200–201. The original recordings are included in his accompanying audio cassette.

Chapter 7

1. See *The Encyclopedia of New York City*, ed. Kenneth T. Jackson (New Haven: Yale University Press; New York: New York Historical Society, 1995), s.v. "cemeteries"; "potter's fields;" Michael Edward Panitz, "Modernity and Mortality: The Transformation of Central European Jewish Responses to Death, 1750–1850," Ph.D. diss., New York, Jewish Theological Seminary, 1989, chap. 1.

2. Panitz, chaps. 2–5. Panitz devotes two whole chapters (2–3) to the controversy over delayed burial.

3. Cited in Hannah Kliger, *Jewish Hometown Associations and Family Circles in New York: The WPA Yiddish Writers' Group Study* (Bloomington: Indiana University Press, 1992), p. 66.

4. The children and teachers of the Workmen's Circle schools erected a tombstone to I. G. Dragunski (1869–1923): "tsum ondenken undzer lerer un khaver" (to the memory of our teacher and comrade). "Lerer" in Yiddish denotes a secular teacher, as opposed to a *rebe*, a teacher of Torah.

5. See Ellen Kellman, "Sholem Aleichem's Funeral (New York, 1916): The Making of a National Pageant," *YIVO Annual* 20 (1991): 277–304; Arthur Aryeh Goren, "Sacred and Secular: The Place of Public Funerals in the Immigrant Life of American Jews," *Jewish History* 8:1–2 (1994): 269–81. I should like to thank Professor Goren for his generous help in researching this essay.

6. Goren, "Sacred and Secular," pp. 271, 281–86; *Forverts*, no. 2, April 1911, as cited by Goren. Twenty-eight years later, in a retrospective essay by M. Ivenski, they are recalled as "the sacrificial victims of the capitalist Moloch." See M. Ivenski, "Di historishe badaytung fun arbeter ring semeteris," Cemetery Department of the Arbeter Ring, *32nd Annual Report* (1939): 12.

7. Goren, "Sacred and Secular," p. 289; Ivenski, "Di historishe badaytung," pp. 12–13.

8. Goren, "Sacred and Secular," pp. 290–97.

9. All biographical data in this essay is taken from the standard Yiddish lexicons.

10. The full epitaph reads as follows: "Vos var un sheyn / vet nit fergeyn— / dem gayst vos shaft / mit kinstler-kraft / un zis gezang— / ervart keyn nakht / fun himslmakht—keyn untergang. / Der dikhter lebt / in zayn gedikht; / zayn zele shvebt / in reynem likht; / in foygls shtim / derkent ir im; / in blits un bren— / zayn sharfe pen. / Azoy iz di reyne neshome fun dikhter / tsu shaynen dort, tsvishn di eybike likhter." [Truth and Beauty / will never wither / no night awaits / the spirit that creates / with artist's craft. / There's no demise / for sweet song / of heaven's might. / The poet lives / through his verse; / his spirit soars / in purest light. / You can know him / in the voice of a bird; / and his ire / in lightning and fire. / The poet's pure soul has risen supernal / to glow there, amongst lights eternal.]

11. Ivenski, "Di historishe badaytung," pp. 11–12.

12. TSISHO stands for the Tsentrale Yidishe Shul-organizatsye, the Central Yiddish School Organization in interwar Poland.

13. Translated by Ruth R. Wisse in her indispensable study of Di Yunge, A Little Love in Big Manhattan, p. 38. In contrast to this exuberant poem, Mani Leib later composed the more muted and self-deprecating "Inscription on My Tombstone," which was declaimed at his funeral. Cf. Wisse, p. 236.

14. "A letste shure fun a lid / a letster bisn fun a moyl / un alts vos iz geven iz gut / un alts vos iz geven iz voyl / a letster zunshpil af di oygn / lesht oys ale regn-boygns." From Tint un leym (New York, 1942).

15. Translated by Adrienne Cooper, in The Tribe of Dina: A Jewish Women's Anthology, ed. Melanie Kaye/Kantrowitz and Irena Klepfisz (Boston: Beacon Press, 1989), p. 155. For the significance of this poem as a key to Margolin's poetics, see Abraham Novershtern, " 'Who Would Have Believed That a Bronze Statue Can Weep': The Poetry of Anna Margolin," introduction to his scholarly edition of her Lider (Jerusalem: Magnes Press, 1991).

16. Premiered on May 6, 1997. Written and directed by Eldad Ziv.

Chapter 8

1. See Yekhiel Shtern, "A Kheyder in Tyszowce (Tishevits)," YIVO Annual of Jewish Social Science 5 (1950): 157 (with the musical notation); and Diane Roskies, "Alphabet Instruction in the East European Heder: Some Comparative and Historical Notes," YIVO Annual 17 (1978): 21–53.

2. The Encyclopedia of New York City, ed. Kenneth T. Jackson (New Haven: Yale University Press; New York: New York Historical Society, 1995), s.v. "Adler, Felix."

3. Ibid., s.vv. "Amalgamated Housing Corporation," "Kazan, Abraham."

4. Naomi Caruso, ed., Folk's Lore: A History of the Jewish Public Library 1914–1989 (Montreal: Jewish Public Library, 1989), p. 53 [text in English and Yiddish].

5.   Yoel Entin, "Di naye yidishe dertsiung (der onheyb fun di yidishe folks-shuln)," *Yidish natsyonaler arbeter farband 1910–1946 (geshikhte un dergrey-khungen)* (New York: Jewish National Workers Alliance, 1946), pp. 145–46; Joseph Kage, "Tsvey hundert yor yidishe dertsiung in Montreal," *Shloime Wiseman Book,* ed. Shimshon Dunsky (Montreal: Jewish People's School, 1961), pp. 160–80 [text in Yiddish, Hebrew, and English].

6.   Quoted in Chaim Leib Fuchs, ed., *Hundert yor yidishe un hebreishe litera-tur in Kanade* (Montreal: Chaim Leib Fuchs Book Fund Committee, 1980), p. 277.

7.   Symcha Petrushka, *Mishnayes mit iberzetsung un peyresh in yidish. Seder Zeraᶜim* (Montreal: Northern Printing & Stationery Co., 1945), preface.

8.   David Rome, "On the Jewish School Question in Montreal 1903–1931," *Ca-nadian Jewish Archives,* n.s. 3 (1975): 61–88.

9.   Jonathan Frankel, *Prophecy and Politics: Socialism, Nationalism and the Russian Jews, 1862–1917* (Cambridge: Cambridge University Press, 1981), pp. 281 and passim.

10.   See Itamar Even-Zohar, *Polysystem Studies, Poetics Today* 11:1, special is-sue (1990): 121–30; Dan Miron, "Sifruyot hayehudim: bein mamashut lemisha'lot lev," *Im lo tihye Yerushalaim: masot ᶜal hasifrut haᶜivrit behek-sher tarbuti-politi* (Tel Aviv: Hakibbutz Hameuchad, 1987), pp. 93–171.

11.   Arie Leyb Pilovsky, *Tsvishn yo un neyn: yidish un yidish-literatur in Erets-Yisroel 1907–1949* (Tel Aviv: Veltrat far yidish un yidisher kultur, 1986), chap. 1.

12.   Emanuel S. Goldsmith, *Architects of Yiddishism at the Beginning of the Twentieth Century: A Study in Jewish Cultural History* (Rutherford: Fair-leigh Dickinson University Press, 1976), chap. 8.

13.   Mordecai Soltes, *The Yiddish Press: An Americanizing Agency* (New York: Columbia University Press, 1925).

14.   Rome, "On the Jewish School Question," p. 69.

15.   Reprinted in *Perets-shuln-bukh aroysgegebn tsum 25 yorikn yubiley,* ed. Jacob Zipper (Montreal: Peretz Schools, 1938), pp. 104–105.

16.   Quoted in Rome, "On the Jewish School Question," p. 79.

17.   Shloime Wiseman, "Yidishe tog-shuln in Montreal," in *Shul-pinkes,* ed. I. Chaim Pomerantz, Yudl Mark, Shloime Bercovich, and M. Brownstone (Chicago: Sholem Aleichem Folk Institute, 1948), pp. 216–52, or in *Shloime Wiseman Book,* pp. 107–44.

18.   Shloime Wiseman, "A memuar fun mayn lebn," *Kanader yidisher zamlbukh,* ed. Jacob Zipper and Chaim Spilberg (Montreal: National Com-mittee on Yiddish—Canadian Jewish Congress, 1982), pp. 391–92.

19.   Reprinted in *Kanader yidisher zamlbukh,* ed. Zipper, pp. 407–409.

20.   Shloime Wiseman, "Yidishe tog-shuln in Montreal," *Shul-pinkes,* pp. 45–52.

21.   See Jean-Marc Larrue, *Le théâtre yiddish à Montréal/Yiddish Theatre in*

Montreal, with a foreword and postscript by Dora Wasserman (Montreal: Éditions Jeu, 1996) [text in French, English, and partially in Yiddish].

22. Ruth R. Wisse, "A Goles Education," *Moment* 2:4 (1977): 28, 62.

23. Shloime Wiseman, "Amerike in undzer yidisher dertsiung," rpt. in *Shloime Wiseman Book,* pp. 72–82. The relevant passage is on p. 78.

24. Wiseman, "Amerike in undzer yidisher dertsiung," p. 78. Horace Kallen's writings on cultural pluralism seem to have greatly influenced Wiseman's thinking.

25. In their desire to maintain the historical link between Yiddish and Hebrew, the Montreal Yiddish educators never adopted the modern Yiddish orthography that was officially launched in 1937 by the network of Polish-Yiddish secular schools, with the blessings of the YIVO Institute for Jewish Research in Vilna. Although designed to be a compromise with the radical spelling reform carried out in the Soviet Union, Wiseman and his colleagues rejected the so-called "YIVO-spelling," for in their eyes it tried to make Yiddish culturally autonomous. For a partisan history of this ideological debate, see Hirshe-Dovid Katz, *Tikney takones: fragn fun yidisher stilistik* (Oxford: Oksforder yidish pres, 1993), pp. 71–128. Lest this strike the reader as merely arcane, I should point out that my own adolescent rebellion began at the age of fifteen when I taught myself the "YIVO-spelling," in defiance of my Folkshule teachers, and began to spread its use.

26. See Roskies, *A Bridge of Longing.*

Chapter 9

1. Hirsh Mac, *Kurerter un turistik in Poyln* (Warsaw: TOZ, 1935); Zalmen Szyk, *Toyznt yor Vilne,* vol. 1 (Vilna: Gezelshaft far landkentenish in Polyn, Vilner opteyl, 1939). Volume 2, already typeset, never appeared.

2. See *Blue and White in Color: Visual Images of Zionism, 1897–1947,* ed. Rachel Arbel (Tel Aviv: Nahum Goldman Museum of the Jewish Diaspora, 1996), where the map is not reproduced.

3. See Orit Ben-David, "*Tiyyul* (Hike) as an Act of Consecration of Space," in *Grasping Land: Space and Place in Contemporary Israeli Discourse and Experience,* ed. Eyal Ben-Ari and Yoram Bilu (Albany: State University of New York Press, 1997), pp. 129–45. While Ben-David provides a sound anthropological study of the role of hiking in Israeli society, her one-sentence-long history of the movement is woefully inadequate.

4. Arthur Green, "The Zaddiq as *Axis Mundi* in Later Judaism," *Journal of the American Academy of Religion* 45 (1977): 327–47; Elliot R. Wolfson, "Walking as a Sacred Duty: Theological Transformations of Social Reality in Early Hasidism," in *Hasidism Reappraised,* ed. Ada Rapoport-Albert (London: Littman Library of Jewish Civilization, 1997), pp. 180–207.

5. My thanks to Dr. Allan Nadler for this information.

6. See Arnold M. Eisen, *Galut: Modern Jewish Reflections on Homelessness and Homecoming* (Bloomington: Indiana University Press, 1986). The quotation is from the Shemoneh Esreh prayer. See Philip Birnbaum, *Daily Prayer Book* (New York: Hebrew Publishing Company, 1949), p. 88.

7. Lukács, as quoted by John Neubauer, "Bakhtin versus Lukács: Inscriptions of Homelessness in Theories of the Novel," *Poetics Today* 17:4 (Winter 1966): 537.

8. "Introduction I: The Perception of Space," in *A Historical Atlas of the Jewish People from the Times of the Patriarchs to the Present*, ed. Eli Barnavi; English ed. Miriam Eliav-Feldon (New York: Schocken Books, 1992), p. ix.

9. Zvia Ginor, "Cul de Sac: Exile, Exodus, and the Death of Myth in Israeli Literature of the 90's," paper read at a conference on "Makkom: Spirit and Space in Modern Israel," New York City, March 2, 1998.

10. Sidra DeKoven Ezrahi, "State and Real Estate: Territoriality and the Modern Jewish Imagination," *Studies in Contemporary Jewry* 8 (1992): 52.

11. "Creativity and Exile: European/American Perspectives," ed. Susan Rubin Suleiman, *Poetics Today* 17:3–4 (1996). The genealogy appears in the lead article, "Exsul," by Christine Brooke-Rose, pp. 290–91.

12. Mendele Moykher-Sforim [Sholem-Yankev Abramovitsh], "Of Bygone Days," trans. Raymond P. Scheindlin, in *A Shtetl and Other Yiddish Novellas*, ed. Wisse, p. 273.

13. See Eric Hobsbawm, "Mass-Producing Traditions: Europe, 1870–1914," in *The Invention of Tradition*, ed. Eric Hobsbawm and Terence Ranger (Cambridge: Cambridge University Press, 1983), pp. 270–72.

14. See, for instance, Isa. 1:21; 23:15–18; Jer. 2:2–3; 2of.; 3:1f.; Ezek. 23:30.

15. See Yirmiyahu Frenkel, *Perush le'Susati' shel Mendele Mokher-Sefarim* (Tel Aviv: Yavneh, 1946); Ruth R. Wisse, "The Jewish Intellectual and the Jews: The Case of *Di Kliatshe* (The Mare) by Mendele Mocher Sforim," the Daniel E. Korshland Memorial Lecture, San Francisco, Congregation Emanu-El, 1992.

16. See "National Cultures before Nationalism," ed. Carla Hesse and Thomas Laqueur, *Representations* 47, special issue (Summer 1994).

17. S. Y. Abramovitsh, "Brief Travels of Benjamin the Third," trans. Halkin, in *Tales of Mendele the Book Peddler*, pp. 301–91.

18. Karl Emil Franzos, "Nameless Graves" (1873), in *The Jews of Barnow*, trans. from the German by M. W. Macdowall (New York: D. Appelton & Company, 1883), p. 298.

19. I. L. Peretz, "The Dead Town," trans. Hillel Halkin, in *Peretz Reader*, ed. Wisse, p. 163. For another iteration, see Sholem Aleichem, "The Great Panic of the Little People" (1904), chap. 9.

20. See my *Against the Apocalypse*, pp. 141–43.

21. Sholem Asch, "Kola Street," trans. Guterman, in *A Treasury of Yiddish Stories*, ed. Howe and Greenberg, p. 261.

22. "As it were" does not appear in the Yiddish original. Cf. "Dos koyler-gesl," in Sholem Asch, *Fun shtetl tsu der velt*, ed. Shmuel Rozhansky (Buenos Aires: Ateneo Literario en el IWO, 1972), p. 101. Guterman's otherwise admirable translation does leave out one important sentence, however. After the climactic face-off between our hero and a frenzied mob of Catholic Poles, the presence of other Kola Street irregulars defuses the potential for greater violence as one Pole says to another (in Polish): "Why, those guys aren't Jews at all!" The ultimate compliment. Cf. the Rozhansky ed., p. 124. For a discussion of the *baʿal-guf*, see Roskies, *Against the Apocalypse*, pp. 141–62.

23. Paul Breines, *Tough Jews: Political Fantasies and the Moral Dilemma of American Jewry* (New York: Basic Books, 1990), p. 254, n. 57. See I. M. Weissenberg's "Father and the Boys," and Zalman Schneour's "The Girl," in *Treasury of Yiddish Stories*, ed. Howe and Greenberg, pp. 295–307, 316–24.

24. Ruth R. Wisse, *The Schlemiel as Modern Hero* (Chicago: Chicago University Press, 1971), p. 39.

25. See especially *The Family Moskat* (1950) and *Shadows On the Hudson* (1957). "Gimpel the Fool," in Saul Bellow's memorable translation, was pre-published in the *Partisan Review* 20 (May 1953). It achieved canonical status the next year by appearing in the Howe and Greenberg *Treasury of Yiddish Stories*.

26. For the obstacles in explaining the schlemiel to North American students, see Wisse, *The Schlemiel as Modern Hero*, p. 68. For the Israeli perspective, see Dan Miron, "Passivity and Narration: The Spell of Bashevis Singer," *Judaism* 41:1 (Winter 1992): 6–17.

27. See Roskies, *Against the Apocalypse*, pp. 144–47; "Superfluous man," in *Handbook of Russian Literature*, ed. Victor Terras (New Haven: Yale University Press, 1985).

28. Y. H. Brenner, "The Way Out," trans. Yosef Schachter, in *Modern Hebrew Litrerature*, ed. Robert Alter (New York: Behrman House, 1975), pp. 145–57.

29. Hayyim Hazaz, "Rahamim," trans. I. M. Lask, in *Modern Hebrew Literature*, ed. Alter, pp. 257–64. Lask translated the first version of the story. In its final recension, Hazaz played down some of Rahamim's baʿal-guf-like features.

30. Yaacov Shavit, *The New Hebrew Nation: A Study in Israeli Heresy and Fantasy*, trans. Fern Seckbach (London: Frank Cass, 1987).

31. Both Yizhar's "The Prisoner" and Yehoshua's "Facing the Forests" are anthologized in Alter's *Modern Hebrew Literature*.

32. Nurit Gertz, *Ḥirbet Ḥizʿeh vebokker lemoḥorat* (Generational shift in literary history: Hebrew narrative fiction in the sixties) (Tel Aviv: Hakibbutz Hameuchad, 1983).

33. *Siaḥ loḥamim: pirkei hakshavah vehitbonenut*, 3rd rev. ed., ed. Avraham Shapira (Israel: A Group of Young Members of the Kibbutz Movement, 1968); trans. as *The Seventh Day: Soldiers' Talk about the Six-Day War* (New York: Scribner, 1971).

34. Ruth R. Wisse, "Jewish Guilt and Israeli Writers," *Commentary* (January 1989): 25–31; and more generally, in her *If I Am Not for Myself.*

35. Yaakov Shabtai, *Zikhron devarim* (Tel Aviv: Hakibbutz Hameuchad, 1977); trans. Dalya Bilu as *Past Continuous* (Philadelphia: Jewish Publication Society of America, 1981). The interpretation that follows draws heavily from Deborah Steinhart, "Shabtai and Gnessin: A Comparative Reading," *Prooftexts* 14 (1994): 233–47.

36. Gershon Shaked, "Avot uvanim, ḥayyim vamavet: ʿal yetsirato shel Yaʿakov Shabtai," ʿItton 77 204 (February 1997): 34–42.

37. David Williams, "The Exile as Uncreator," in *The Literature of Exile, Mosaic* 8:3, special issue (Spring 1975): 1.

38. Zali Gurevitch, "The Double Site of Israel," in *Grasping Land*, ed. Ben-Ari and Bilu, pp. 203–16.

39. Sidra Ezrahi, "Our Homeland, the Text . . . Our Text, the Homeland: Exile and Homecoming in the Modern Jewish Imagination," *Michigan Quarterly Review* 31 (1992): 463–97.

40. See Gershom Scholem, "Toward an Understanding of the Messianic Idea in Judaism," in *The Messianic Idea in Judaism and Other Essays in Jewish Spirituality* (New York: Schocken Books, 1971), pp. 1–36.

41. See Eisen, *Galut*, pp. 78–105.

42. See Roth's *The Counterlife* and *Operation Shylock* and Sidra Dekoven Ezrahi, "The Grapes of Roth: 'Diasporism' between Portnoy and Shylock," *Studies in Contemporary Jewry* 12 (1996): 148–58.

43. A. M. Klein, *The Second Scroll*, introduction by M. W. Steinberg (Toronto: McClelland & Stewart, 1969).

Afterword

1. See *The Invention of Tradition*, ed. Eric Hobsbawm and Terence Ranger (Cambridge: Cambridge University Press, 1983); Benedict Anderson, *Imagined Communities: Reflections on the Origin and Spread of Nationalism*, 2nd rev. ed. (London: Verso, 1991).

2. See Nina Tumarkin, *The Living and the Dead: The Rise and Fall of the Cult of World War II in Russia* (New York: Basic Books, 1994).

3. See Slobin, *Tenement Songs*, chap. 3.

4. See James Loeffler, "*Di Rusishe Progresiv Muzikal Yunyon No. 1 fun Amerike:* The First Klezmer Union in America," in *Klezmer: History and Culture, Judaism* 47:1, special issue (1998): 29–40.

5. See David N. Meyers, *Re-Inventing the Jewish Past: European Jewish Intellectuals and the Zionist Return to History* (New York: Oxford University Press, 1995).

6. Jonathan Boyarin, *Storm from Paradise: The Politics of Jewish Memory* (Minneapolis: University of Minnesota Press, 1992); Nurit Gertz, *Shvuyah beḥa-*

lomah (Captive of a dream: National myths in Israeli culture) (Tel Aviv: Am Oved, 1995); Anita Shapira, "Historiography and Memory: Latrun, 1948," *Jewish Social Studies* 3:1 (1996): 20–61; Yael Zerubavel, *Recovered Roots: Collective Memory and the Making of Israeli National Tradition* (Chicago: University of Chicago Press, 1995); *Israeli Historiography Revisited*, ed. Gulie Ne'eman Arad, special issue of *History & Memory* 7:1 (1995). For an excellent overview, see Oren Baruch Stier, "Memory Matters: Reading Collective Memory in Contemporary Jewish Culture," *Prooftexts* 18 (1998): 67–82.

Index

Locators that include an f (e.g., 76f) refer to figures.

Israel: as covenantal space, 169–71; the *talush*, exile in the promised land, 165–69
Israel Ba'al Shem. *See* Ba'al Shem Tov
Ivenski, M., 144
IWO (International Workers' Order), 121

Jewish Daily Forward (*Forverts*), 89
Jewish Folk Encyclopedia (Pietruszka), 149
"Jewish Holidays and Jewish Education, The" (Wiseman), 153
"Jewish Letter Carrier, The" (Opoczynski), 29
Jewish literature, 46–49, 72, 74, 170
—literature of destruction and: *Destruction of Galicia* and, 19–20; Kishinev pogrom, 17–18; Oyneg Shabes archive and, 20–23; World War I and, 17, 18–19; "Yizkor, 1943" and, 23–24, 37–39, 180n.17
Jewish memory, 1, 172–73
—free market of pasthoods, 14–16
—ideology and, 7–9, 14–16
—literature and, 12–14
—nineteenth-century kulturkampf and, 2–3; change in remembrance and, 3–4; historical themes in, 4–7; ideological rift in memory and, 7–9
—Sholem Aleichem and, 9–10; *Tevye the Dairyman and the Railroad Stories*, 10–12
—*See also* covenantal memory
Jewish memory, shtetl in, 41–44
—between fact and fiction, 44–46
—ideology and the Polish shtetl, 54–56
—shtetl as covenantal landscape: in American-Jewish writing, 65–66; Brańsk, 65; Felshtin shtetl, 57–61, 58f, 60f, 62f, 63f; Konin, 64–65; *yizkor* books and, 61–64
—shtetl as protagonist, 46–49
—shtetl through the eyes of the Other, 49–54
Jewish National Arbeter Farband, 121. *See also* Poalei Zion
"Jewish People's Library," 149
Jewish schools. *See* Yiddish culture, in Montreal
Jewish Society for Exploring the Countryside. See *landkentenish*

Jewish song, 3, 27
Jewish Teachers' Seminary, 155
Jewish Theological Seminary, 173
Jewish-Gentile relations, 46, 49–54, 61
Jews
—exodus from Russia, 145
—group memory and, 172–73
—ideological divisions among, 14–16
—loss/dislocation and, 9, 59
—representation of, 163; ba'al-guf, 164–65; schlemiel, 165; *talush* and, 165–69
—self-criticism of, 35
Joseph, Rabbi Jacob, 127
Judaism, ideological divisions within, 14–16

kahal (Jewish community council), 6, 44, 52; *kohol-shtibl* (meeting place), 41
Kalmanovitsh, Zelig, 37
Kaplan, Chaim, 29–30, 33
Katzenelson, Yitskhak: *Song of the Murdered Jewish People*, 35; *Vittel Diary*, 35
Kaufman, Yehuda, 149
Kazan, Abraham, 147
kehillah kedoshah (covenantal community), 44
Kemelman, Harry: *Friday, the Rabbi Slept Late*, 88
Kfar Habad, 160, 161
khadorim. See heder
Khayim Gravitser (Schneourson), 75–76
khevres (voluntary societies and professional guilds), 44
Khurbm Galitsye (The destruction of Galicia) (Ansky), 19–20
"Khurbm Varshe" (Perle), 34–35
Kiddush Hashem, 14, 17, 19, 180n.10
Kiddush Hashem (Huberband), 35–36
kinnus (anthologizing of the Diaspora), 8
Kipnis, Itsik, 52–54
Kishinev pogrom, 17–18
Klein, A. M.: *The Second Scroll*, 170
Dos kleyne mentshele (The parasite) (Abramovitsh), 70
Klezmer Union, 174
Di klyatshe (The mare) (Abramovitsh), 8, 163

Kobrin, Leon: *Ore di bord*, 164
"Kola Street" (Asch), 29, 50, 51, 201n.22
Kompert, Leopold, 4
Konin, as covenantal landscape, 64–65
Konin (Richmond), 64–65
kool-shtibl. See *kahal*
Korczak, Janusz, 33, 34
Korn, Rokhl: *Erd*, 55
Kosovsky, Vladimir, 136
Kotsk (Kock) shtetl, 78
Kotsk in the Struggle for Truth
    (Heschel), 86–87
Krantz, Phillip (Yankev Rambro), 133
kulturkampf, nineteenth-century, 2–3;
    change in remembrance and, 3–4;
    historical themes in, 4–7; ideological
    rift in memory and, 7–9
Kurski, Franz (Shmuel Kahn), 138

labor groups, 13, 149. *See also* Old
    Mount Carmel Cemetery
Labor Zionism (Poalei Zion), 150–51.
    See also Jewish National Arbeter Far-
    band
Ladies' and Men's Society of Konin,
    Inc., 64–65
Landau, Zishe, 133
landkentenish (Jewish Society for Ex-
    ploring the Countryside; knowledge
    of the landscape), 26–27, 54–55, 159,
    175
landsmanshaft, 13, 121, 129; First Felsh-
    teener Benevolent Association, 59;
    Ladies' and Men's Society of Konin,
    Inc., 64–65
language, use of, 46, 68; in Hebrew lit-
    erature, 47–48; ideology and, 150–51
law: lost art of, 74–76; rabbi as up-
    holder of, 83–86, 87
Lebedeff, Aaron, 115–18, 119; *Der lit-
    visher Yankee*, 117
Leichtsinn und Frömellei (Frivolity and
    hypocrisy) (Wolfsohn), 3
Leivick, H. (Leivick Halper), 110, 140,
    142
Lejpuner, I., 54–55
Lekert, Hirsh, 127, 138
"letter to Mama, A" ("A brivele der
    mamen") (Shmulewitz), 108, 109f
Levi Yitskhok of Berdichev, Rabbi, 91
Levine, Charles A., 118–19
Levitan, Isaac, 145

Lewin, Abraham, 18, 33
Leyeles, A. Glantz, 140
Liberman, Aaron Shmuel, 127, 128f,
    133, 138
Liberman, Khayim, 138
library of Jewish catastrophe, 17, 24–25
—the Holocaust and, 25
—literature of destruction and: *Destruc-
    tion of Galicia* and, 19–20; Kishinev
    pogrom, 17–18; Oyneg Shabes ar-
    chive and, 20–23; World War I and,
    18–19; "Yizkor, 1943" and, 23–24,
    180n.17
Lichtenstein, Israel, 33
Lifschutz, Ezekiel, 59
Linetzky, Isaac Joel: *Polish Lad*, 69
literary cafés, 112
literature of destruction, 19; *Destruc-
    tion of Galicia* and, 19–20; Kishinev
    pogrom, 17–18; Oyneg Shabes ar-
    chive and, 20–23; World War I and,
    18–19; "Yizkor, 1943" and, 23–24,
    180n.17
Der litvisher Yankee (Lebedeff), 117
Lodz ghetto, 18, 27, 28–30
London, Meyer, 129
Lord's Jews, The (Rosman), 44
loss: awareness of, 9, 59; emblems of,
    55–56
Love of Zion, The (Mapu), 8
love songs, 112
Low Goyish, 46, 52
Lubavitsh Hasidim, 160
Lublin ghetto, 33
Lyessin, Avrom (Avrom Valt), 133

magic realism, in literature, 13, 66
Maharsha (Rabbi Samuel Eliezer
    Edels), 67
Maimonides, Moses, 15, 67
Makel no'am (The Staff of Beauty)
    (Zbarzher-Ehrenkrantz), 95–97
Mandelkern, Shlomo: *Divrei yemei
    Rusia*, 5–6
Mani Leib, 112, 140, 142
Mapu, Abraham, 5; *The Love of Zion*, 8
mara d'atra (rabbi as halachic author-
    ity), 68
Mare, The (Di klyatshe) (Abramovitsh),
    163
Margolin, Anna (Rosa Lebensboym
    Ayzland), 142–44, 143f

studyhouse (besmedresh), 41, 42, 51, 66
Sutzkever-Kazcerginski Collection, 25
symbolism, in literature, 13
synagogues, 41, 44, 52
Szajkowski, Zosa, 20
Szyk, Zalmen: 1000 Years of Vilna, 159

talush (uprooted intellectual/super-
fluous man), 72, 165–69
Tcherikower, Eliyohu (Elias), 14, 20
Tevye the dairyman, 10–12
theater. See Second Avenue; Yiddish
Stage, The; Yiddish theater
Third Temple ("bayyit shlishi"), 160
Der tilim-yid (Asch), 80–81, 190n.35
time, in Holocaust literature, 30–31; bi-
furcated time, 32–33; duration, 31–
32, 183n.18
"Tip of the Yud, The" (Gordon), 69–70
tiyyul, use of, 158, 160
Tokheha (Mosaic Curses), 20
Torah, contradictions in, 169
Treblinka, 22–23
Triangle Shirtwaist Company Fire, 127–
29
Trunk, I. J., 138
Tsemakh Atlas (The Yeshiva) (Grade),
86
Turski, Marian, 31, 35

Ukrainian civil war, 17, 20, 52–53, 57–
59, 58f
Uncle Tom's Cabin (Di shklavery oder
laybeygnshaft) (Stowe), 5
Uptown Jews, 152
usable past, 1
—free market of pasthoods, 14–16
—literature and, 12–14
—nineteenth century: change in remembrance and, 3–4; historical
themes in, 4–7; ideological rift in
memory and, 7–9
—nineteenth-century kulturkampf
and, 2–3
—Sholem Aleichem and, 9–10; Tevye
the Dairyman and the Railroad Stories, 10–12

Vaad Ho'ir (Jewish Community Council of Montreal), 151–52
Vilna ghetto, 18
"Visual Images of Zionism, 1897–1947"
(exhibition), 159–60

Vittel Diary (Katzenelson), 35
Vladeck, Boruch Charney, 129, 131

Walinsky, Rosa, 142
walking, as religious act, 160
Wanderer, The (Der geyer) (Boraisha),
86
Warsaw ghetto, 18, 27–28, 31
Warshawski, Oyzer, 30
Wasser, Hirsh, 23
Wasserman, Dora, 155
"Way Out, The" ("Hamotsa")
(Brenner), 166
weddings, Yiddish song and, 92–93, 94
Weinreich, Max, 21
Weissenberg, I. M., 30, 51–52, 54
Wiadomości, 39
Winchevsky, Morris (Leopold
Benedict; Lipe Ben-Tsiyon Novakho-
vitsh), 110, 131, 132f, 133–34
Wiseman, Shloime, 149, 152–55, 156,
174; "The Jewish Holidays and Jew-
ish Education," 153
Wishing Ring, The (Abramovitsh), 47–
48
Wisse, Ruth R., 35, 112, 165, 167; "A
Goles Education," 156
Wolfsohn, Aaron Halle: Leichtsinn und
Frömellei (Frivolity and hypocrisy), 3
women: Hasidism and, 80; Yiddish lit-
erature and, 5–6, 87; Yiddish song
and, 90f, 91–92, 99, 104
Workmen's Circle, 121, 122f, 127, 129.
See also Old Mount Carmel Ceme-
tery
World War I, 17, 18–19

Yablokoff, Herman: "Papirosn" (Ciga-
rettes), 115
Yechiel of Gostynin, 80–81
Yehoshua, A. B., 167
Yeshiva, Rosh, 68
Yeshiva, The (Tsemakh Atlas) (Grade),
86
Yeshiva University, 173
Yiddish Art Theater, 12
Yiddish culture, in Montreal, 148–50,
155–57; ideology and, 150–51, 157;
Jewish community council and, 151–
52; Shloime Wiseman and, 151, 152–
55; Yiddish language and, 150–51,
152–57
Yiddish Drama Group, 155

Yiddish lament, 97

Yiddish language, 8, 23, 46, 52, 68; women and, 5–6; Yiddish culture in Montreal and, 150–51, 152–57. *See also* Yiddish culture, in Montreal

Yiddish literature, 13–14, 69, 73, 77–79, 86–87; contradiction of exile and, 163–66; romance with the *ba'al-guf*, 29–30; shtetl in, 41–44; women and, 5–6, 87

Yiddish schools, 146–48, 149–50, 154–55

Yiddish song, 89–91, 94, 101–102, 107, 114–15, 173–74

—Abraham Goldfaden and, 104–107, 106f

—Brody singers and, 94–95

—Mikhl Gordon and, 97–101, 100f

—parody and, 117, 118–19

—Shloyme Shmulewitz and, 107–108, 109f

—shund and, 115–18

—socialist songwriters and, 108–10

—in traditional settings, 91–92; Purim, 93–94; weddings, 92–93, 94

—Velvl Zbarzher-Ehrenkrantz and, 95–97, 96f, 98f

—women and, 90f, 91–92, 99, 104

—the Youngsters (*Di Yunge*) and, 110–14

Yiddish Stage, The, 102

Yiddish theater, 9, 12, 102, 155; musical theater, 104–107, 106f

YIVO Institute, 20, 21

Yizhar, S., 167

"Yizkor, 1943" (Rokhl Auerbach), 23–24, 37–39, 180n.17

yizkor books. *See* memorial books

Yomen, Ben, 112

Yoshe kalb (I. J. Singer), 79, 80

Youngsters (*Di Yunge*), 110–14, 133, 140–44, 141f, 143f

Di Yunge (the Youngsters), 110–14, 133, 140–44, 141f, 143f

zaddik, 2, 68, 79, 160

Zbarzher-Ehrenkrantz, Velvl, 95–97, 96f, 98f; "Dos gute kepl," 95–97; *Makel no'am (The Staff of Beauty),* 95–97

Zelkowicz, Yozef, 27–28, 181n.7; *In yene koshmarne teg* (In those nightmarish days), 28

Zerubavel, Yael, 174

Zhitlowsky, Chaim, 150

Zikhron devarim (Past Continuous) (Shabtai), 167, 168–69

Zionism, 8, 156, 158–60, 161–62, 164, 165, 174; creativity and exile and, 162; end of the dream, 168–69; ideology and, 170; Marxism and, 161; opposition to, 174

Zionist schools, 13

Zionist youth groups, 159

Ziv, Eldad: *'Al hahayim ve'al hamavet* (A matter of life and death), 145

Zonabend Collection, 25

Zunser, Elyokum, 101–102, 103f, 107; "In sokhe," 101–102

Zunz, Leopold, 4

Zygelboim, Artur (Shmuel Mordecai), 138, 139f

DAVID G. ROSKIES is Professor of Jewish Literature at the Jewish Theological Seminary. His books include *Against the Apocalypse: Responses to Catastrophe in Modern Jewish Culture* and *A Bridge of Longing: The Lost Art of Yiddish Storytelling.* He is a founder and editor of *Prooftexts: A Journal of Jewish Literary History.*